DRIVE USA

A ROAD TRAVELLERS SURVIVAL KIT

DRIVE
>>
USA

Andrew Vincent

VACATION WORK
PUBLICATIONS

Published by Vacation Work, 9 Park End Street, Oxford
www.vacationwork.co.uk

DRIVE USA

A Road Travellers Survival Kit

By Andrew Vincent

Editor: Andrew James

First published 2002

Copyright © Vacation Work 2002

ISBN 1-85458-281-X

Cover design by Miller Craig & Cocking Design Partnership

Typeset by Brendan Cole

Maps by Nicola Averill and Andrea Pullen

Printed and bound in Italy by Legoprint SpA, Trento

Contents

Preface

As a mollycoddled motoring writer and broadcaster, travel in the USA holds no fears for me. Public relations folk ('PRs') usher me from the business class section of the silver bird to my car and thence to my five star hotel. Every move is planned and my sensitive eyes are shielded from anything that might offend. It's stress free travel that I've got used to these last twenty odd years. Emphatically though, it was not ever thus. I've also visited God's Own Country as a punter, as well as pundit. Unfortunately, during my earlier explorations Andrew Michael Vincent was still in diapers, rendering his splendid book, Drive USA, unavailable at the time; and boy, did I need the variety of help this book now offers.

They may call it The Land of the Free, but for the uninitiated, the USA can be intimidating. Just like anywhere else in the world, human sharks bask out there, ready to take a sizeable bite out of the unsuspecting traveller's wad.

We may share a common tongue but local terms and ways of communicating can be very different. Not knowing that when a waiter offers a 'sun kiss,' orange juice is available or that when an oncoming driver flashes his lights he is claiming right of way, could turn a social nicety into an awkward situation.

Drive USA will transform the naïve visitor into a seasoned road tripper. It's all about getting you on to the World's greatest network of roads with the confidence to enjoy it. Andrew's book is stunningly researched and written with the panache and humour you might expect from a man who's been there, done that.

Painstaking detail that's never boring covers everything from the law to carjacking, from turnpikes to bikes and from the frozen Sierra Nevadas to the relentless heat of California's gruesome Death Valley. Drive USA is a must-have item in your suitcase, especially if you're on a budget! You'll take so much more away from your experience if you know what you're doing, and with this information absorbed you'll look a lot less wet behind the ears.

I too shall pack a copy of this confidence-inspiring tome, just in case I run clean outta PRs to hold my hand.

Zog Ziegler
Motoring correspondent & Broadcaster

Introduction

'The motor car will never usurp the place of the horse.'
                                                    The Economist, 1911.

When you are in Los Angeles you are closer to outer space than you are to New York. Space is just an hour's drive away, if you had a car that went straight up. New York is ten days and nearly three thousand miles away. *En route* you will pass through some of the world's most inspiring scenery, sample the best (and the worst) of America's culinary heritage, hear music to open the mind and see cultural icons which epitomise the United States of America.

America is a vast collage of mountains, deserts, lakes, rivers, prairies, valleys and plains. It boasts 54 National Parks - from Arcadia in Maine to Zion in Utah. They stretch from the Gates of the Arctic in Alaska down to the Everglades in Florida. (If you want to drive between those two, you'll cover more than five thousand miles).

On a cross-continent journey you can be driving with the air conditioning on and watching tumbleweed bouncing off your car in the morning and be wrapped up with the heater blasting and snow settling on your windscreen by the afternoon. There are times when you will come round a bend on a mountain road to be greeted by a valley as if it's dropped down on one knee, thrown its arms out wide and shouted, 'Ta-da!'

The country is a maze of roads and each one has its own mystique; the Pacific Highway which hugs the west coast from Seattle to San Diego, Highway One which island-hops along the Florida Keys, Highway 50 - America's Loneliest Road - and of course the Mother Road, Route 66. Dirt roads will take you into the heart of an isolated community and six-lane freeways will sweep you into the buzzing centre of a metropolis.

The American road trip is the one great adventure *anyone* can enjoy; an expedition to the North Pole, a crossing of the Sahara Desert or an ascent of Everest all require years of preparation, a massive support team and a *lot* of money. All *you* need to cross the United States is a car, a driving licence and a map. Anyone can be Thelma and Louise, Jack Kerouac, John Steinbeck or Hunter S. Thompson. On the American road trip a traveller can step in to the pages of a book or on to the movie screen and live the fantasy, whether it be …

Gunning along a ruler-straight road in the blazing Mojave sun

 Cruising the Las Vegas Strip, with the top down, basking in the neon and the glitz

 Winding north along the Pacific Highway with the hills rolling away on your right and the ocean lashing the coast on your left

 Driving the white roads of a snow-covered Yosemite Valley in the winter

 Pulling in to the parking lot of a chrome diner along Route 66 or

 Visiting towns with poetic names like Sonora, Baton Rouge, Carmel or Key West ...

...these experiences are open to anyone - and you will not need a team of sherpas or oxygen to achieve them.

To get the best out of an American road trip, you need to know the ropes. That is where *Drive USA* will prove invaluable. A desert road is not so romantic when the radiator bursts and a mountain pass is less than picturesque when badly fitted snow chains tear the tyres to shreds. That Corvette bought in New York could become a liability when it fails an emissions test in California and the whole road movie romance can become a horror film when the guy you bumped at a traffic light sues you for neck injuries.

Drive USA tells you all you need to know about driving in the United States: how to get the best deal when renting or buying a car, the law, the Highway Code, and how to cope with the extremes of terrain and weather (*nothing* can prepare you for a Florida thunderstorm). It tells how to escape from a submerged car, how to avoid hitting the wildlife, how to cope with driving on the wrong side of the road and *even* where the speed traps are.

So take it easy the first time you drive in America. With a little patience it will not be long before you are breezing into LA on the freeway with the top down, the wind in your hair and some serious driving sounds on the stereo. Pack this book, keep it in the glove compartment and have it handy when you are trying to work out whether you need snow chains or snow tyres, whether you want to take the PIP or get the SLI when buying car insurance or you want to know when it is legal to drive through a red light. It will provide the hints, the tips, a few of the scams and the inside information which will make sure your trip is more Kerouac than calamity.

First, though ..

How It All Started

In 1919 a young United States Army lieutenant was given a mission - to take a convoy from Maryland to San Francisco to see if such a journey was possible and to test how quickly the armed forces could respond to an emergency. It took the officer two months at an average speed of seven miles an hour. (Picture the tailback trying to overtake *that*).

34 years later that lieutenant was the President of the United States and Dwight D. Eisenhower decided that America needed a network of interstates criss-crossing the country. The federal government pumped 75% of its transport budget into road building (and a paltry 1% into public transport) and the result is that today the United States boast more than four million miles of paved roads and highways, 200 million vehicles and 175 million drivers travelling more than two trillion miles every year. The United States of America is Gasoline Alley and, like it or not, the car rules.

A lot of people have invested a lot of time, money and effort so that *you* can enjoy America from the comfort of a car. Travelling coast to coast will not take two months (unless you want it to), you will be able to go faster than seven miles an hour, supper can be picked up at a drive-in diner rather than hunted down in the woods, and America's spectacular landscape can be watched whizzing by from the comfort of a modern car with the delights of a loud stereo, air conditioning, leather seats, power-steering, cruise control and even a global navigation system to keep you behind the wheel and on the right road.

Enjoy the ride.

American Place Names

American place names can be both poetic and prosaic. You can visit Sweetgrass in Montana, Heaven Heights in Massachusetts and even Poetry in Texas. Or try more prosaic-sounding destinations like Toad Suck in Arkansas, Bumble Bee in Arizona or Bummerville in California. There is also a town called 'Why' in Arizona and another one called 'Why Not' in Virginia – a drive of about 2,300 miles.

✦ Bell, California to Ding Dong, Texas - about 1900 miles ✦

Cars

'The automobile has practically reached the limit of its development.'

Scientific American, 1909.

A Brief History

Stink Chariots and Bugmobiles

No other country or culture has embraced the automobile as warmly as America; it is more than a product, more than a means of transport - it is an icon. Over the years some of the names of classic American cars have read like engineering poetry - the Torino, the Bel Air, the Mustang, the Thunderbird, the Elderado Seville, the Corvette. Even some of the manufacturers' names hint at the exotic - Chevrolet, and Pontiac and Cadillac (which is actually named after the founder of Detroit, Antione de la Mothe Cadillac).

The United States is dedicated to making itself as accessible as possible by car. The automobile has inspired literature, music and film. It is as firmly fixed in the American psyche as the horse and the railroad.

It took a little time for America to be won round to the idea of the automobile or even to agree what to call this new type of machine. Among the names suggested at the end of the 19th Century were stink chariot, road engine, locomotor, motor buggy, bugmobile and the locomobile. Eventually, 'automobile' established itself as the favoured moniker.

The society which is, today, so in love with the car was less than enthusiastic when the technology was first developed back in the 19th Century. In 1875 the US Congressional Record reported in its study of the 'so-called internal combustion engine' that *'...the discovery with which we are dealing involves forces of a nature too dangerous to fit into any of our usual concepts.'*

The idea of propelling people along by means of a series of small explosions inside a metal chamber must have seemed positively suicidal. In fact one engineer warned, 'You can't get people to sit over an explosion.'

Charles and Frank Duryea built the first American motor car in Springfield, Massachusetts, in 1893. Two years later they formed the Duryea Motor Wagon Company and sold the first gasoline-powered cars. The same year the first automobile race was held in America; the 50-mile race around Chicago was won by a Duryea with an average speed of (hold on to your hats) five miles an hour. After that it was just a roller coaster ride of technological innovation.

In 1900 the steering wheel replaced the tiller, oil was discovered in Texas in 1901 and Oldsmobile invented the speedometer in the same year (not that there was much speed to measure). In 1903 Henry Ford set up the Ford Motor

Company. That year a Dr Horatio Jackson, and his dog Bud (both wearing goggles) drove the first coast-to-coast road trip to win a $50 bet. Dr Jackson had to drive backwards over the Rockies because the petrol drained away from his engine if he went forwards over the mountains. The journey took them more than two months.

In 1903 Dr Horatio Jackson and his dog Bud drove coast to coast to win a $50 bet

In 1907 America's first gas station opened in St Louis. The Model T, the first mass-produced car, rolled off the production line in 1908. A year later Alice Ramsay brought the cross-country time down to 41 days. By 1915 there were two and a half million cars on America's roads and the country's first coast-to-coast highway - the Lincoln - opened.

Six and a half million cars were on the road by 1920 and Route 66 opened in 1926 between Chicago and Los Angeles. (Bobby Troup, incidentally, composed the song in 1946 and Nat King Cole was the first, among many, to have a hit with it).

The Golden Age

The Golden Age of American motoring was the 1950s and 1960s. During this period of post-war prosperity the car became *the* must-have status symbol. By 1956 Lieutenant Dwight Eisenhower had become President Eisenhower and he pledged $27 billion to create an Interstate Highway network. The expansion of the Interstate network opened the United States up to the automobile. America's population doubled between 1950 and 1980. The number of cars increased four-fold over the same period.

High above America's roads its test pilots were pushing at the limits of space in the new fast jets and the United States and the Soviet Union were vying for first place in the space race. Cars reflected that age of technological development. Fins and farings were all the rage. New cars gleamed with chrome and looked like aircraft or space rockets. In fact, several manufacturers recruited aeroplane designers to develop new models.

The style was known as the 'Forward Look' and the names of cars echoed themes of power - the Firedome, the Thunderbird and the Tempest. It was not enough for the exterior fittings to reflect the space age. Inside the cars bristled with gadgets like Prest-O-Justment Seats and Console-Key Instrument Panels. In the 1950s Chrysler developed an in-car Phonogram which played specially-designed vinyl records - the multi-CD changer of the day. (Chryslers were also built with characteristically high roofs so men could drive them without removing their hats).

Cars were built for the future, looking ahead to the days when we would all be wearing silver suits, living on Mars and saying 'affirmative' to each other.

Unfortunately, there was just one small problem; it was all a complete waste of money. Performance-enhancing innovations that drivers really wanted came in later years - disc brakes, fuel injection and front-wheel drive - all developed in Japan and Europe. American cars had the glamour, foreign cars had the guts.

The End of An Era

Years ago American manufacturers dominated their back yard and foreign manufacturers were seen as strictly small-time. In 1958 *Business Week* reported that imported car sales were unlikely to beat the 425,000 they reached that year. Ten years later it breezily claimed, 'the Japanese auto industry isn't likely to carve out a big slice of the US market.' By the 1980s Japanese cars accounted for nearly a third of the American market.

For years American manufacturers built cars as if there was an endless supply of fossil fuels and exhaust emissions had absolutely no effect on the environment. The American automobile was big and thirsty - the Cadillac the length of a football pitch or the De Soto the size of a small battleship.

The 1973 oil crisis was a wake-up call for the car industry and as gas prices went up, automobiles were scaled down. The 55 miles-an-hour speed limit was introduced to save fuel (making a road trip an even longer affair) and gradually Americans came to accept, grudgingly, that their cars had to reflect leaner times. A growing awareness of environmental issues added to that momentum.

Size Matters

P. J. O'Rourke is a seasoned travel writer and driving enthusiast with down-to-earth opinions and expedient solutions to driving sensibly and safely. Like most Americans, he still has a love for and recommends driving a BIG CAR ...

'... Because when something bad happens in a really big car ... it happens very far away - way out at the end of your fenders. It's like a civil war in Africa; you know, it doesn't really concern you too much. On the other hand, when something happens in a little bitty car it happens right in your face.'

P.J. O'Rourke, Republican Party Reptile, Picador, 1987.

☠Tales of the Tailpipe ☠

'A tree's a tree. How many more do you need to look at?'

Ronald Reagan, 1966.

In the 1900s the average American city had to clear 133 tons of horse manure from its streets every year. A century later and only the nature of the output has changed. According to traffic researchers in Vermont, the average driver will cover 17,000 miles in a year and during that time their car will pump into the air:

- ☠ 935 lbs (424 kg) of carbon monoxide
- ☠ 13,600 lbs (6,169 kg) of carbon dioxide
- ☠ 114 lbs (51.7 kg) of hydrocarbons
- ☠ 68 lbs (30.8 kg) of nitrogen oxide

The Environmental Protection Agency says there are steps drivers can take to help reduce pollution:

- ☠ **Plan journeys.** Plan several tasks for one trip, park in a central location and walk between destinations. Call ahead to check items to be purchased are in stock rather than make a wasted trip.
- ☠ **Maintain your car**. Keep the engine properly tuned and the tyres at the right pressure.
- ☠ **Avoid idling.** If the car is stationary for any length of time, switch off the engine.
- ☠ **Drive smoothly.** Avoid sudden acceleration and deceleration as it increases the load on the engine and try to anticipate changing traffic lights and traffic speeds.
- ☠ **Air conditioning makes the engine work harder.** The EPA advises drivers to open windows or to use the fresh air vents rather than the air con.
- ☠ **Refuelling. Spilled gasoline evaporates and causes pollution so avoid 'topping off' when filling up,** especially in hot weather.

A survey once asked Americans how far they would be prepared to walk before using a car. The average distance was about 1,500 metres.

How To Drive an American Car

Driving on the Right

For anyone used to a right-hand drive vehicle, driving a left-hand drive American car can take some getting used to:

Perception. Some people might have difficulty adjusting to the fact that the bulk of the car is on their right with the result that they pass dangerously close to objects on that side.

Mirrors. Looking up at the rear view mirror on the opposite side takes time to get used to.

Blind spots. In America you must learn to look over your left shoulder before starting any manoeuvre, such as a lane change.

Why Do Americans Drive on the Right?

It goes back to the days before the car or the internal combustion engine were invented, when the choice of transportation was more limited; you could have any colour as long as it was a horse. The horse was a versatile engine - you could simply strap a saddle on it for a sports model or you could attach it to a cart to make a family saloon. Other models included a buggy, a stagecoach, a dray, a landau, a trap or a wagon. There was one design element common to all these vehicles; the brake was always positioned on the left of the long bench-seat up front. So the driver sat on the left-hand side of the seat where the brake was within easy reach.

When driving along the crude, unmade tracks which passed for roads it made sense to keep to the right so that the driver was positioned near the middle of the highway for the best view ahead. That's how the practice of driving on the right evolved.

In Britain horse-drawn vehicles were built with their brakes on the other side so the practice of driving on the left of the road evolved. By the time the automobile came along the practice of driving on the right in the United States was already well established.

Power Steering

Most cars in America come with power steering and cruise control fitted as standard. Power steering gives even the biggest car the feel of a small runabout. Drivers who are unfamiliar with power steering may need a little time to adjust; the car will be unexpectedly sensitive and the effort needed to turn a conventional car could send a vehicle with power steering bumping up on to the curb.

Cruise Control

Cruise control can be a mixed blessing on long journeys. It does mean you can sit back and relax and take your foot off the accelerator. Also, cruise control makes the car more fuel-efficient because you maintain a steady speed. The disadvantage is that even if you think you are driving safely you will be slower to respond to changing situations. You might feel it is safe to set the cruise at 10 miles an hour above the speed limit on a clear stretch of interstate but with your foot away from the pedal your reaction time will be a fraction of a second slower; as the author realised when a highway patrol's radar recorded his speed before he had time to react to its presence.

Most cruise controls are mounted on a stalk on the steering column. The driver finds the desired speed and flicks a switch that makes the car keep to that speed. The cruise control can be over-ridden simply by accelerating or braking. On some versions the car will not fall below but return to its pre-set cruise control speed when the foot is taken off the accelerator. Braking tends to disengage cruise control all together. It can also be disengaged with an off switch on the stalk.

Gerry Brown on cruise control

'In some parts of America there is nothing to do apart from making sure the car is going in the right direction. Kansas is deadly dull to cross - the I-70 has barely a curve for hundreds of miles at a stretch. Fields of cereals fan out on either side of the road and there aren't even many hills to capture your interest. It's like Norfolk, in Britain, repeated a hundred times. If you are heading West, once you are clear of Topeka there's not much to do until you reach Denver in Colorado. At one stage I drove for 90 minutes without touching the brake or the accelerator. The road was straight and the traffic was light enough to overtake without accelerating or braking to allow other vehicles past. I think I only used the pedals twice in Kansas - to stop for gas and food.'

Gears and Transmission

Once visitors from some countries have got used to everything being the wrong way round in American cars there is the transmission to work out. Most American cars are automatics and the manual, or stick shift cars tend to be foreign imports.

How to Drive an Automatic

Despite its name an automatic transmission does have gears you can use manually and these are for occasions when you need to over-ride the automatic gear selection. The gear stick in an automatic is a T-shaped stick on the driver's right. Some older cars have the stick mounted on the steering column. There is usually a button on one end of the T-bar at the top of the stick and this needs to be pressed in before the stick will move.

Automatics do not always have a hand brake. Instead they may have a foot brake which is a pedal located on the far left of the driver's footwell. Push it all the way to the floor to engage the parking brake and let it up to release the brake. Most automatics have another fail-safe to prevent the car from being started in gear and lurching forward; you will only be able to disengage Park when your foot is on the brake pedal.

On setting off, most automatic cars will move even without any pressure on the accelerator. An automatic's tendency to creep forward as soon as Drive is engaged is something you will have to be aware of at Stop signs or traffic lights. Remember to engage the brake or to select Neutral or Park.

Once on the open road, the right foot should be used for both the accelerator and the brake pedal. Using both feet could lead to the accelerator and the brake being applied at the same time straining the engine and wearing down the brake pads.

That is about all there is to driving an automatic. There are, though, a **few disadvantages to** automatic transmissions:

☞ They are **less fuel-efficient** than manual gearboxes. In an automatic there is always a slight lag between the driver applying more gas or decelerating and the automatic selection of the appropriate gear. Furthermore, automatic transmissions are much heavier than manual gearboxes and this can affect fuel consumption.

☞ Automatics sometimes **lack 'poke'**; they do not respond immediately to acceleration, which can be a pain when you want to nip into another lane or zip past a truck. They also have an annoying tendency to lurch if the gas pedal is pressed suddenly - at first there is no response and then suddenly there is a surge of power which can take you by surprise.

☞ Automatic transmissions are much **more complicated** than manual gearboxes so when they go wrong be prepared for a huge bill.

Apart from those few disadvantages, however, an automatic is easy to drive- no gears or clutches; just slip it into 'Drive' and do just that.

How to Drive a Stick-Shift

Many foreign visitors seek out stick-shift rental cars (which are very rare) or cars to buy because that is what they are used to. However, driving a left-hand-drive stick shift can present an unexpected problem for some foreign nationals; after years of changing gear with the left hand they will find themselves groping for a stick which is not there or trying to change gear with the window handle. The secret is to **keep** your hand on the gear stick even though this goes *against* the advice of driving instructors who will tell you to keep both hands on the steering wheel.

On a right-hand drive car, first gear is away from the driver. On a left-hand drive it is towards the driver. Some stick-shift cars in America also have failsafes to prevent them from being started in gear. Some will not start unless the clutch is depressed.

Air Conditioning

Air conditioning is a 'must-have' in the United States and fortunately it is fitted as standard to most cars. Without it, driving can be an uncomfortable experience in places like Florida and southern California. If the air con is on the **windows should be shut** otherwise all the cool air just escapes.

There are three *disadvantages* to air conditioning. Approximately 10% of the engine's power is diverted to the air con when it is switched on, leading to an increase in fuel consumption. The second disadvantage is that the engine may overheat as it is working harder. This leads to the ironic situation that the air con may have to be turned off in the very conditions where it is needed most. The third disadvantage is that a car may have a reduced top speed and more sluggish acceleration as the engine's power is directed away from moving the car forward.

With Knobs On

American car makers are now much more concerned with substance than they were back in the 1950s and 1960s, when style was more important than small matters like safety, efficiency or performance. In the 21st Century car owners demand all three and manufacturers have had to respond in order to maintain sales. Most of the gadgets and systems described here are available on new or rental cars.

Satellite Navigation

Two of the big developments in recent years have been satellite navigation - or Sat Nav - and Global Positioning Systems, or GPS. These tell the driver exactly where he or she is and, if the vehicle has been stolen, exactly where it is even if they are not in it.

These innovations come with a potentially life-saving safety feature. General Motors' **OnStar** system, for example, not only acts as a basic Sat Nav system but it will also alert the emergency services when the air bag is deployed. The system will locate the car using satellites and direct rescue crews to the scene even if no 911 call has been made. This optional system costs around $900 to buy, another $100-$200 to install, and then there is a monthly fee of about $22 on top of that. Mercedes-Benz has developed a similar system called **Tele Aid**. OnStar's sister system is called **MedNet** that relays all your medical details to the paramedics who are administering First Aid.

Other manufacturers have developed their own brands of automatic rescue system: BMW and Motorola offer the **Mayday Cellular Phone** which works like Mercedes' Tele Aid system but with the added feature of remote door unlocking; Ford and Mercury have developed **VEMS, or Vehicle Emergency Messaging System.**

Since the early 1990s high-tech safety devices have filtered down from the top-of-the-range cars into the cheaper end of the market. It is now possible to buy cars with state-of-the-art safety features for less than $15,000.

The Acura Navigation System allows the driver to plan a route on a display screen and gives voice prompts along the way. That comes in at $2,000.

Reverse sensing systems will detect anything, including a child, which may be in the path of a reversing car and alert the driver with a warning beep. These are fitted as standard on some models such as the Nissan Micra and are becoming more common.

Ford and General Motors have developed an emergency **release handle inside the trunk.** This could also prove a lifesaver for adults who may be bundled into their own trunk during a carjacking or for children who have chosen a foolish place to hide.

Cadillac is working on **Night Vision,** a thermal imaging system that will allow a driver to see better in the dark.

Most new models have air bags fitted as standard. More and more models are now also available with **side air bags** to protect occupants from a collision to the side. Mercedes-Benz and Volvo have produced a side curtain that drops down from the ceiling to protect both front and rear occupants. BMW has developed an inflatable tube that deploys diagonally across the windows to protect driver and passengers from side impact.

One problem with air bags is that you have to sit a certain distance from the unit otherwise you can suffer serious injury when they deploy. This has been a problem for shorter people who find it difficult to reach the pedals and remain at a safe distance from the bag. Ford has come up with power adjustable pedals that can be moved to allow for shorter legs.

In-car entertainment has moved on from the days of Chrysler's Phonogram and its specially designed vinyl records. Oldsmobile and Pontiac are fitting some of their people carriers with passenger **video screens.** Daewoo offer the option of a DVD player and screen or a Sony Playstation in their Tacuna model and other manufacturers look like following suit.

In the 1950s and `60s cars simply *looked* like aircraft. The high-tech equipment now fitted as standard is turning the driver's seat into something resembling a cockpit. The fashion for cars to mimic aircraft is making a comeback.

The Car's the Star - Films and TV

The automobile has been the star, or at least the second lead in hundreds of films and TV programmes. One such star, the Batmobile, was actually a real car and not something dreamt up by the prop department. Bruce Wayne's alter ego drove a Lincoln Futura - a prototype sports car from the 1950s that never went into mass production.

Starsky and Hutch's famous red and white car was a Ford Torino whose hood was regularly buffed to a sheen by the behinds of the two cops as they slid across it. In the 1990s Don Johnson, as San Francisco cop, Nash Bridges, preferred a 1971 Plymouth Barracuda. In his earlier persona as Sonny Crockett in Miami Vice he drove a Ferrari Daytona before switching to a Ferrari Testarossa. Where Sonny Crockett's clothes were boutique, Columbo's were car boot. The scruffy detective drove a beat-up 1959 Peugeot 403 convertible (although if you are really into television trivia, it is actually *supposed* to be a 1950 model in the series).

The General Lee in the Dukes of Hazzard was a 1969 Dodge Charger that had its doors welded shut to allow Bo and Luke the chance to show off their athleticism by diving through the windows. Barry Newman's character, Kowalski, also opted for a Dodge in the 1971 movie Vanishing Point. He bets that he can deliver a Dodge Challenger from Denver to San Francisco in 15 hours. In Knightrider the high-tech supercar, called Kitt, was actually a Transam.

Perhaps the definitive car chase movie is Bullitt, starring Steve McQueen, in which cars race up and down the hilly streets of San Francisco. McQueen drives a 1968 Ford Mustang Fastback, although computer wizardry put him behind the wheel of a Ford Puma for a television advertisement in 1997.

Cars that appear in films or television programmes become collectors' items but the problem is identifying which is the genuine article. When Columbo returned to the screen in 1989, Peter Falk wanted the car from the original series. Claims came in from around the country before his original Peugeot 403 was tracked down in Ohio. The problem is that film companies often use more than one car because they take such a hammering. The A-Team, for example, used three black GMC vans - the numberplate was just swapped around. A vehicle that has featured in a film is a potential money-spinner and while there was only one Steve McQueen there are probably a few 1968 Mustang Fastbacks around. So beware forgeries.

Museums and Festivals

A nation so in love with the automobile will, inevitably, have more than its fair share of museums devoted to the machine. The man who pioneered mass production of the motor car has a museum in his name at Dearborn in Michigan, about 20 miles south of Detroit. The **Henry Ford Museum** boasts an extensive collection of vehicles - among them the limousine in which John F. Kennedy was shot in Dallas in November 1963. Attached to the museum is Greenfield Village that offers a potted American history.

The **Museum of Automobile History**, in Syracuse New York, achieves the seemingly impossible - a fascinating account of the automobile in America but without any cars. What it does have is an extensive collection of memorabilia related to the car - advertising, road signs, gas pumps and toys.

Indiana has an impressive collection of car museums. Studebaker was one of the car makers that failed to survive the 20th Century and went under in 1963. The company's home town, South Bend, contains the **Studebaker National Museum** and hosts a **classic car festival** every Labor Day, attracting upwards of 200,000 people. In Auburn there is the **Auburn-Cord-Duesenberg Museum** which houses many classic makes including a collection of models designed by Errett Cord – some of the most beautiful cars ever to grace America's roads in the 1920s and 1930s. Meanwhile Elkhart, Indiana has its own - if rather less glamorous - museum. **The RV Hall of Fame** tells the story of the Recreation Vehicle and its place in American folklore.

The full list of automobile museums and festivals is too extensive to cover here but you can access most of their websites through **www.carstuff.com**.

Where Can I Find Out More?

Car Makers

Audi: ☎ 1-800–FOR-AUDI (367-2834); www.audiusa.com.

BMW: www.bmwusa.com.

DaimlerChrysler: ☎ 1-800-992-1997 (International 1-248-512-7730); www.chrysler.com.

Daewoo: www.daewoous.com

Ford: Ford also manufactures Aston Martin, Jaguar, Lincoln, Mazda, Mercury and Volvo. ☎ 1-800-392-3673; www.ford.com.

General Motors: General Motors also manufactures Buick, Cadillac, Chevrolet, Oldsmobile, Opal, Pontiac, Saab and Vauxhall. ☎ Inside USA 1-800-462-8782. International 1-905-644-4112; www.gm.com.

Honda: www.honda.com.

Hyundai: ☎ 1-800-826-CARS (2277); www.hyundaiusa.com.

Infiniti: ☎1-800-662-6200; www.infiniti.com.

Isuzu: ☎1-800-255-6727; www.isuzu.com.

Kia: ☎1-800-333-4KIA (4542); www.kia.com.

Mazda: ☎1-800-222-5500 www.mazdausa.com.

Mercedes: ☎1-800-FOR-MERCEDES (367-6372); www.mbusa.com.

Mitsubishi: ☎1-714-898-0485; www.mitsubishicars.com.

Nissan: ☎1-800-NISSAN-1 (647-7261); www.nissandriven.com.

Saab: www.saabusa.com

Subaru: ☎1-800-SUBARU-3 (782-2783); www.subaru.com.

Suzuki: ☎1-877-MYSUZUKI (697-8985); www.suzukiauto.com.

Toyota: ☎1-800-GOTOYOTA (468-6968); www.toyota.com.

Volkswagen: ☎1-800-DRIVEVW (374-8389); www.vw.com.

Volvo: ☎1-800-458-1552; www.volvocars.com.

Environment

American Council for an Energy Efficient Economy (ACEEE): 1001 Connecticut Avenue NW, Suite 801, Washington DC 20036. (☎202-429-0063; www.aceee.org)

Environmental Protection Agency: 2565 Plymouth Road, Ann Arbor, Michigan 48105. (☎734-214-4333; www.epa.org)

See also; **www.thegreenscene.com** and **www.greenercars.com**

History

Ark-La-Tex Antique and Classic Vehicle Museum: 601 Spring Street, Shreveport, Louisiana (☎318-222-0227; www.softdisk.com).

Auburn-Cord-Duesenberg Museum: 1600 S. Wayne Street, Auburn, Indiana 46706 (☎219-925-1444; www.adcmuseum.org).

Henry Ford Museum: 20900 Oakwood Boulevard, Dearborn, Michigan 48124-4088 (☎1-800-835-5237; www.hfmgv.org).

Museum of Automobile History: 321 North Clinton Street, Syracuse, New York 13202 (☎315-478-CARS (2277); www.museumofautomobilehistory.com).

The Harrah Collection - National Automobile Museum: 10 Lake Street, Reno,Nevada 89501. (☎775-333-9300; www.automuseum.org).

Petersen Automotive Museum: 6060 Wilshire Boulevard, Los Angeles, California (☎213-930-CARS (2277); www.petersen.org).

RV Hall of Fame: 801 Benham Avenue, Elkhart, Indiana 46516 (☎1-800-378-8694; www.rv-mh-hall-of-fame.org).

Studebaker National Museum: 525 S. Main Street, South Bend, Indiana 46601 (☎219-235-9714; www.studebakermuseum.com).

Virginia Museum of Transportation: 303 Norfolk Avenue, Roanoke, Virginia 24016 (☎540-342-5670; www.vmt.org).

For links to hundreds of car museums in America; **www.car-stuff.com/carlinks/museums**

✦ Peculiar, Missouri, to Odd, West Virginia - 844 miles ✦

Driving Licences,

Licence Plates & Taxes

'The automobile is only a novelty - a fad.'
Horace Rackham, president of the Michigan Savings Bank, 1909.

(A few years later Rackham sold his $5,000 shareholding in the Ford Motor Company for more than $12 million).

The Driver's Licence

The driving licence is one of the most important personal documents in the United States. It confers more than just the right to operate a vehicle - it is also the universally accepted form of identification in America. Whether you are making a purchase with a credit card, writing a cheque or simply trying to prove you are old enough to buy alcohol, that piece of plastic with your picture on it is the proof of identification requested. So important is the driver's licence that it is the Department of Motor Vehicles (DMV) that issues alternative identification cards for non-drivers. They cost about $5 and are marked, 'This is not a driver's permit' and they are accepted as official identification in the same way as a licence.

- For Visitors

Foreign visitors to the United States are permitted to drive on their licences from their home countries. However, the police, car rental companies and anyone else who needs to verify a driver's identity will ask to see a driving licence written in English and carrying a passport-sized photograph. If your national licence does not meet these criteria, it is worth getting an International Driver's Permit - or IDP - before departure.

An IDP costs about $6 (£4) and is available through any motoring organisation such as the AA or the RAC (for Britain). The IDP is valid for one year, explains in several languages that you hold a valid driver's licence in your home country and it carries your licence number and your photograph.

The law requires you to carry your driver's licence whenever operating a vehicle. Some states may confiscate your car if you do not have your licence on you when stopped by the police.

- For Residents

Anyone planning to live or work in the United States for more than a year will have to get an American licence. Most states insist you apply for a driver's licence from that state within 10-30 days if you take up residence.

On application for a licence some states will require a written test to be taken and a vision test to be conducted but holders of foreign or out-of-state licences will probably not have to take a new driving test. The local Department of Motor Vehicles will be able to advise on the state rules.

Legal Driving Age

The legal age for driving in most states is 18 although it is as low as 15 in Mississippi and as high as 21 in Colorado and Georgia. Teenagers can, however, start lessons from as young as 14 in some states, but usually from 16, if they obtain a Junior Licence or a Learner's Permit which is equivalent to the British provisional licence. Certain restrictions may apply; for example, the owner of the licence may only be allowed to travel to and from schools. The applicant may also need a parent or guardian's consent before obtaining a junior licence or a learner's permit. The state's legal driving age will apply in precedence over an IDP or foreign national driving licence that a foreign visitor may have.

Unlike in some other countries, where a licence is valid until a driver is 70, American licences are valid for four to six years and drivers must renew them. The requirement to re-sit the written test varies from state to state so check with the local Department of Motor Vehicles. In some states drivers are allowed to renew licences without re-taking the exam, some insist on a new test and some allow drivers to renew their licences by post twice before taking the exam again.

Obtaining an American Driving Licence

• **1. Get a Social Security number**

It is possible to obtain a number even if you are not a resident in the United States. However, it will not entitle you to work. There are three categories of Social Security card:

- The **first** entitles the owner to work without restriction.
- The **second** is for foreign visitors admitted for temporary employment and reads, 'Valid for working with INS (Immigration and Naturalisation Service) authorisation.'
- The **third** is available to almost anyone who applies and it is clearly marked, 'Not valid for employment.' This is the one you will need. It will allow you to apply for a driver's licence *and* to open a bank account or apply for a credit card.

An application form will be available at the nearest Social Security office: valid identification in the form of original documentation (passport, birth certificate, insurance policy, etc.) and an American address - a friend's will do - for the Social Security card to be mailed to will be required.

- **2. The Written Exam**
Some states insist on a minimum number of hours in the classroom before you can take your test - somewhere between 30 and 36 hours.

The exam will cost $10-$15. Tests vary from state to state both in terms of difficulty and the number of questions. Applicants will be tested on:
- **Basic highway code - road signs etc.**
- **Safety – e.g. braking distances**
- **Understanding of the law – e.g. the state's drunk-driving limit.**

- **3. The Vision Test**
The fee for the written exam covers the vision test. The two tests are carried out at the same location by Department of Motor Vehicles staff. Once the written exam *and* the vision test have been passed, a learner's permit is issued and it is time to get behind the wheel. Glasses and contact lenses are permitted.

- **4. Lessons**
Learner drivers should expect to spend between 15 and 20 hours behind the wheel. Prices for lessons start at around $230 for a full course of 30 hours of theoretical and 20 hours of practical tuition. Driving schools are listed in the Yellow Pages.

Insurance for Lessons.
Some insurance companies will only offer cover to car owners. In many states, however, you are only allowed to buy a car if you have a licence. Fortunately, the motor insurance industry is waking up to this anomaly and now offers 'non-owned' policies that cover a driver but not a particular car.

- **5. The Test**
Arrive for your test with your Learner's Permit, proof of identification and proof that you are insured to drive the car. You must also bring a qualified driver with you to drive you home if you fail.

A pass will be achieved by not falling below a certain mark on a scorecard set by the state DMV. The examiner will deduct points for bad driving in any area of the scorecard, weighting the deduction according to the seriousness of the error. Hence, cautious drivers with no particularly outstanding faults will be the ones who can blithely complete the test, snatch the pass certificate from their examiner's hand and head straight into the DMV office to have their mugshot taken for their American licence.

Licence Plates & Taxes

Although states get a grant from central government every year, road maintenance is predominantly left to the individual states. So there is no federal road tax but there are a number of state and local taxes and fees for keeping a vehicle on the road.

The **registration fee applies to the licence plates,** or 'tags' as they are known in America and varies from $10 to $50 a year depending on the state. Registration has to be paid annually, either on the owner's birthday or on a date assigned to the first letter of the family name. Payment is indicated by a sticker attached to the tag on the rear of the vehicle that shows the expiry date. Carrying 'dead' or out of date plates will attract a fine and there will also be penalties for late renewal.

Vehicles must be registered in the state in which their owners live so people are given up to 60 days to register after they take up residence. If an owner is planning a prolonged stay in a state, say a month to three months, then the vehicle may have to be registered temporarily on a visitor's permit.

In some states the licence plates belong to the owner rather than the car so he or she may keep them when the vehicle is sold. This is certainly the case when the car carries personalised or 'vanity' plates. Check with the local Department of Motor Vehicles for state regulations; a new owner may have to apply for new tags for the car.

When you get your annual renewal notice the registration fee will be itemised and made up of the following: registration, licence, weight, special plate (optional), county/district and owner responsibility fee. The Licence Fee part of the registration may be deducted from income tax - check with your local Internal Revenue Service office.

Smog and Safety Checks

Annual Safety Check

Twenty-five states insist on an annual safety check for vehicles. They are Alaska, Arkansas, Delaware, Hawaii, Louisiana, Maine, Massachusetts, Mississippi, Missouri, New Hampshire, New Jersey, New York, North Carolina, Oklahoma, Pennsylvania, Rhode Island, South Carolina, Texas, Utah, Vermont, Virginia, West Virginia and the District of Columbia. Test fees vary from $15 to $40.

The parts of the car which must be checked every year will vary from state to state but are likely to include the lights, brakes, wipers, horn, tyres, chassis, body and seat belts. Local Departments of Motor Vehicles will explain their state's requirements.

In some states the sale of a car depends on an annual safety check and transfer of ownership will not be complete until the test has been passed. The buyer will have the right to treat the transaction as void and seek reimbursement.

If a car does fail its safety check the owner is given some time to get it fixed or take it off the road.

Emissions or Smog Tests

As with safety tests the rules for emissions or smog tests vary across America but California sets the toughest standards. A car that passes California's emissions test will probably pass in any other state. A car must pass a test the first time it is registered and on every change of ownership although, generally, older cars do not have to meet the same standards as new vehicles. The fee is between $10 and $20.

A smog test must be carried out at a Department of Motor Vehicles approved garage and a copy of the pass certificate must be mailed to the local DMV. Cars that pass are issued with a sticker that must be displayed on the windshield or the licence plate. If the car fails, the DMV will issue a temporary registration with a date by which the car must pass if it is to stay on the road.

Smog Impact Fee

Many states have introduced Smog Impact Fees for cars bought out of state and in some cases these could run in to hundreds of dollars. Check your state's rules before buying a car from out of state because you could be landed with an extra bill. *The Impact Fee will be in addition to the cost of getting the car through an emissions test.*

Personalised, ELP &
Special Interest Plates

Owners can apply for **personalised, or vanity plates** on payment of an additional fee of around $50 plus an annual renewal fee of $20 to $40. The plates usually have space for around seven characters but must meet local DMV guidelines; they must not be offensive, in bad taste or misleading (for example, 'POL1CE' would be unacceptable) and they must not already be in use. The Department of Motor Vehicles will have a register of personalised plates that are already in use. Application forms are available from the DMV office.

Vehicle owners can also help local charities by buying **Environmental or Special Interest Plates.** These cost more than standard plates but a portion of the fee goes to local groups. In California, for example, the $41 purchase fee and $25 a year renewal fee for an Environmental Licence Plate, or ELP, helps organisations working for the environment.

Other Californian organisations which could benefit from the sale of Special Interest Plates include the California Arts Council, the Coastal Commission (which works for the protection of whales), University of California at Los Angeles (UCLA), Child Health and Safety Fund, Lake Tahoe Conservancy, Olympic Training Centre Fund and Yosemite National Park Restoration Projects.

It is also possible for members of certain organisations to buy Special Interest Plates (upon proof of eligibility) - for example, Californian Fire Fighters. Each of these plates costs between $20 and $50 and carries a design representing the organisation the fee is helping. Each state's Department of Motor Vehicles will advise on the list of Special Interest Plates that are available.

Disabled Drivers

Drivers may be eligible for either temporary or permanent disabled person plates and parking placards. Temporary plates and placards are valid for six months and permanent ones have to be renewed every two years (for example, on June 30th in every odd-numbered year in California). Foreign visitors will have to make a new application to obtain disabled plates and parking placards in the United States.

A doctor's certificate is needed for the initial issue of the plate and will be needed again on renewal of a temporary registration. No new certificate is required for the renewal of a permanent plate or parking placard - once the records have been verified they will be renewed automatically every two years.

Disabled person plates carry a white pictogram of a person in a wheelchair on a blue background. When parking, space should be left around vehicles carrying such a pictogram to allow for wheelchair access.

Again, individual DMVs will explain which conditions are eligible for disabled plates and parking placards and the application procedures. Abuse of the system carries fines of anything between $250 and $1,000.

Where Can I Find Out More?

The Insurance Institute for Highway Safety: 1005 North Glebe Road, Arlington, Virginia 22201 (☎ 1-703-247-1600: www.hwysafety.org)

The Insurance Information Institute: 110 William Street, New York City, New York 10038. (☎ 1-800-221-4954; www.iii.org)

The Centre for Auto Safety: The Motorist Safety Information Bureau, 2007 Woodland Way, Deerfield Beach, Florida 33442-1219. (☎ 1-954-428-MSIB (6742); www.autosafety.org)

American Association of Retired Persons: 601 E St., NW, Washington DC 20049. (☎1-800-424-3410; www.aarp.org)**www.iDMV.com**. This website will take you to the sites for the Departments or Divisions of Motor Vehicles for all 50 states

Zero, Mississippi, to
One Horse Store, Arkansas -
Two Egg, Florida, to
Three Trees, South Carolina, to
Fourway, North Carolina, to
Figure Five, Arkansas, to
Six Lakes, Michigan, to
Seven Rivers, New Mexico, to
Number Eight, Missouri, to
Number Nine, Missouri, to
Tenville, Indiana...

...and on through Camp Twelve, Oregon, to

Sixteen Springs, New Mexico, to
Seventeen, Ohio, to
Nineteen, Kentucky, to
Twentynine Palms, California, to
Thirty, Indiana
Forty Fort, Pennsylvania, to
Fifty-Six, Arkansas, to
Eighty Four, Pennsylvania, to
Eighty Eight, Kentucky, to
Ninety One, Oregon, to
Ninety Six, South Carolina, to
Old Hundred, North Carolina, to
Thousand Oaks, California...
...and right up to Million, Kentucky

...a few thousand miles!

Renting

'Some say a front-engined car; some say a rear-engined car. I say a ***rented*** *car. Nothing handles better than a rented car. You can go faster, turn corners sharper and at a...higher rate of speed ... You can also park without looking, and can use the trunk as an ice chest.'*
P.J. O'Rourke, Republican Party Reptile, Picador, 1987.

About Renting

Car rental is God's way of telling tourists that they don't have to use a bus. Why spend 36 hours on a cramped bus, with a fellow traveller who has some serious personal hygiene issues, breathing in the aroma of a broken chemical toilet as the driver stops at every lamp post between Chicago and Anaheim?

Renting From Outside the US

Car Hire

Although it is *extremely easy* to hire a car in the US, it *may* simplify matters to organise it from your home country. You can go through either the main multi-nationals (Hertz, Budget, etc.) or through car hire brokers who shop around for you. The competition is cut-throat and several promise to undercut any deal you come across. Remember when comparing prices that all-inclusive deals will appear much more expensive than basic ones, but by the time the various insurance top-ups are added, may turn out to be cheaper (see rest of this chapter). The very cheapest inclusive rate will start at $35 a day in Florida and increase in California and again in New York. Often there is a stiff high season surcharge of $30-$45 per week plus a further $7.5 a day. All-inclusive deals usually include all the relevant insurance for foreign visitors but it is best to check.

Here are the main car hire firms with their UK booking numbers, although their equivalents will be just as easy to find in the telephone directories or using the web search engines of other countries. You can also find out about car hire and place a reservation on more general websites, for example on www.travelocity.com or www.expedia.com:

- **Hertz** - 08705-906090. www.hertz.co.uk
- **Avis** - 08705-900500. www.avisworld.com
- **Budget** - 0800-181181. www.budget.com
- **Dollar** 0800-252897. www.dollar.co.uk or www.dollar.com
- **Thrifty** - 08705-168238
- **Alamo** - 08705-994000. www.goalamo.com

The main *car hire brokers* can sometimes do better than any of the above:

- **Holiday Autos** - 08705-300400 or 08704-000000
- **Pelican** 8-10 Trafford Road, Alderley edge, Cheshire SK9 7NT (01625 586666). Also have a brochure on motor homes.
- **Hire for Lower,** 25 Saville Row, London W1X 1AA (0207-4911111. Guarantee the lowest prices.
- **Suncars** - 08705-005566. www.suncars.com
- **Park & Go** - 01904-652400. www.parkandgo.co.uk
- **Premier Car Hire**, Short House, Riverway, Harlow, Essex CM20 2DW (01279-641040; www.premiercarhire.co.uk)

Van Hire

Two specialists in motor home or RV rental (which usually cost in the neighbourhood of $150 a day) apart from Pelican listed above are:

- **Hemmingways**, 56 Middle St, Brockham, Surrey RH3 7HW (01737-842735.www.hemmingways.co.uk). Has brochures
- **Motorhome Holidays**, Oak House, Cliff End, Pett Level, East Sussex TN35 4EF (01424 814100). One of the UK agents for Cruise America

Motorcycle Hire: see Hemmingways just above.

Finding The Best Deal

The rented car may cost more than other modes of transport, like the bus or the train, but it puts you in control. There are hundreds of rental agencies to choose from so remember two things:

They're all desperate for *your* business…so be choosy and haggle.

   A little preparation goes a long way and helps you detect the flannel and the flim-flam. Agents are trained for the hard sell and sometimes it pays to be a hard customer to sell to. From $20 a day to $2,000 a day, from compacts to convertibles, from vans to V8s and from Lambrettas to Lamborghinis - it is possible to find the right agency with the right set of wheels to make a road trip memorable.

When renting a car in the United States, remember this checklist:

- ☞ **Plan ahead** - rates will be cheaper if a car is **booked early**
- ☞ **Take time to find out who is offering the best deal** but once a bargain is found, go for it; offers change and might not be available next week
- ☞ **Check your own holiday insurance** to see if you need to take out any of the options being offered by the agency and be absolutely clear what you are covered for
- ☞ **Choose the right vehicle for the type of journey** you will be taking and the number of people and the amount of luggage you will be carrying

Car rental is big business in the United States with operators to satisfy every budget from the big companies like Hertz and Alamo to the economy end of the market like Thrifty or Rent-A-Wreck. No one company is consistently cheaper or better than any other; the cheapest rental firm may vary from week to week as new packages and deals are announced and competitors try to match them.

The key to a good deal is to **shop around** - there will be a full list of local rental agents in the Yellow Pages. Rates often vary by as much as 50% across companies in the same location and by as much as 100% at the popular tourist destinations like Florida or Las Vegas.

Beware, though, of ads that offer cars 'from as little as $X a day.' Those prices are often the stripped-down deals that just about let you drive the car round the block. The rate might also only apply to a minimum rental period. By the time all the added extras and the 'options' are included the original price could treble.

⌁Surfing the Prices⌁

⌁ You can get a snapshot of airport rental rates from **BreezeNet** (www.bnm.com) which offers a sample of prices from a number of companies, allowing you to compare the best deals. The rates shown are the rental-only prices and don't include additional charges like airport fees, sales taxes or other options. The site does warn that prices change quickly so the rate you are quoted when you contact the agent may differ from the one you have seen on BreezeNet. It does, at least, give you an idea of prevailing prices. Try also www.rentalcarguide.com.⌁

The Rental Companies

The bigger operators, like Alamo, Hertz or Dollar can be found at nearly all the airports and major downtown locations. They are high profile and easy to find. At the budget end of the market are Rent-A-Wreck and Thrifty but they are not as downmarket as they sound; their cars are only about four years old, not the rusting bangers the names imply. Despite its name, Rent-A-Wreck *does* also rent out new vehicles. *One advantage* the bargain basement companies have over the larger operators is that they can often be *found in smaller locations* (🖐) where choice is limited. One *disadvantage* is that the limited free mileage the small agents offer, coupled with the age of the cars (although they are thoroughly serviced and mechanically sound) makes them *less suitable for longer journeys* (🖐).

The Cars

Rental cars are categorised according to body size and not engine capacity. You need to weigh up what sort of driving you are going to be doing. A Geo Metro, equivalent to a Vauxhall Corsa, might be the ideal runabout for pottering around

Boston but it will not be the best car when there are five people crammed into it in Death Valley in the middle of July. Similarly, a Chrysler LHS, equivalent to a Mercedes 3.5 litre, may be the car of choice for cruising along the Interstates but see what consumption you get out of it in New York during the Friday night gridlock.

These are the most common types of car on offer from the major auto rental agencies. These companies also offer other models in the same range:

	Alamo	Dollar	Hertz	Rent-A-Wreck
Economy (Equivalent to: Vauxhall Corsa or Ford Ka)	Chevrolet Metro	Hyundai Accent	Ford Focus	
Compact (Vauxhall Astra or VW Golf)	Chevrolet Cavalier	Chrysler Neon	VW Golf	Dodge Neon. Ford Escort
Intermediate (Vauxhall Cavalier)	Pontiac Grand Am	Dodge Stratus	Chevrolet Cavalier Ford Contour	Nissan Altima. Toyota Corolla
Full-Size (Vauxhall Carlton)	Chevrolet Malibu	Dodge Intrepid	Chevrolet Monte Carlo Ford Taurus.	Pontiac Grand Prix. Toyota Camry
Premium (Vauxhall Omega)	Buick Le Sabre	Chrysler Concorde		
Luxury (Mercedes 3.5 litre)	Cadillac Sedan de Ville Buick Park Avenue	Chrysler LHS	Lincoln Town Car	Cadillac Sedan de Ville Lincoln Town Car
Convertible (BMW Series 3)	Chevrolet Cavalier	Chrysler Sebring	Ford Mustang	

Age Limits for Renting

The age limits applied by auto rental firms are slightly different from the legal driving age. Most companies will not rent to anyone younger than 21 and they will charge a supplement for drivers aged between 21 and 25 (sometimes as much as $20 a day) because, of course, we all become the perfect models of safe driving on our 25th birthdays. If you are in the twilight of your driving career you will not be much better off with most companies refusing to rent cars to anyone over 71 years old.

Driving Licences

Most rental companies will accept a valid national driver's licence and will only require an International Driver's Permit (IDP) if the national licence is not written in English. It is worth investing the £4 for an IDP, anyway, just in case a rental company representative or a police officer is unfamiliar with a particular type of licence and needs extra proof that an individual is qualified to drive a car.

What is A Rental Agreement?

When you reserve a car you are actually reserving the rental rate, not the car, so the agent will not be able to guarantee you a specific make and certainly not a specific colour. Companies may offer a number of models within a category and you will be allocated whatever is available when you collect the car.

More Than You Bargained For

The competitive American market has led to a highly developed sense of customer service. As Lisa Becker found out, this can work in your favour when an agent over-books its more popular models:

'A group of us clubbed together at the Fort Mason hostel, in San Francisco, and decided to rent a car to visit Yosemite National Park. Five of us headed downtown on the Wednesday afternoon to book a car for the weekend. We decided on a mid-size Toyota, signed all the paperwork there and then and left. When we returned on the Friday to pick up the car we were told that the company had over-booked and all the mid-size cars were out. So they offered us a Lincoln Town Car – a huge American saloon, like one of the top-of-the range Mercedes. There was more than enough room for five backpackers and their rucksacks. We looked like backpackers, too, but the rental company wasn't bothered - a deal's a deal. So we spent four days touring Yosemite, Sequoia and Big Sur in this plush car. In fact we found the delivery docket in the glove compartment - the Lincoln was only three weeks old. Driving out of San Francisco was a bit hairy - trying to steer this huge shiny car through unfamiliar streets. But once we got used to it, it was great.'

What You Get For Your Money

Taking as an example renting a mid-size Pontiac Grand Am, with two drivers over 25 years old plus a child under 2 years old and driving from Los Angeles Airport to San Francisco over two days.

Here is what a traveller would normally expect for a basic rental-only price:

- A car with automatic transmission, radio, air-con and power steering
- Unlimited mileage
- Limited third-party insurance
- A free map!

Here is what the customer will have to pay extra for:

- $ Collision Damage Waiver ($10-$17 per day)
- $ Loss Damage Waiver (include this with Collision Damage Waiver)
- $ Supplementary Liability Insurance ($12 per day)
- $ Personal Injury Protection ($6 per day)
- $ Underinsured Motorist Protection ($6 per day)
- $ Additional Drivers ($6 per driver per day)
- $ Child Safety Seats($3.50-$5 per day)
- $ Drop-off Fees ($50-$500 per day)
- $ Airport/Handling Fees (various)
- $ Local Taxes (various)

The added extras can soon eat in to your budget but there are ways to bring the cost down. All the major rental companies offer 'all-inclusive packages', which include Collision Damage coverage and Supplementary Liability. But even these deals could exclude things like additional drivers, local taxes and a tank of gas so ask the rental company to explain what exactly all-inclusive means.

OK to sign you up for CDW, SLI, PIP, LDW as well as giving you the UMP?

As soon as you say you want to rent a car the salesman seems to stop speaking English and he's asking you whether you want CDW, SLI, PIP, LDW as well as giving you the UMP. That attractive offer got you through the door and that's where the rental company wants you. Now it's time to deal. Do you need all those extras though? What do they mean?

"Hey, Big Spender ... !"

For travellers with a fistful of dollars or a tenuous grip on reality (or both) there are rental companies offering something a little more exotic than the standard economy cars, saloons or people carriers. There is top-of-the-range and then there is beyond-most-pockets. A couple of companies specialise in expensive, classic or unusual vehicles.

Las Vegas-based Dream Cars will rent you a 1959 Cadillac Convertible if you want to return to the days of the big gas-guzzlers when the environment could go hang. If you are looking for real nostalgia, Dream Cars also rents a 1932 Ford - the kind seen in Chicago gangster films. How about an armoured personnel carrier - a Hummer? Dream Cars also offer sports cars.

Rent-A-Vette, also based in Vegas, specialises in exotic sports cars. (Vette is an abbreviation of Corvette - a classic American sports car). They will rent you a Porsche Boxster for $300 a day or a Ferrari 348 Targa for $449 a day. If you have just won the lottery you can rent a Lamborghini Diablo VT Roadster (top speed 200mph, 0-60 in 4 seconds) for $2000 a day. There is no free mileage and you will be charged $2 for every mile you drive.

All of these prices are for rental-only - the various insurances and options will vapourise what is left of your pocket after the initial fee has burned a hole in it. If you want to save some money (although if you can afford to rent a Lamborghini money is obviously no object), Dream Cars do half-day deals. You can rent a Ferrari Testarossa for five hours for $450. The Lamborghini Diablo will cost you $900 for five hours.

Insurance

Not all states require rental companies to provide basic Third Party cover on their vehicles so **always ask what insurance is provided.**

The figures quoted assume you buy all the elements separately. But the rate offered by the rental company may include the basic rental of the car, limited Third Party Liability and Collision Damage Waiver. In addition, you might not need Personal Injury Protection because it may already be provided by your own holiday insurance. Of all the other covers offered, customers should seriously consider Supplementary Liability Insurance to bump up their Third Party Cover.

Many rental companies will not accept insurance coverage provided by another company. Dollar, for example, says in its literature - 'Dollar does not accept or recognise any substitute to the LDW/SLI other than the LDW/SLI product provided by Dollar' (Source; Dollar Rent A Car USA Tariff 2001).

Rental agents will offer a range of coverage to their cutomers:

Collision (or Crash) Damage Waiver - CDW. This offers peace of mind and rental company staff will push this option heavily. Customers who take out CDW do not have to pay for any collision damage to the car - even if it is their fault. Strictly speaking, CDW is optional but rental agents will try to convince customers that it is the answer to all their prayers and anyone who does not take it is condemned to burn in Hell for eternity - or words to that effect.

Travellers who choose to decline this 'option' could be asked to pay a large deposit up front and to provide evidence of credit worthiness including a credit card with a limit of at least $1,500. In some states, like New York, CDWs are illegal so the rental companies will charge an excess - something like $200.

CDWs can be very expensive, sometimes putting as much as £25 a day on the cost. So check your own holiday insurance first to see whether you are covered for damage to vehicles you drive. Check, also, with your credit card company, which may also cover you.

Loss Damage Waiver - LDW. Collision Damage Waiver should not be mistaken for Loss Damage Waiver. **These are not the same.**
Be specific when discussing your coverage with the agent and ask if you are covered for Collision Damage and Loss Damage.

Collision Damage cover will *only* cover collision damage, whereas Loss Damage will cover for collisions *and* other types of damage - for example, windshield or tyre damage or vandalism. So LDW offers wider protection.

It is up to you to ensure the car is kept locked and secure because you could be liable if any loss or damage was proved to be down to carelessness. If the rental company has to send the car away for repairs it may continue to charge you while it is out of action. A Collision or Loss Damage Waiver will be void if you drive on unpaved roads and it does *not* give you third party coverage. So while you may avoid the bill for your rental car, you might still be stung for the cost of repairs to the vehicle you hit.
Approximate additional cost of combined CDW/LDW - $17 a day.

Supplementary Liability Insurance - SLI. Also known as Extended Protection Insurance, or EPI. Rental companies need only provide a bare minimum of third party coverage and in some states, like Florida, that could be as little as $20,000 which will not go far if you write off someone else's car and put them and their passengers in hospital. Supplementary Liability Insurance can take Third Party coverage up to $1 million. Again, check if your own holiday insurance covers you. Taking out SLI is recommended for peace of mind.
Approximate additional cost of SLI - $12 a day.

Personal Injury Protection - PIP. This used to be called Personal Accident Insurance. In about half the states you will have to sue the person responsible for your injuries to get your money. Other states have adopted a no-fault insurance law; in other words you can claim from your insurance company without having to prove the other person was at fault. That's where Personal Injury Protection comes in.

PIP covers hospital or medical expenses, loss of income, the provision of services arising from your injuries - for example, home care - and funeral expenses. Loss of income and the provision of services will be payable for a period of up to three years. You should be covered for personal injury on your holiday insurance but if you buy the coverage from the rental company…
Approximate additional cost of PIP - $6 a day.

Underinsured (or Uninsured) Motorist Protection - UMP. The penalties for driving without insurance in some parts of America are pathetic - sometimes only a couple of hundred dollars, so there is little incentive for drivers to take out any cover. Even then they might only get found out when they have an accident so they take a risk in the knowledge that even if they do get caught they will not be out of pocket too much. UMP is useful protection, with coverage up to $1 million, if you are injured by an uninsured driver. Check whether you are covered in other policies. **Approximate additional cost of UMP - $6 a day.**

Other Charges

On top of those charges there a few other costs to take into account:

Drop-off Fees. You might not want to return the car to the same office where you picked it up. Most rental companies will charge a drop-off fee and this could range from $50 up to $500 if you are leaving the car on the other side of the country.

Additional Drivers. Most rental companies will charge in the region of $6 a day per additional driver. (Around $20 a day for drivers under 25).

Child Safety Seats. These are compulsory in all states for children under 4 or weighing under 40lbs. The average cost is between $3.50 and $5 a day with a $50 deposit.

Local Taxes. These vary from state to state and even from city to city. Sales Tax is charged on the retail rental value. For example, in Los Angeles the Sales Tax is currently 8.25%.

There is also a **Rental Licence Tax** of between 71 cents and $1.75 a day, depending on the size of the car. In **Nevada** Sales Tax is 7% and then there is a **Vehicle Tax** of 6%. **San Francisco has a City Tax** of $2 a day if you pick up your car from a city centre office rather than the airport. There may also be **Airport or Handling Fees** to pay which could be in the region of 10%.

Payment

Rental companies usually ask for payment by credit card with all the charges being deducted on the return of the car. The rental company will 'block off' the amount you are due to pay from your card. In other words, although the money is not deducted from your account your credit on the card is reduced by the amount to be debited. That could cause problems when you want to use your card to pay for hotels, and so on, if you are already close to your credit limit. The company will also deduct other charges from a card - parking and speeding fines, damage not covered on insurance.

Credit Card Crisis

Few people realise it but when details of a credit card are put down on a standard car rental contract, any changes to the amount billed have effectively been authorised. This means that if there are any errors by the rental company you may end up footing the bill.

Maggie Drummond was recently reported as renting a car in New York and dropping it off a week later in Boston. She must have been horrified when her credit card was later charged for about $15,000 for the price of the unreturned car. Apparently, there had been a breakdown in communications and the Boston car rental branch had not informed the New York branch of the car's safe return.

The moral of this story is that one should ensure that slips with card details taken for security should be returned when a hire car is returned. Also, when a drop-off is made the driver should ideally phone the branch where the pick-up was made to ensure that they are aware of the car's safe return.

Most operators will accept payment from a debit or bank card when you bring the vehicle back but they will not accept them to book the car in the first place. If you do not want to use a credit card you could be asked for a large cash deposit, which could exceed the cost of renting the car, and you might even be asked to fill in a detailed and probing questionnaire which will be verified.

If you want to pay with cash you will have to 'cash qualify' - and even then only if the company allows it. This involves a thorough check into your financial reliability and can take anything up to 30 days, so it is not usually worth the effort.

Ways to Save Money

Read the rental agreement before you sign anything and be clear about your own liability and what you will be charged for.

Big Brother

Big Brother could be watching you. Modern technology enables some rental companies to keep track of their cars, even when they are out there in the wilderness as James Turner found out to his cost. He returned a mini-van to a rental company in New Haven, Connecticut, only to be presented with a $450 surcharge. Unknown to James the vehicle was fitted with a Global Positioning System that transmitted information, via satellite, back to the agent. The GPS told the agent that James had clocked over 90mph on three separate occasions incurring a surcharge of $150 per offence - even though he was not caught by the police. When he challenged the charge the agent pointed to the warning in the small print of the rental contract.

So if you are prone to exceeding the speed limit, ask if the car is fitted with GPS (put it as if you are interested in case the vehicle is stolen rather than because you want to burn some rubber) and check the small print for any surcharges.

Finding a good deal takes time and effort but it will be worth it. When the author wanted to rent a mid-sized car for eight days from Los Angeles Airport (LAX) one way to San Francisco these were the rates quoted over the phone by some of the leading companies:

Company	Basic Rental + Tax	Collision Damage Waiver	Drop-off Fee	Total
Alamo	$346.34	$9/day	Zero	$474.34
Avis	$224.10	$9/day	Zero	$305.10
Budget	$231.66	$9/day	Zero	$312.66
Dollar	$225.14	$9/day	Zero	$306.14
Thrifty	$299.89	$8.95/day	$250	$622.49

So on that particular day Avis just edged it over Dollar by $1.04 and rates were so fluid that there were variations in prices of up to 100%. On the day the car was picked up the agent offered the author a full-size category Pontiac Grand Prix for just $4 a day more than the smaller Grand Am.

Rental companies are constantly jostling for customers so at best you can just grab the best option when it comes up. Incidentally, the author was able to reserve each of those rates over the phone without any cost or commitment. So it is possible to pin a quote down at one company and take a better offer from another if it comes up. To reserve a rate you are simply allocated a reservation number that you give at the desk when you collect the car. If you do not show up, you will not be charged as no credit card details are taken.

There are other ways to bring down the cost:

$ Promotions. The advice from the American Society of Travel Agents is to ask your travel agent about any offers or deals which may not be advertised to the general public; if you don't ask, you don't get. But beware of 'blackout days' - days when offers, promotions or discounts do not apply.

$ Drop-Off Destinations. Some destinations are more popular for one-way rentals than others so cars may start gathering at depots, leaving others short of vehicles. Florida offices, for example, may find themselves with a glut of returned cars. You might be able to get a cheap deal if you are willing to return a vehicle to its original depot. This type of rental car is known as a 'dead-head'. Call agents and ask if they have any returns. If they are really desperate they might even offer to pay for fuel.

$ Book early. Rental companies calculate their rates on the basis of supply and demand and in the busiest locations prices can change hourly (usually increasing rapidly as the drive date approaches and the number of available cars decreases). Try and book your car at least a week in advance and rent it at a weekly, rather than a daily rate.

$ Shop around. It's a competitive market and you could find a wide variation in prices between companies. The American Society for Travel Agents adds a note of caution, though; beware of deals that offer a low rental rate and check the small print because the agreement's restrictions could outweigh the savings.

$ Late Returns. Rental companies operate on a 24-hour clock so if you take out a car for one day at 10 in the morning you will have to return it by 10 o'clock the following morning. You will probably be allowed a 59-minute grace period after which you will be charged by the hour - anything up to $20 an hour. So if you are likely to be more than four hours late you might as well **arrange to rent the car for another day** because it will work out cheaper.

If you fail to tell the rental company you will be late, you could be driving without insurance. Worse still, the agent might presume you have stolen the car. **So call the company.**

$ Free mileage. You will be offered free unlimited mileage for extended rental periods of a week or so but in other types of deal you may have to pay so much per mile you drive - say up to 30 cents a mile. These deals could actually save you money if you know roughly how far you will be driving, especially if you only need the car for a day. Rent-A-Wreck, for example, offers a typical free mileage of 50-100 miles a day. If you drive fewer miles than that you could save up to $15 a day. Say you agree to a deal giving you 150 free miles a day; the rental rate might be around $10 cheaper and you might only pay 25 cents a mile for every mile over the limit.

$ Rent longer. Generally the longer you rent the car, the cheaper the daily rate. There could be a wide variation in prices within the same company because of local conditions; phone around other offices within a reasonable travelling distance. If Washington DC is too expensive it is only a short train ride to Baltimore. It will also turn out cheaper if you rent a car for the longer period and bring it back earlier rather than renting it for a shorter period and paying for the extra days as you will be charged higher rates for those extra days.

Collecting and Returning Your Rented Car

⌷ Collecting Check List ⌷

⌷ **Check the car for interior and exterior damage** and point out any faults to the member of staff issuing the car. Have the member of staff describe the damage on the contract and include his/her name or staff number

⌷ Get a **spare key** if possible

⌷ If you have signed a limited mileage deal, **make a note of the car's mileage** before you leave and agree it with the company representative

⌷ If you are **not satisfied with the car, ask for another one**

⌷ If you are collecting the car from the airport it may be parked in a lot with hundreds of other rental vehicles, many of them might be an identical make and colour to your own. **Check that the licence plate number tallies with the one on the paperwork.** If you take the car which the key fits but it isn't the one you have signed for, you might not be covered on insurance

☞ **Set the seat and the mirrors** to positions that are comfortable for you

☞ **Find the controls** for the lights, wipers, indicators, cruise control, wing mirrors and radio. Figure out how to open the hood, trunk and petrol cap. Locate the horn and the controls for the de-misters and the air conditioning

☞ **Read the free map**

☞ **Make a note of the location of the rental depot;** a surprising number of drivers return to a city with no recollection of where they picked up the car

☞Returning Check List☞

☞ **Return the car with a full tank.** Rental companies will charge you to refill it themselves at a hefty per-gallon price – sometimes twice the normal price. Try to avoid gas stations near the rental depot - they sometimes cash in on drivers keen to avoid the rates charged by the hire companies

☞ **Check the trunk, the glove compartment** and any other compartments to make sure you haven't forgotten anything

Safety and Security

Rental cars carry no obvious markings or logos to show that they are rented to avoid advertising the fact that you are a tourist with a trunk full of luggage and a pocket full of cash.

Accidents

If you have an accident in the rental car you should make **three phone calls**, in this order:

☎ **The Police.** State laws vary on the need to call the police but if it is serious they need to be called. The number for all emergency services is **911**

☎ **The Rental Company.** Notify the agent as soon as possible and act on their instructions

☎ **The Insurance Company.** If you have not taken the rental company's Collision or Loss Damage Waiver you will need to notify your insurer or your credit card company that a claim will have to be made

You will also need to **get the following information**:

• **The name, address and telephone** number of the other driver
• **Drivers Licence number and insurance details** of the other driver
• **Licence plate numbers** and a description of the other vehicle(s)
• **Time, date and location** of the accident
• **Witnesses' contact details**
• **A copy of any police report**

If the damage is minor the company may tell you to keep the car until you are due to take it back. It is your responsibility, though, to make sure it is safe and legal to drive - be careful you don't get a ticket for a broken tail light. You will also need to allow extra time when you return the car to fill out an accident report so take this into account if you have a flight to catch. If the car is undriveable the agent may deny you a replacement or, if it does provide a new vehicle, it may refuse you permission to drive it and insist one of the other named drivers take over.

Breakdowns

If you break down there should be a telephone number for a recovery service on the dashboard. If you are on a major freeway or an Interstate a regular highway patrol or the state police will spot you eventually and stop. Raising the car's hood is recognised across the United States as a call for assistance but women should beware of doing this. Rental companies now also offer mobile phones - they only charge a small fee until it is actually used. As an added security measure, 911 is often already programmed in on speed dial.

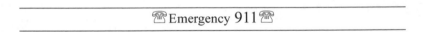

☎Emergency 911☎

In some states it is possible to contact the emergency services from mobile phones by dialling #77.

Losing the keys

The whole point of security systems on cars is to keep people out so if you lose the keys you will have problems getting back in. This is why you should ask for a spare set. Your car may not have originated from the office where you collected it so the agent may not have a spare key. The police will not break in if you lock the keys inside because of liability claims.

Some cars have a key code panel in the driver's door and the rental company may give you the code over the phone. Sometimes the manufacturers print the code on a sticker inside the trunk so if that is open you might be able to find it.

If you do have to call the agent, ask how much you will be charged if someone has to be sent out to help. Losing the keys or locking them inside the vehicle is likely to be seen as your fault so there is a good chance you will be charged. Check if your credit card offers a free locksmith service.

Remember that damage you cause to the car in trying to get back in is unlikely to be covered on any insurance you took out.

Old Boot in a Boot

A local newspaper in Minnesota reported the case of a 68-year-old woman who locked herself out of her car. She had the bright idea of climbing into the trunk and trying to kick down the passenger seats and crawling through. Unfortunately, the lid slammed shut, trapping her inside for four hours before her cries for help were heard.

Seatbelts

Seatbelts are compulsory in all states and children under 4 or weighing under 40lbs must travel in child safety seats.

Drugs and Booze

All insurance is invalidated if you drive under the influence of alcohol or drugs.

Special Needs

Disabled drivers are well catered for by rental agents. Companies should be able to provide hand controls and other equipment on request, although they will need advance notice to make any special arrangements. Many companies' fleets also include people carriers with low-floor wheelchair access and transfer seats.

Recreation Vehicles

The car is not the only way to see America - you could combine your transport and your accommodation in a Recreation Vehicle - or RV. Thousands of Americans sell their homes at retirement and plough their money into a Recreation Vehicle in which they tour their country. You can spot them on the roads, usually towing a car, or parked up in Florida's RV parks for the winter. It is as if there is a vast nomadic tribe of retired Americans roaming the country not on horseback or in wagon trains, but in diesel-engined behemoths.

RVs can be fun to rent but even the Recreation Vehicle Rental Association admits there is a downside as well as an upside to driving a motor home:

The Upside:

- You are **closer to nature** because you do not have to stay in hotels
- You get to sleep in beautiful campgrounds and national parks
- You never have to look for a bathroom
- You get to **meet other friendly people** who share your interests
- You can easily **pack the whole family** on a vacation
- **Freedom** to go where you please

The Downside:

☞ It's not always possible to **find a parking space** in an RV park (especially in Yellowstone)

☞ If you park where there is no power, the RV soon **heats up without a generator**

☞ If you do breakdown most **repair shops don't have the space** to work on a 36 foot RV

☞ **Repairs can take a long time,** especially if the garage has to send out for parts

☞ **Gas consumption** is 8-10 miles per gallon on the freeway. Ouch!

☞ You might need to **tow a small car** as a runabout

☞ It's so damn big!

Several companies specialise in renting motor homes so that you, too, can cause a tailback of traffic as you wind along a country road.

RVs range in length from 19 feet to 36 feet and they can accommodate up to five adults and three children. They come with power steering and power-assisted brakes (which you'll need when trying to drive or stop something that big), cruise control and automatic transmission. You can also expect to find air conditioning, a stove with an oven, a fridge, a freezer, a microwave, a water heater, a shower and a flushing lavatory. Some companies also throw in a colour television.

Unlike a car, a Recreation Vehicle is not something you can hop into and drive away immediately. You need time to familiarise yourself. Many agents will not allow you to pick up a motor home on the day of your arrival in the United States; an RV is too big a piece of machinery to take out on to the road while you are still jet-lagged. You may also be expected to attend a familiarisation session during which all the controls, equipment and handling characteristics will be explained. This will last about an hour and may also include a video.

The principles for renting a Recreation Vehicle are the same as for renting a car - shop around. The prices quoted will be for rental-only and you will have to budget for insurance coverage and other optional extras.

Kampgrounds of America - or KOA - runs hundreds of camp sites across America, Canada and Mexico. The organisation caters for holidaymakers who want to stay in tents, cabins, cottages or Recreation Vehicles. KOA also operates a Value Card that offers members a 10% discount on camping fees and a 15% discount on Budget car rentals

RVs can be fun to rent

$2,600 for Freedom

An RV may not be the most stylish mode of transport but it can open up America for you. Australian backpacker, Cam Smith, bought a 1974 Dodge Overlander for $2,600 in Los Angeles;

'It was a heap - a great big box-shaped body with all the aerodynamic qualities of a brick. Its sides were a kind of clapboard so it looked like a wooden shack on wheels. Inside the décor was a little piece of 1974 frozen in time; it had yellow and brown Paisley curtains, fawn leather seats and a thick green carpet with lemon flecks in it. In fact, when I visited Graceland I noticed that Elvis had the same sort of carpet in his living room, which he called the Jungle Room. So I named the RV the Jungle Room.

'It may have looked a bit rough but it took me all over America, down into Mexico and up into Canada. I had the scam to save money on campground fees; I made up a 'For Sale' sign and at night I would try to find an RV dealer's lot. I would park up among the other vehicles and put the sign on the windshield. As long as I was away before the staff arrived in the morning, no one was any the wiser. The Jungle Room had a stove and a fridge, cupboards and a dining table. The toilet was in the shower cubicle so you had to sit on the toilet while you had a shower. It was state-of-the-art for 1974 but a bit basic by today's standards. It was reliable though - the only problem I had was a leak in the power steering in Mexico, which was easy to fix.

I was sorry to let it go but I got $3,000 for it when I sold it back in LA.'

Age and Licences

The same age limits apply as for cars - the minimum age is 21. You can drive a motor home on a national licence, although an International Driver's Permit is also recommended.

Cost

There are more than 400 RV rental outlets across America with companies like El Monte and Cruise America the best known. Many campgrounds also now offer on-site rentals. You can expect to pay between $70 and $120 a day for a motor home and $50-$120 a day for a trailer (a caravan). Again, these are rental-only prices and there are those dreaded added extras to think of.

What you might get for your **basic price**:
- **The motor home** with all the facilities listed above
- **Basic liability insurance plus Collision Damage or Loss Damage Waiver.** You may have to pay the first $5000 in the event of accidental damage, theft and vandalism
- **500 free miles**
- **Reimbursement for accommodation and car rental** in the event of the RV breaking down
- **Kampground of America campground guide**
- **KOA Value Card**

What is not included - and will cost you extra:
$ **Deposit.** You could be asked for up to $500
$ **Free mileage**
$ **Food**
$ **Bedding**
$ **Cooking utensils**
$ **Generator**
$ **Campground fees**
$ **Propane gas** for cooking and heating. (You may be given the first bottle)

Additional Charges

The RV agent will offer a **Provisioning or Vehicle Departure Kit** which might include kitchen utensils, cookware and saucepans, broom, torch, can opener, bottle opener and a coffee percolator all for between $85 and $100 per vehicle.

It is also possible to buy a **Personal Kit** containing a sleeping bag, pillow, sheet and pillow case, a bath towel, laundry bag, cutlery set, plate, bowl and a cup at around $35 per person.

The larger Recreation Vehicles will need a **110-volt generator** to run the facilities. You can either pay in the region of $3 an hour or buy unlimited use for about $5 a day.

Many agents allow you to pre-purchase **1000 mile 'packs' of mileage**. Cruise America, for example, offers 1000 miles for about $266. Renting a Recreation Vehicle demands more advance route planning than renting a car to avoid pre-buying more miles than will be travelled. Otherwise RV customers could end up paying excess mileage charges on their return. Your rental agent or Kamp of America will be able to advise you.

Insurance and Taxes

Vacation Interruption Protection - VIP. The CDW or LDW offered in the basic price only gives you protection above an excess - you could still face a bill of up to $5000 for any damage to the vehicle. VIP can reduce your liability to $300. Taking out VIP will also reduce the amount of the deposit you will be asked to pay.
Approximate additional cost of VIP - $12 a day.
(But you can only take out VIP for a maximum of 35 days in some cases).

Vacation Interruption Protection Plus - VIPP. This reduces your liability to zero and provides Supplementary Liability Insurance of up to $1 million plus reimbursement for expenses in the event of a breakdown. VIPP also includes Personal Accident Coverage, Personal Property Coverage and Physical Damage Responsibility Reduction, or PDRR. PDRR reduces the renter to zero liability for accidental damage to the vehicle no matter who is at fault. PDRR is, however, void if the damage is caused by negligence.

Approximate additional cost of VIPP - $24 a day. (Up to 35 days).
Local Taxes. As with car rentals local Sales Taxes are not included in the rates and range from zero to 15%, according to state.

Insurance Restrictions

Make sure you know the height of the RV because your coverage might be limited or lost if you damage it by **hitting an overhead object.** Similarly, you could also be liable for **damage caused while reversing.** When you are backing up a 36 feet long motor home make sure you can see where you are going or someone is guiding you. Other restrictions on your cover might include **interior damage**, **damage to wheels and tyres**, **damage caused by overheating** or freezing the vehicle's systems or damage **caused off the highway**, such as unpaved roads, campgrounds, parking lots, service stations and garage forecourts.

Some companies also impose restrictions on where you can take the motor home. Death Valley, or other **desert areas**, might be off-limits in the summer months. **Logging areas** could be declared out of bounds and some agents do not allow their vehicles to be taken in to **New York City or Mexico**. If you are allowed to take your rented Recreation Vehicle in to Mexico you might have to take out Mexico Liability Insurance at about $12 a day. Rental companies may impose special restrictions on driving vehicles in **potentially hostile environments** such as Alaska, the Yukon and the Northwest Territories.

Saddam in a Motor Home

During the Gulf War, Iraqi television showed pictures of Saddam Hussein meeting his generals inside a motor home. American intelligence identified the vehicle as a Winnebago and for the remainder of the conflict US pilots blasted away at every hapless RV they spotted on Iraqi roads in the hope that Hussein might be inside.

Further Charges on Return of an RV

You could be presented with other charges, most of which are avoidable. **Late return** of the RV could cost you upwards of $25 an hour. It is your responsibility to **clean the interior** of the RV - if you do not, you could be charged up to $100.

One downside of living out of a Recreation Vehicle is that you are producing a lot of waste on board and all this goes in to the holding tank. This will have to be emptied regularly at designated dumping stations in campgrounds. Illegal dumping carries stiff penalties. If the rental company has to **empty your holding tank** it could charge you $100.

Drop-Off Fees. As with car rentals, drop-off fees depend on where you are returning the vehicle. For example, if you rent the RV in Florida and return it somewhere else within the same state it will cost you $50. Within California the drop-off is $150. From anywhere in America into California it is $500.

Motorcycles

For the truly adventurous the *only* way to see America is from the back of a Harley-Davidson. Check out Tom Cunliffe's excellent book, *Good Vibrations - coast to coast on a Harley*, for a taste of what biking across America is really like. Now anyone with a motorcycle licence can feel the sun on their face and the wind in their hair - helmets are not compulsory in some states.

For the truly adventurous the only way to see America is from the back of a Harley Davidson

Age of the Rider

Most rental agencies will not rent to anyone under 21. As regards the laws regarding legal riding age, many states seem to have a very relaxed view. You can hop on a 50cc moped at 10 in Arkansas or at 13 in New Mexico. For machines over 50cc the minimum age is 14 in Alabama and 15 in Florida. Some states require riders under the age of 18 to take rider education lessons.

Licences

You can ride a machine up to 125cc on a normal car licence. Unlike Britain you only need pass your initial test to be allowed to ride a powerful bike so you could graduate from a moped to a 750cc machine without any experience or special training. Moped riders are not required to take any test.

Crash Helmets

25 states insist that riders wear helmets, others only require riders aged under 18 or 19 wear them. A few states require helmets only to be carried and not necessarily worn. In Rhode Island only the passenger has to wear a crash helmet. The states' Departments of Motor Vehicles will be able to advise on local laws.

The laws are slightly more relaxed for moped riders - helmets are compulsory in around 20 states and 10 of those only require riders under 19 to wear them.

Other Laws

There are a few other legal considerations you need to be aware of when riding a motorbike in the United States.

- 🚲 If your bike has no windshield some states require you to wear goggles
- 🚲 You are required to ride with your low beam headlights on at all times in some states
- 🚲 You are not allowed to ride between lanes of traffic in all states
- 🚲 Some states do not permit riding two abreast

The Rental Companies

Several years ago four Harley-Davidson enthusiasts realised that people were looking for adventure on their holidays - travellers wanted to travel, not simply to arrive. So Chris McIntyre, Jeff Brown, Peter Wurmer and Robert Pitts set up Eagle Rider, an agency specialising in renting out Harleys. Now they operate a fleet of more than 500 motorbikes out of offices across the United States. Eagle Rider isn't the only motorbike rental agency in America but it is the largest.

The same rules apply as for cars and RVs - shop around; rates and offers change. It should be possible to find an agency to help you live out your fantasy of riding an Electra Glide or a Softail Classic across America. Rental prices begin at around $100 a day but comes down if you hire for a week.

When you make a reservation for a car or an RV you are likely to lose your deposit if you cancel the reservation. Deposits paid to Eagle Rider are similarly non-refundable but the company will give you a raincheck - allowing you to take up the confirmed reservation again within one year.

For the basic rental-only price you get:

- Unlimited mileage
- Basic liability insurance
- A helmet for rider and passenger
- Saddlebags
- Locks

Additional Costs

What is not included - and will cost you extra:

Damage Liability Waiver - DLW. This will cover you for damage caused by accident, collision, vandalism or theft. However, you will normally have to pay the first $1,000 for damage and $2,000 for theft.

Approximate additional cost of DLW - $14 a day.

Enhanced Coverage. You can bring the excess down to $500 for damage and $1,000 for theft by taking out Enhanced VIP Coverage.

Approximate additional cost of Enhanced Coverage - $20 a day.

Deposits. You will also be expected to pay a hefty deposit and if you do not take out coverage offered by the agent that could be **as high as $3,000**. It comes down to $2,000 with DLW and $1,000 with Enhanced Coverage.

Drop-Off Fees. If you are returning the bike to an office within the same state it will be in the region of $100. Between neighbouring states it goes up to $200 and beyond that the drop-off charge is $375 and upwards.

Late Returns. Up to **$25 an hour.**

Where Can I Find Out More?

Car Rental Agencies

Advantage; ☎ 1-800-777-5500; www.arac.com
Alamo; ☎ -800-354-2322; www.goalamo.com
Avis; ☎ 1-800-331-1212; www.avis.com
Budget;☎ 1-800-527-0700; www.budgetrentacar.
Dollar; ☎ 1-800-800-4000; www.dollarcar.com
Enterprise; ☎ 1-800-325-8007; www.pickenterprise
Hertz; ☎ 1-800-654-3131; www.hertz.com
National; ☎ 1-800-227-7368; www.nationalcar.com

Payless; ☎ 1-800-729-5377; www.paylesscar.com
Rent-A-Wreck;☎   1-800-421-7253;www.rent-a-wreck.com
Thrifty; ☎ 1-800-367-2277; www.thrifty.com
Value; ☎ 1-800-468-2583; www.valuecarrental.com
This website will direct you to a range of rental agencies;
www.travelsource.com

This company specialises in vans with wheelchair access:

Rainbow Wheels; ☎ 1-800-910-VANS (8267); www.rainbowwheels.com

Recreation Vehicle Rentals

Camper Tours; This a German-based website, but in English. It offers advice on booking campers and RVs around the world as well as the United States. ☎ 49-6196-940-877; www.campertour.com

Cruise America; ☎1-800-327-7799; www.cruiseamerica.com

El Monte; ☎ Inside United States 1-888-337-2214. Outside United States 562-483-4956; www.elmonte.com

Recreation Vehicle Rental Association; 3930 University Drive, Fairfax, Virginia 22030. ☎1-800-336-0355; www.rvra.org

Kampgrounds Of America; KOA, PO Box 31734, Billings, Montana 59107-1734. ☎406-248-7444; www.koa.com

RV Roadhelp is like a Triple A service for Recreation Vehicle drivers. Membership means all the other vehicles you own will also be covered - including motorbikes.
☎1-800-214-5135; www.rvroadhelp.com
This website covers RV rentals, sales, spares and repairs; **www.rvrentalnet.com.** ☎ 925-673-9016

Motorcycle Rentals

American Dream; ☎1-888-235-7190; www.americanryder.com

Budget; ☎1-888-736-8433; www.budgetharley.com

Eagle Rider; ☎1-800-501-8687; www.eaglerider.com

Texas Motorcycle Rentals; ☎210-805-0777; www.alamotorcycle.com

This website will direct you to all of the main motorcycle rental agencies in the United States: **www.motodirectory.com**

Exotic/Classic/Sports Cars and Motorcycle Rentals

Dream Cars; www.dreamcarrentals.com, ☎1-877-373-2601

Rent-A-Vette; www.rent-a-vette.com, ☎1-800-372-1981

Rental Tips and Advice

These sites offer information and advice on renting a range of vehicles - cars, RVs and motorcycles;
www.auto-rental.net
www.bnm.com
www.destinationusa.net

✦ Sunrise, Florida, to Sunset, California - 3,350 miles ✦

Buying

'Try novelties for salesman's bait,
For novelty wins everyone.'

Goethe, Faust Part 1.

Why Buy?

An American newspaper recently asked its readers which was the sleaziest way to earn a living. Selling cars came top, ahead of drug dealing. Certainly the American car salesman is in need of an image makeover - traditionally being portrayed as dishonest and manipulative and armed with a thousand ways to part the hapless customer from his cash. The truth may be different – it may not.

For many people buying a car in the United States can seem more than a little daunting. It is important for the customer to keep his goal in mind - to buy a safe, reliable vehicle at a reasonable price - and to filter out the hard sell.

Car Salesmen are not best Known for their sympathy

Deciding to Buy

First of all, decide whether buying is the right option for you. The major advantages and disadvantages are as follows:

The Advantages of Buying

☞ **Fewer rules.** You do not have to worry about all those rules and regulations imposed by rental companies and driveaway agents

☞ **Less cost.** There are no on-going daily rental charges to worry about

☞ **Freedom.** You can go where you want, when you want. There are no no-go areas, no deadlines to meet, and no bus timetables and routes to follow

☞ **Personal space.** You can be as messy as you like. If you want to smoke, light up, if you want to cover the floor in fast food packaging, feel free, get lucky in the back seat - it is *your* personal space to do with what you will

☞ **The American Dream.** By buying your own car you become a shareholder in the American Dream. There is something that connects you to the United States more directly than renting or delivering. You are almost an honorary American

The Disadvantages of Buying

☞ **A Dud Buy.** There is the danger that you will make a bad choice and car salesmen are not known for their sympathy when a dissatisfied customer comes back

☞ **Inflexibility.** Although the United States has some beautiful scenery, there are vast stretches that are utterly monotonous to drive through. Other forms of transport may allow you to hop between the good bits more quickly or at less cost

☞ **Red tape.** Once the ideal car has been chosen and the financing has been arranged, there is the bureaucracy to deal with; registration, insurance and taxes

☞ **Time.** Finding the right car and selling it can take up valuable travelling/ holiday time. Before sale, a car will have to pass the state's emissions tests before it can be sold and that can be a headache if it was bought in a part of the country where standards were lower

Buying a car could be a viable option, even if your stay in America will not be that long; it might be worth buying an old banger, or 'junker' as a runabout or for a road trip. That way the financial loss will not be so big when it is time to sell.

Buying A Used Car

Used, second-hand, pre-owned, previously cherished, pre-possessed, nearly new - salesmen will come up with any number of euphemisms to describe an old car.

The used car market in the United States is huge - about 41 million were sold in 2000 compared to 17 million new cars. The average price of a used car was $8,700 with an average price for a new car coming in at a shade under $22,000. Generally, used cars offer good value for money in America and you can pick up a decent one for a lot less than the average if you know where to look, what you are looking for and if you know how to negotiate.

Different Types of Car

Choosing Your Car

You are on the threshold of the American Dream, at the starting point of your Great American Road Trip and you do not want to be chained to a ton of useless metal rather than breezing down the highway without a care in the world: **the importance of choosing the right car cannot be stressed enough.** You will need to weigh up purchase cost, reliability, fuel consumption and repair costs. It is not always easy to strike a balance between these factors. For example, foreign imports, such as Toyotas, are cheap to buy on the second-hand market but finding spares can be expensive. Older V-8 cars are extremely reliable but drink fuel like there is no tomorrow.

A used car is obviously more likely to break down so **go for a popular make with dealers nationwide and easy access to spares**. That British Mini might have seemed a quirky buy at the time, but try getting spares in Minnesota. If you are on the backpacker circuit Beetles and VW Campers have a certain caché and are relatively easy to sell. The air-cooled engine of a Beetle is also well suited to hot weather which makes it particularly useful in the South West. **Be realistic.** Before you part with your cash, switch off your emotions and focus on the practicalities; you may have dreamt of driving across the United States in a 1966 Corvette, but is it actually feasible?

Ask yourself:
1. Can I afford it?
2. Is it the right car for the type of driving I will be doing?
3. What features do I want? Automatic or manual? Two-door or four-door?
4. How much trunk space?
5. What is the fuel consumption like?

Lemons

Whatever type of car you are looking for, this is the one type which should be avoided at all costs.

A lemon is a car with either a recurrent problem or a litany of faults, which means it has its own personal parking space at the repair shop. A lemon is trouble. How can you tell whether the second-hand car you are planning to buy is dodgy? You can **run a 'Lemon Check'** through the Internet.

Log on to www.carfax.com and for a small fee you can enter the vehicle's details to see if it has any skeletons in its cupboard - whether it is a salvage vehicle, whether there were any manufacturer recalls on that model and even if the mileage is suspicious. The information is updated every two months although there is no guarantee that the vehicle has been entered onto the site.

All states have strict Lemon Laws that offer strong protection for buyers of new cars. Dealers will be forced to offer a refund or a replacement if they fail to fix a recurrent problem. Many also extend that protection to the buyers of used cars and to those who have a leasing agreement. Each state's Better Business Bureau website will explain the local Lemon Law.

Essential reading for anyone planning to buy a used car in America is *The Lemon Book* by Ralph Nader and Clarence Ditlow, available from Amazon, price $17.50. This is an invaluable A to Z handbook with advice on how to avoid being ripped off and what to do if you do find yourself the less-than-proud owner of a lemon.

Another useful publication is the quarterly magazine, *The Lemon Times*, published by the Centre for Auto Safety. The magazine offers regular updates on safety issues such as recalls, defects, salvage vehicles sold as new and Lemon Laws. It costs $25 a year outside the United States and is available through www.autosafety.org.

Buying Used Cars from a Dealer

Anyone who is to enter into negotiations with a dealer for a used car should read the following sections which appear later in this chapter: *How Much Should I Pay, Beating The Dealer* and *Dealers' Tactics and Scams*. These relate to dealers of new car dealers but provide essential preparation for coping with any car dealers.

If you choose to buy a used car from a dealer, rather than a private seller, there are **five 'types'** of used car you might see for sale in addition to the straightforward second-hand models:

🚗 **Program cars.** These are cars given by manufacturers to their employees for company business. After all, Ford wants its staff to be seen driving Fords and Chrysler wants its workers in Chryslers. Once these cars clock up 10,000 miles they are sold to the company's own dealers at closed auctions and put on the sales lot as 'Program Cars'. These are popular with both dealers and customers; the dealer can make a big profit while still selling it at a low price. The customer gets a well-maintained car at a bargain price. The only downside is that you do not know how much the dealer paid for it at auction so you are negotiating in the dark when trying to hammer out a price.

🚗 **Rental cars.** Buying an ex-rental car which has been flogged from Connecticut to California and back again by hundreds of tourists might not seem the most sensible purchase. However, not all rental cars have been abused - most of them are well maintained. They are also dirt cheap because of their high mileage and because the rental companies get a good deal from the manufacturers in the first place. A typical ex-rental car might be a year old with 15-25,000 miles on the clock. Prices from dealers specialising in ex-rentals are usually very competitive with very little room for haggling but the bonus is that the manufacturer's warranty is still valid.

🚗**Salvage Titles.** This means the car has, at some stage, been an insurance write-off. Any garage or dealer which buys an insurance write-off has, by law, to give it a 'salvage title' to alert any future buyers as to its history and status. However, problems may occur when a salvage car is sold out of state because it is possible to 'lose' the salvage title when the vehicle is re-registered and issued with new plates. As a rule of thumb, salvage titles are generally offered at a 50% discount. So if a deal seems too good to be true, it probably is. Even if you do knowingly buy a salvage vehicle you might have trouble finding someone else willing to take a risk when you want to sell it. In terms of performance, the biggest dangers with these types of vehicles are poor wheel alignment and a bent frame. A bent frame will cause uneven tyre wear and poor handling.

Generally, the only type of salvage car worth buying is where the car has been stolen, the insurance company has paid out and then the vehicle has turned up virtually undamaged. You could be lucky and save up to $5,000 on this type of car.

Second-hand car dealers also sell these *peace-of-mind* types of car:

🚗**A Certified Used Car.** More and more dealers are now offering certified used cars for sale. These have undergone a thorough inspection and come with a manufacturer's warranty valid for anything up to two years. You will, though, pay for your peace of mind – a certified used car will to cost up to $1,000 more than an uncertified equivalent.

🚗**Used cars still under warranty.** New cars come with a three-year/36,000 miles manufacturer's warranty. So if you buy one less than three years old or with less than 36,000 miles on the clock the manufacturer will fix it for free.

Where Do I Find My Car?

🚗**Publications.** There is a host of magazines available for people looking to buy a used car. The local Saturday and Sunday newspapers also carry extensive supplements listing cars for sale.

🚗**The Internet** is another good source - try **AutoTrader.com** or **Classifieds2000.com**, both of which carry ads for cars that might only be a few blocks away. The Internet has the advantage of enabling you to refine your search by entering the make, model, age and price range of the car you are looking for.

A word of warning about searching for used cars on the internet; the people who operate these sites and contribute to them want to sell you something, so maintain a healthy scepticism. It also helps to know which sites are tied in to dealerships and which are just for private buyers and sellers. **Cars.com,** for example, is a joint effort by the major newspaper chains and includes a lot of ads from dealerships. **Classifiedonline.com** has a massive audience and has the advantage of being free for people trying to sell their cars. **Autotrader.com** includes more than half a million vehicles directly registered on the site but it does not include dealerships.

🚗**Auctions.** Another source of cheap cars is the repossession auction - cars which have been taken back by finance companies. Check the local press for dates and venues.

🚗**Noticeboards.** If you are staying at hostels during your visit check out the noticeboards. There is usually a varied selection of vehicles being sold by backpackers about to leave the country. But what you see is what you get - these will be older cars that have already been round the block a few times. They may have been sold on from traveller to traveller a few times already. Their big selling point is they will be cheap and if the owner's departure date is approaching they may be prepared to accept whatever price they can get. Beware, though, of buying a car from someone who could be on the other side of the world in 24 hours time.

Bulletin boards in local supermarkets and in schools, colleges and universities will also carry a selection of vehicles for sale.

🚗**Dealers.** You could take time to tour used car lots. Many of them are grouped together at out-of-town business parks so you can see a selection within easy walking distance. The upside of visiting sales lots is you can check out the cars there and then. The downside is you will be harassed by salesmen.

Ugly Duckling is a well-known nationwide used car dealership. Dealers specialising in new cars are another potential source of reliable used cars. They often have trade-ins for sale. Trade-ins have often cost the dealer next to nothing so you might find a low offer accepted if it leaves the salesman with some profit.

You can check how many complaints have been made against a dealer through the local Better Business Bureau (www.bbb.org).

How Much Should I Pay?

Help on the Net

Several sites will claim to evaluate the price of your used car if you are planning to sell, possibly using a depreciation calculator. In a country as large as the United States, though, the prices quoted can at best be an approximation of value as local market conditions vary and the specific condition of any one car will impact on its price. Prices are often calculated on the values being reached at auctions so they should not be taken as an accurate reflection of what a car will fetch if sold by other means.

If you are trying to get a value for your second-hand car on-line, avoid any website which asks you to 'certify' that the information you have given is correct. You could be making yourself legally liable for any problems the dealer might have when he subsequently tries to sell your car on.

Generally, websites that offer evaluations or appraisals will be operated by used car dealers. The price they quote for your vehicle might not be as good as you could get by selling it privately.

The most reliable site is www.kelleybluebook.com or www.kbb.com. Others include www.edmunds.com, www.nadaguides.com, www.theautochannel.com and www.cars-online.com

Price Variations

Prices vary from state to state according to various factors. For example, used cars tend to cost more on the West Coast because the emissions laws are stricter. That is something you will need to consider when you want to sell the car; a vehicle bought in California will have no problem passing New York's emissions test but the same can't be said for a Big Apple car in Big Sur.

Recommended Reading

The four Bibles of used car prices;

- The Kelley Blue Book Auto Guide
- Consumer Reports magazine
- Used Car Price Guide published by the National Automobile Dealer's Association (NADA)
- Edmund's Used Car Prices

Inspecting the Car

If buying from a **private seller:**

- **Call before you go** to save a wasted journey
- **Ask for the car's mileage**
- **Verify the asking price when you call** to avoid any unexpected surprises.
- **Take someone who knows about cars** if what goes on beneath the hood is a complete mystery to you.

Be careful when buying a car in the northern states which are prone to heavy snowfall because a lot of states prefer salt to grit when roads ice up and that can have a corrosive effect on cars. Generally, the sunnier the state the better the bodywork which makes Florida and California good places to find decent cars.

By and large, American car owners are less diligent about routine maintenance than Europeans. Filters, fluids, plugs and points could go unchanged for tens of thousands of miles and a car might only be taken for a tune-up to sort out a problem rather than as a periodic check. So do not expect the same standards of maintenance as you would buying a car back home.

⌁Carry out a Lemon Check before Committing⌁

⌁ **Prepare a list of points to check** and questions to ask before you go so you do not miss anything when you inspect the car

⌁ **See the car in daylight** - darkness can obscure a multitude of sins

⌁ **Make an overall visual check** of the car first, looking for signs of rust, corrosion and any mismatches in the shade of paint which might indicate repair work or even two halves of different cars welded together

⌁ **Look from the level of the front fender** along the surface of the car for any ripples or dents in the body work which might indicate crash damage

⌁ **Look for uneven gaps between the doors** and the hood which, again, may point to crash damage

⌁ **Check the ground** over which the car is parked. If it is parked there regularly telltale stains might indicate leaks - green for coolant, black for oil, pink for transmission fluid

⌁ **Transmission** fluid should be pink and not brown. It should not smell burned

⌁ **Oil**. Beware if it looks metallic

⌁ **Exhaust**. Gunk on the inside of the tailpipe could indicate worn valves or piston rings

⌁ **Fan belt**. Is it tight? Does it look worn?

⌁ **Check all the doors,** the hood and the trunk for dents and ease of opening

⌁ **Test all the lights,** indicators, heaters and air conditioning - even the sound system

⌁ **Look at the pedals** - extensive wear indicates how much use the car has had

⌁ **Listen for any unusual sounds** when the engine is running - knocking, hissing, ticking or whining

⌁ **Tyres**. Check they match and there is sufficient tread

The Test Drive

Before you take the car out for a spin make sure you are insured either on your own insurance or the owner's.

Try and re-create the conditions in which you will normally be driving the car. If you will be doing a lot of freeway driving, take it out on to the open road and take it up to speed. If you will be using it as a runabout, take it through town and if you will be driving through the mountains, put it through its paces up and down some hills.

🚗 **First thing in the morning** is the best time for a test drive; it will be a good test of how the car starts when it is cold. Starting a car which has been parked up overnight can reveal any serious problems it might have. White or blue smoke from the exhaust is a bad sign and sudden noises which disappear within a few seconds could be symptoms of a worn timing belt

- **Adjust the seat** and the mirrors to suit you. You could be spending a lot of time in this car, whether it is in a New York gridlock or crossing the Wyoming prairie, so make sure you will be comfortable
- **Switch the radio off.** It can drown out some interesting noises

White or blue smoke from the exhaust is a bad sign

Once you move off, check these performance characteristics:
- **Acceleration** from a standing start
- **Engine noise** - is it running smoothly, is there a misfire?
- **Gear changes** – are they smooth?
- **Rattling noises** from the body – annoying when driving five hours daily?
- **Hill-climbing power**. It is worth conducting this part of the test drive with the air conditioning switched on and turned up full as the air conditioning uses up about 10% of an engine's power
- **Brakes**. When it is safe and convenient, try an emergency stop. The car should not pull to the left or the right
- **Steering**. On a straight stretch of road, relax your hands on the wheel. The car should continue in a straight line and not drift to either side
- **Interior controls** – do they work?

> ## Verifying age
>
> The Certificate of Title will say how old the vehicle is. However, there is another way to verify its age. Every vehicle carries a Vehicle Identification Number (VIN) which is located on top of the dashboard, on the driver's side, and visible through the windscreen. (All VINs have to be in this position to help the police find them quickly when carrying out a check) The tenth character in the 17-character sequence, which was introduced in 1981, refers to the model year;
>   B 1981, C 1982, D 1983, ...Y 2000
>
> From 2001 until 2009 the year will be indicated by a number, 1-9, before reverting to letters again, starting with A in 2010.

After the Test-Drive

🚗 **Check the service history** 🚗 Ask to see any receipts for work that has been carried out. A car should have its oil changed every 5,000 to 7,500 miles so check this has been done. Beware of any major work which has been carried out such as transmission replacements or engine overhauls.

🚗 **Get a mechanic's opinion** 🚗 To be absolutely sure that the car you want to buy is safe and sound, take it to a mechanic. It will be down to you to persuade the owner to let you take it to a garage although some mechanics will carry out on-site inspections. You can expect to pay between $50 and $100 for a mechanic to give a car the once over. The advantage of getting an expert second opinion at a garage is that the car will be lifted up on to a ramp. This will allow a more thorough examination and a garage can also carry out a compression test to check engine wear. A mechanic will be familiar with problems relating to particular makes and models. (Advice on locating a reliable mechanic can be found in the *Garages, Gas, Grub & Goodnight* chapter).

Financing A Purchase

There are several financing options open to the prospective car buyer.

Credit Rating

To find out your credit rating, refer to the Consumer Reporting Agencies – or CRAs listed at the end of this chapter.

Cash

If you have the notes to spare, paying cash is quick and painless - and once the transaction is complete the car is yours and there are no further financial ties to the deal to worry about. The only caveat to be aware of is that if the vehicle is to be used wholly or partly for business then payments will be tax deductible and you will not be able to claim against tax if you paid cash.

A Bank Loan

See the section on obtaining a social security card under *Obtaining An American Driving Licence* in the *Driving Licences* chapter before trying to open a bank account. Banks are most peoples' first port of call when financing the purchase of a car. If they already have an account then they are likely to pre-qualify for a loan and that eliminates the anxious wait while their financial background is investigated by a loan company. Competitive interest rates may be offered to existing customers.

The car you are buying may be the security against which the loan is offered in which case it will effectively be the bank's property until the last payment is made. If you want to sell the car before all the payments are complete you will have to pay off the balance of the loan first.

Dealer Financing

The prospect of signing a financial agreement with a car dealer makes many people worried. It comes back to that image problem mentioned at the beginning of the chapter.

However, there are **advantages:**
- 👍 You stand a good chance of being approved for financing
- 👍 You can buy the car and sort out financing at the same location
- 👍 The dealer may offer a more attractive buying price if you arrange financing through him

On the downside, **disadvantages** include:
- 👎 The dealer might offer a good buying price but then claw the money back in a complicated loan agreement
- 👎 The dealer might persuade a customer to agree to a longer term in return for lower monthly payments and effectively gain more money in the long-term.
- 👎 The car may depreciate in value faster than it is being paid for so that when the owner wants to sell the car he may find it is worth less than he still owes for it

Credit Unions

Credit Unions are building societies; they are much smaller operations than banks and often serve much more localised areas. Nationally, credit unions hold 10% of customer savings and yet they account for 25% of car loans. Their main advantage is that they can often offer more competitive interest rates than banks. Their disadvantages are that they may sometimes only lend to existing customers and savings may be used as security so your nest egg could be frozen if you default.

Independent Finance Companies

There has been a massive expansion of independent finance companies in the United States, over recent years, especially those operating on the internet. The problem for the customer is that the market is fragmented making comparisons and cross-references more difficult.

Leasing

A lease is like a long-term rental agreement - usually over 24, 36 or 48 months. The main benefit is that you get to drive a new car for monthly payments that are usually lower than for loans.

In a hire purchase (or 'financing') lease the customer ends up owning the car at the end of the lease. Otherwise, the leasing company will own the car at the end of the lease, although there may be an option to purchase.

Leasing has the advantage of financing the use of a new car at a low monthly price. The disadvantage is that the terms of the lease are usually fairly inflexible so that the customer may be constrained to certain annual mileage, a level of service and maintenance of the vehicle. Interest rates and second-hand car values have been predicted and set in the monthly lease payments. Should these change during the term of the lease, the customer may 'gain' or 'lose' with regard to the level of monthly payments set at the start of the lease.

Closing the Deal

Buying From A Dealer

What is Included in the Price?

All used car dealers must display a 'buyer's guide' sticker on the vehicle's windshield. That tells the customer who is responsible for repairs, whether there is a service contract and what type of warranty is offered. The car could be sold with no warranty, a full or limited warranty or an implied warranty. The latter applies in states where customers' rights are protected by law.

Essential Paperwork

The Sales Contract. This should include the price you are paying, a smog fee (see below), a charge for the smog certificate, sales tax and license fees. Some less than honest dealers might try and slip in a few hidden extras so inspect the contract with a fine toothcomb.

Insurance. You have to provide proof of insurance before you are allowed to drive the car away. Once you have agreed to buy the car call your insurer and ask for a temporary policy to be faxed to the dealer. You will normally only have to provide the vehicle's identification number (VIN) over the telephone.

The Due Bill. This is an agreement by the dealer to carry out any work before you take delivery. Make sure you get any such promises in writing in a Due Bill.

The Smog Test. In some states a car has to pass an emission, or smog test the first time it is registered and then every two years or so. It must also be tested every time it changes ownership. Fees and acceptable emissions levels vary across the country but the costs are usually between $10 and $20. California has the toughest smog test and people are actively encouraged to 'shop' smoking vehicles to the authorities. Cars that have passed their smog test must carry a sticker on the windshield or licence plate.

The Safety Inspection. This is the American equivalent of the UK's MOT and covers pretty much the same areas of the car. Again, rules vary from state to state but generally cars must be tested every year and on change of ownership. Often the sale of a used car is not complete until it has passed a safety inspection. The cost of the test is up to $40 and if the used car you are planning to buy fails you have the right to walk away from the deal.

Sales Tax. Rates vary across the country. For used cars the tax is levied on the balance of the sale after the value of any trade-in has been deducted. Sometimes Sales Tax will only apply if the car was not previously registered in that state.

Pink Slips. See below for further description. One of these must be obtained from the dealer.

Buying from a Private Seller

Most private sellers will want paying in cash or with a cashier's cheque. If you pay by cheque you may have to be prepared to wait for it to clear before the vehicle is handed over. This is only a sensible precaution and one you should take when you sell the car on.

Transfer of Title. Make sure the person selling the car actually owns it - did they buy it with a loan and are they still making payments? If they are still paying for it the car, the Certificate of Title will be held by the bank or the finance company and it is the seller's responsibility to pay off the balance before the transaction is complete. **Do not hand over any money until you see the Certificate of Title.** Once the lender has been paid the outstanding balance, only then can the car be signed over to you.

The Pink Slip. The most important document of all is the Certificate of Title or 'pink slip'. This is the record of ownership or registration certificate. Without the pink slip you have no proof that you own the car. The seller must notify the local Department of Motor Vehicles (DMV) that they have sold the car by filling in the relevant part of the pink slip. The new owner must also notify the DMV. You might have to pay a small fee to register the car in your name.

Licence Plates (or 'tags'). The car must be registered in the state in which it is being bought and carry that state's licence tags. If you are planning to sell your car after your trip around America, bear in mind you might not be flying out from the same state in which you bought it. So you face the choice of either allowing enough time before your departure to re-register the car in the state or accepting a lower price to compensate the new owner for the chore of doing it themselves.

Another peculiarity of buying a car in America is that the vendor can keep the licence plates if he wants which leaves you the added cost of getting new ones. Personalised, or 'vanity' plates are popular in the United States and people like to hang on to them when they change vehicles. If the vendor wants to keep the plates take this into account when negotiating a price for the car.

Finally the taxman gets his cut even from a private sale. While the local Sales Tax may not apply, you will have to pay a **Use Tax**, which will vary from state to state.

Buying a New Car

The obvious benefit of buying a new car is the reliability (well, in theory anyway). Obviously, you are paying for that privilege - several thousand dollars, in fact. You are buying two things - peace of mind and that unmistakable new car smell. ($20,000 or more for a smell really is paying through the nose).

A driver should be sure of several years of trouble-free driving with a new car but he will also suffer its rapid initial depreciation in value. A car is said to lose 10% of its value as soon as it is driven off the sales lot and a further 20-30% in its first year. So an average-priced car which cost $21,800 new will be worth $15,250 a year later - that is a depreciation of $6,550.

> Those who are compulsive spenders and cannot stop buying new cars should contact **Debtors Anonymous**, General Service Board, PO Box 920888, Needham, Massachusetts 02492-0009. (Tel 781-453-2743; www.debtorsanonymous.org)

What Type of New Car Do I Want?

As with buying a used car, do your research and ask yourself two questions:
- Can I afford it?
- Will it meet my driving needs?

However, you should also ask yourself a third question when considering a new car –
- Will it meet my *future* driving needs?

You need to take the longer view - how will your lifestyle change? Will you need room for more children? Pets? Will you be living in a different part of the country with different driving conditions?

Do Your Research; study the market, consider the terrain and weather conditions that you are likely to encounter, look at the numerous car magazines and surf the net.

Options, Added Extras and Gadgets

To make matters even more confusing many of the 'options' (CD-players, heated seats, etc.) you will be offered may not be optional at all and you will have to pay extra. Japanese imports are good value for money in America with many of the extras included as standard. When all the optional extras are included, the price is advertised as *'fully loaded'*.

Where Do I Find My New Car?

New cars are usually sold through manufacturer-authorised dealers that can be found in the Yellow pages or by searching the internet.

Beating the Dealer

The Essentials

Know your minimum requirements and the maximum you can pay and do not negotiate outside of these boundaries.
Inspect the car and inspect the paperwork, whether you are buying a used car or a new one - especially when you are buying it with a loan or finance deal.
Make sure your bill is itemised - know how your monthly repayments are made up.
Beware of added extras and options. Be clear - you just want the car.
If you are not happy - walk away. The most powerful weapons you have in your negotiating arsenal are your feet.

How Much Should I Pay?

Below is a guide to how much car you can expect to get for your dollars. However, there will be a wide variation in prices across the country because of local economic conditions. The list below is based on a search of the Kelley Blue Book (**www.kbb.com**) for cars in the New York City area in March 2002. The values are those listed for used car dealers - the same vehicles should cost less if bought through private sales. The guide offers a cross section of sizes of cars as well as a range of American, European and Japanese manufacturers.

Under $2,000	$2,000-$4,000	$4,000-$6,000
1990 Geo Metro $1,060	1988 Pontiac Grand Am $2,175	1992 Toyota Corolla $4,175
1982 Toyota Corolla $1,475	1988 Volkswagen Golf GL$2,865	1992 Saab 900 $4,550
1988 Ford Escort $1,750	1987 Honda Prelude $2,985	1992 Volkswagen Jetta $4,650
1986 Pontiac Grand Prix $1,875	1990 Ford Mustang LX $3,265	1993 Dodge Intrepid $4,905
$6,000-$8,000	$8,000-$10,000	$10,000+
1993 Nissan Altima SE $6,065	1992 BMW 3 Series 318 $8,100	2000 Mitsubishi Mirage $10,120
1997 Geo Prizm $6,775	1997 Ford Probe $8,225	1998 VW New Beetle $12,300
1994 Pontiac Firebird $6,990	1996 Subaru Impreza L $8,675	1996 Toyota Convertible $4,335
1997 Chevrolet Lumina $7,400	1998 Pontiac Grand Am $9,325	2001 Lincoln Town Car $29,765

Generally, new cars in America are much cheaper than in Europe. However, when you buy a new car in America, remember two things:
$ No one pays full price
$ Haggling is a long-established tradition in car showrooms

The price you see on the windshield of a new car is known as the 'sticker price'. New cars in the show room will have two stickers in the windshield.

The advertised price of a new car may bear no relation to what you will actually pay. The dealer makes his profit on the added extras, not the basic car, so be prepared for the hard sell when you walk in to the show room.

The Base Sticker Price. This shows the basic price with the manufacturer's installed options. It should also include transportation charges and the fuel economy.

The Dealer Sticker Price. This is usually attached to the Base Price sticker. It shows the base price plus the dealer installed options. The sticker will also display the Additional Dealer Mark-up, or ADM (or 'Additional Dealer Profit – ADP').

Be warned - the ADM may seem a legitimate part of the deal because it is on a sticker and clearly displayed, but it can be a way of wringing more money out of you. See below for scams on the Additional Dealer Mark-up.

What are not included in the sticker price are sales tax, licence plates and registration. Dealers often like to charge an administration fee for processing the paperwork, which is a bit of a cheek seeing as you are paying thousands of dollars for the car. The fee could be as high as a couple of hundred dollars, but it is often negotiable.

The book *Don't Get Taken Every Time* by Remar Sutton is a recommended book on this subject. You can also check out his website on **www.dontgettaken everytime.com.** Sutton explains every step and pitfall of car buying in America - how to haggle, how to research your car and how to avoid the cons and scams.

The Basics of Negotiation

If you want to buy a car you have to be a tough negotiator. Good negotiation is a matter of good preparation - know what you want and what you have to offer and know what your 'opponent' has to offer and what value it is to you.

With this in mind, prepare to deal:
$ **What is it crucial to obtain (your most basic car)?**
$ **What is the maximum you are prepared to pay for this?**
$ **What is the minimum the dealer is prepared to accept?**
$ **What extra negotiating options does the dealer have and of what value are they to you?**
$ **Be firm** - do not deal below your most basic demands of a car or above your maximum price, and don't be misled by extras that are of little value.

The rest is a matter of determination and haggling - good deals are won and lost on who blinks first. Most car dealers are honest; they want to make a profit as much as you want to negotiate them into a loss. In most cases you will meet somewhere in the middle.

Knowing how much profit a dealer is making gives the customer an edge. Typically, dealers add between 5% and 20% to the price they have paid for a car. Several car magazines and websites show the prices paid to the manufacturers (the 'invoice price').

However, you will never negotiate a car dealer into making a loss - if you can cut into his profit on one part of the deal, he will claw it back somewhere else, usually on the added extras, or in a financing deal.

Dealers' Tactics and Scams

Car dealers in America have a range of tactics to get you in to their show rooms and once you are there, prices have a habit of going up.

Low-Balling. This is the practice of advertising prices as being ridiculously low, barely above cost price. The catch is that when you walk in to the show room you find you have to pay for those non-optional options.

High Balling. Dealers will offer you an unfeasibly high trade-in price for your old car. Again, things change once you are in the show room and you find your car is not as valuable as you were led to believe.

Moving the Goalposts - Squeezing the Buyer

Monthly repayments. The salesman will have to show a break-down of the costs and the terms of the financing deal but he will be banking on the customer being tempted by lower repayments if he extends the agreement and the number of payments. **Do your sums and take your time to understand the financing scheme** and make sure the monthly repayments add up to the price you have agreed for the car.

Free First Payment. The salesman says he will pay the first instalment for you, so you do not pay anything for two months. He will even write you a cheque for that first payment. This is known colloquially as the 'Christmas Club'. What actually happens is that first month's payment is added to the over-all price you pay off over the duration of the agreement.

Trade In Values. He offers you $5,000 on your old car when you only expected $3,000. He will make up that lost $2,000 by adding it to the price of the new car.

Free Membership of a Buyer's Club. Amongst pretty much nothing else, your membership will include periodic free oil changes (big deal!) and early notification of new products and services (i.e. junk mail).

Offering to pay off your existing loan. Sounds attractive but all you are doing is transferring your current contract to a new financier and end up paying for two cars in your monthly repayments.

Changing Interest Rates. You sign the finance agreement, take the keys and drive the car home. A couple of weeks later you get a call saying the interest rate on your loan has changed *and* you have to pay an extra $1000. Most people think that once they have signed the loan agreement it is set in stone. There is a phrase in the small print - 'subject to financing' or 'subject to loan approval' which allows some dealers to move the goalposts.

The Rip-offs and Being 'Back-ended'

High-balling and low balling get customers through the doors. The sharp salesman will also have a range of scams for squeezing a few more dollars out of the customer once a deal has been agreed. It is known as being **back-ended** - costs suddenly appear at the back-end of the deal when the final details are being sorted out. The hope is that the customer will be too blinded by the prospect of driving off in a new car to notice or feel too far down the line to withdraw from the deal.

Dealer Prep. They tell the customer that the car needs to be prepared - waxing, vacuuming, etc. Even if this is pre-printed on the invoice *it is avoidable - it is an entirely made-up charge.*

The Optional Extras. *Window etching* is a popular one and entirely gratuitous. Other 'Options' include charging a couple of thousand for a *car alarm,* which only costs $100 or so, and $400 for *seat cover protection* which you can do yourself with a $10 can of aerosol spray bought at a supermarket.

The Forced Warranty. The dealer tells the customer that he has to take out an extended warranty for a couple of thousand dollars, otherwise the bank or finance company will not approve the loan. Rubbish. No loans are dependent on taking extended warranties.

Forced Credit Life Insurance. The salesman tells the customer he has a poor credit rating and that by taking out a Credit Life Insurance Policy he can approve the finance but in fact, the finance application might be rejected anyway.

The Disappearing Deposit. The salesman says he needs to get approval for your offer from his manager and asks you to write a cheque for a deposit so the manager will be convinced you are serious about buying the car. The salesman returns looking embarrassed saying the manager rejected your offer. You ask for your cheque back and the salesman makes a show of having forgotten it. He goes back to his manager's office only to come back claiming his boss has since gone to lunch for two hours and in an unfortunate mix-up the cheque has been endorsed and banked. You, meanwhile, have nothing in writing to prove the cheque was not supposed to be cashed. Do not hand over any money until you get an agreement on the price on an official buyer's form.

Shipping A Car Home

It is something we have all experienced - the holiday romance. For the briefest of times we have fallen head over heals and wondered if maybe, just maybe the relationship could survive in the humdrum work-a-day world back home. Often it can. Shipping your car home is surprisingly easy and cheap.

A freight forwarding agent will handle the delivery - all you have to do is drive the car to a seaport with all the ownership documents and payment for the shipping which is about $1,000 for delivery to a European port.

One thing you need to be aware of is the differing safety regulations for vehicles in the United States and your home country so make sure your car will be able to comply with the law before you pay to ship it home.

Sales Talk

Like all professions car salesmen have their own language in which they speak to each other. Knowing the lingo can give you an insight into how salesmen see you and help you avoid being taken for a ride.

"Bumping." Raising the customer's offer for a car. In other words you say, 'I'll pay a thousand.' The salesman asks, 'Up to?' And you reply, '$1,200'. The salesman has got you to raise your offer without you realising. It's a constant source of amusement (and pleasure) to car salesmen how many customers fall for this one.

"Closer." An experienced salesman who comes in at the end to close the deal.

"Green Pea." A new salesman.

"Grinder." A customer who haggles for hours, grinding out a good price. Be a Grinder!

"Lay Down." A customer who accepts whatever the salesman offers without haggling. Do **not** be a Lay Down.

"Mini." A sale at close to cost price. Good for you, bad for the salesman.

"Mooch." A customer who wants to buy at close to cost price. Car salesmen complain about the growing number of Mooches because the Internet has made customers more aware of fair prices.

"Pounder." A $1000 profit.

"Rip Their Heads Off." Taking a customer for all they have got.

"Roach." A customer with bad credit.

"Spiff." A kickback or bribe.

"Turn Over or Turning." Passing a customer on to another salesman in the hope that the chemistry between the two might be better. This practice also stops customers leaving the lot.

"Up." A customer who walks on to the sales lot. As in, 'Who's up next?.'

"Voucher." The document which tells the salesman how much he has made on the deal. Often they do not know until the sale is finalised.

Where Can I Find Out More?

The 'Grandaddy' of all new and used car price guides is the **Kelley Blue Book.** The guide was first published in 1926 when a new Packard Sedan was listed as being worth $3,825 while a 1921 Nash Tourer would was listed at $50.

The price guide is available from Amazon and all good bookshops, price $9.95

The Kelley Blue Book; 5 Oldfield, Irvine, California 92618. (☎ 949-770-7704; www.kelleybluebook.com or www.kbb.com)

Essential Reading

These publications will tell you everything you need to know about buying a new or used car in the United States. They tell you all the latest safety issues, the current cons and scams and any changes in legislation. All, with the exception of The Lemon Times, are available through Amazon.

Don't Get Taken Every Time by Remar Sutton. $17.50 (Remar Sutton also runs a website at www.don tgettakeneverytime.com)

Little Secrets of the Auto Industry by Clarence Ditlow and Ray Gold. $17.50.

The Ultimate Car Book by Jack Gillis (New edition every January). $30.00

The Lemon Book by Ralph Nader and Clarence Ditlow. $17.50.

The Lemon Times published quarterly by the Center for Auto Safety. $25.00.

Other

More and more new and used car dealers are going on-line. Most websites allow potential customers to search for the car they want by entering the model or the price range. These sites will carry ads for both new and used vehicles.

www.autobytel.com and www.autoweb.com. Customers can enter the details of the car they are looking for and the websites put them in touch with the relevant new or used dealers. Both sites are part of the same organisation and can be contacted at; 18872 MacArthur Boulevard, Irvine, California 92612. (☎ 877-381-7433) **www.autoconnect.com** and **www.autotrader.com** are on-line versions of AutoMart and Auto Trader magazines and carry ads for both private sales and dealerships. **Www.cars.com** carries ads for both dealers and private sellers.

www.edmunds.com Edmund's site lists average prices for new and used cars as well as reviews and advice for the car buyer.

www.stoneage.com Lists all the cars advertised in the Yahoo Classifieds, Ameritech Yellow Pages, Cartrackers and the Classified Network.

Two other useful websites for potential car buyers include;

www.carpoint.msn.com

www.classifiedonline.com

Price Guides

Autofusion Corp; 1940 Garnet Avenue, Suite 104, San Diego, California 92019 (☎ 858.270-9444; www.carprices.com). Set up in 1998, this website compares the prices of thousands of new cars.

Vehicle Information Services

5 French Creek Place, San Mateo, California 94402. (☎ 415-312-9008; www.autoworld.com). The Autoworld website monitors more than 100 car auctions across the USA and draws up average prices.

Safety and Purchasing Advice

Centre for Auto Safety; 1825 Connecticut Avenue NW, Suite 330, Washington DC 20009-5708. (☎ 202-328-7700; www.autosafety.org).

National Automobile Dealers Association; PO Box 7800, Costa Mesa, California 92628. (☎ 888-232-6232; www.nada.com)

Financial Advice

In the United States you have the right to know what records say about your credit worthiness. Records are held by one or more of three main Credit Reporting Agencies - or CRAs;

Equifax; PO Box 105783, Atlanta, Georgia 30348. (☎ 1-800-685-1111; www.equifax.com)

Experian; PO Box 2104, Allen, Texas 75013-2104. (☎ 888-397-3742; www.experian.com)

TransUnion Corp; PO Box 390, Springfield, Pennsylvania 19064-0390. (☎ 312-408-1400; www.transunion.com)

Consumers' credit reporting rights are protected by the Fair Credit Reporting Act. More information is available from the Federal Trade Commission at;

Consumer Response Center, Federal Trade Commission, 6th Street & Pennsylvania Avenue NW, Washington DC 20580. (☎ 202-326-3128; www.ftc.gov)

Bank Rate Monitor; 11811 US Highway 1, North Palm Beach, Florida 33408. (☎ 561-630-2400; www.bankrate.com). This newsletter provides information on hundreds of financial products and services. The website also allows customers to compare bank interest rates.

The National Credit Union Administration: 1775 Duke Street, Alexandria, Virginia 22314. (☎ 1-800-827-9650; www.ncua.gov). The NCUA will help locate a Credit Union in your area.

People who are finding it difficult to meet their credit commitments can get help from the Consumer Credit Counselling Service. The non-profit organisation will offer advice on rescheduling repayments to creditors. Local offices can be found by contacting;**The National Foundation for Consumer Credit:** 8701 Georgia Avenue, Silver Springs, Maryland 20910 (☎ 1-800-388-CCCS (2227); www.nfcc.org)

✦ Lemon, Kentucky, to Lime, Oregon - 1,900 miles ✦

Insurance

'Everything in life is somewhere else and you get there in a car.'
E.B. White, One Man's Meat, 1944.

There are some important differences in the insurance requirements for driveaways and car rentals and these are covered in the chapters relating specifically to those subjects.

Failure to comply with state insurance laws can lead to suspension of your driver's licence and insurance requirements of different states vary widely – checks can be made with the local Department of Motor Vehicles.

> You do not have to have motor insurance in all states. In Alabama, Iowa, Mississippi, New Hampshire, Pennsylvania, Rhode Island, Tennessee, Utah, Virginia, Wisconsin and the District of Columbia drivers need only prove they can meet a moderate claim of around $20,000 if they are involved in an accident. The other big difference in the United States is that **insurance policies do not offer unlimited third party cover.**

The news from states where insurance *is* mandatory may not be much more comforting; in some, the minimum level of coverage could be as little as $10,000 for death or personal injury or $5,000 for property. This means that, should you be the victim, the amount of compensation available to you will be limited to these amounts and anything that can be gained through litigation against the other party (and they may be broke!).

Different Types of Policy and Cover

What is a deductible?

This is an amount up to which a policy holder will pay before claiming against his insurance company. In some parts of America this is called **First Dollar** - other countries call it 'voluntary excess'. Drivers can reduce their premiums by increasing the amount they will pay from their own pocket – the deductible - in the event of a claim.

Bonds and Cash Deposits. In those states, where motor insurance is not compulsory, drivers must comply with 'financial responsibility' laws by paying a bond or a cash deposit to the state Department of Motor Vehicles. Alternatively motorists may provide evidence of self-insurance - in other words, that they personally have the financial resources to cover any damages.

Third Party Liability Insurance. The most basic level of auto-insurance is **Liability Insurance** that is a form of Third Party cover. It provides coverage for injury to another person and for damage to their property. However, the amount paid out is not unlimited.

A typical 'off the shelf' Liability Insurance policy provides coverage of $300,000 per accident. The coverage may be *'general'* or *'specific'*. In other words, the $300,000 may be used to cover claims for death and injury *and* damage to property - general coverage. *Or* that $300,000 might be divided up with so much set aside for dealing with death or injury claims, say $100,000 per victim, and $25,000 for damage to vehicles or property - specific coverage.

That $25,000 might be enough to replace a Honda Civic but not enough to meet the full replacement cost of an $80,000 Ferrari. So you could be sued for the outstanding $55,000. For this reason it is much easier to take out a policy that provides general coverage.

Even $300,000-worth of general coverage might not be enough. **Litigation is a lucrative business and insurance should cover the lower of your personal asset worth and feasible amounts for which you could cause costs and damages to a third party.** So it is worth paying an extra premium or taking out **Supplementary Liability Insurance (SLI) or Liability Insurance Supplement (LIS)** to bump up your coverage to around half a million or a million dollars.

A victim of a crash may sue an uninsured person for any costs and damages not covered by bonds, deposits or self-insurance. The damages sought may be huge so if you have assets worth suing for, it is worth taking out third party liability insurance, even if it is not mandatory to do so. The Golden Rule in motor insurance is never skimp on the amount you are covered for.

The Uninsured Menace

In 1995 the California Department of Insurance estimated that on average 10% of a typical Californian driver's insurance premiums goes towards paying for the problems caused by uninsured drivers.
PIP and Collision Cover offer some peace of mind should you be hit by one.

Personal Injury Protection (PIP) or Personal Accident Insurance (PAI). This covers *your own* **expenses,** even if you are responsible for the accident. PIP or PAI will cover loss of income, the provision of services arising from your injuries - for example, home care - and funeral expenses. Loss of income and the provision of services will be payable for a period of up to three years. *You should be covered for personal injury on your holiday insurance.*

It is possible to buy Personal Injury Protection which will cover *just* medical expenses and not all these other expenses. It is worth investigating the value of extending a PIP to cover you and your family if involved in an accident while travelling in someone else's vehicle, if hit as a pedestrian or if a victim of a hit-and-run.

The advantage of holding PIP is that fault does not have to be proven so it is possible to get paid quickly and without hassle. The main disadvantage is that the right to sue for any additional damages may be restricted.

Collision Cover. This will pay for repairs caused by the owner to his or her *own car* in an accident. Rental and leasing agents will insist you take out Collision Cover through them.

Comprehensive Cover. This offers peace of mind and may offer cover for fire and theft and just about any type of damage whether caused by another vehicle or not. That might include damage caused by hitting an animal, flood damage, vandalism and even windshield damage caused by a stone thrown up from the road.

It should be possible to tailor a comprehensive policy to your particular needs - for example, basic third party, fire and theft cover for a low-value vehicle.

Gap Cover. This applies to certain types of financing arrangements but particularly leased vehicles. This type of cover is designed to protect the finance company and will cover the excess of unpaid finance instalments over and above the insured residual value of the car at the time of it being stolen or written off in an accident. A financing/lease agreement will lay down how much Gap Coverage you must have and who is responsible for paying for it.

Finding the Right Company

Shop around. The array of companies and agents is vast and you will be presented with a wide range of quotes for insurance - possibly from a couple of hundred dollars to a thousand. With such choice, how can you be sure you are getting a good deal?

Firstly, deal with an independent agent, rather than directly with a single insurer or a 'captive' agent who acts on behalf of one insurer, who will shop around on your behalf. To find a good agent, talk to friends and neighbours, trawl the Yellow Pages and the internet, or refer to motoring organisations like the AAA, which may offer good deals or advice to members.

Secondly, once your agent has provided several quotes, take your time to examine what is and is not covered – that means reading the small print. Do not be tempted by the cheapest offer that does not meet your insurance needs and could leave you exposed through insufficient cover. Also, beware of too many frills, which do not really add much to your cover? For instance, a policy offering to pay towing fees of up to $25 is not much help when you are rarely going to pay less than $100 to be towed off the freeway.

Once you have chosen an insurance company you have to hope the insurance company accepts you; some have very strict standards and insist on an exemplary driving record.

Filling in the Form

It is the law in some states that insurance policies must be written clearly and in plain English – if you are unsure about the wording of a policy, reject it.

Be careful when you are filling out the application form; **be accurate and be truthful** because an insurance company may later look for a legitimate reason not to honour a claim. Having said that, it is worth knowing what factors increase insurance premiums and these are considered below.

Cost

Foreign visitors should be able to pick up a basic motor insurance policy, covering third party, fire, theft and accident damage for around $150 for six weeks or $250-$300 for three months. Supplementary Liability Insurance or Liability Insurance Supplement will cost an additional $9-$13 a day.

The American insurer, AIG, offers a reasonably priced policy called Topsure that extends liability cover up to $1 million.

Reducing the Cost

There are a few things you can do to make yourself an attractive proposition to a potential insurer:

♦ Do not be young ♦ Do not be a man ♦

Younger drivers can sometimes benefit from lower premiums when another adult is insured as the principal driver on the policy and the younger friend or relation is insured as an occasional driver.

Goody-two-shoes

Another way young drivers can pay less for insurance is when a company operates a 'good student' policy. To qualify a driver must be at least 16 and in full-time education in high school or college. He or she must rank in the top 20% of the class, have a 'B' grade average, perform well in Standard Assessment Tests and have made it on to the Dean's List or Honour Roll. So it is not only thirty-something females who are assumed to be good insurance risks, but also the goody-two-shoes of the world.

There are a number of other factors that can influence insurance premiums:

$ **Where you live** with areas prone to car theft attracting hefty fees; try to avoid living in an inner city area

$ **Keeping a car in a locked garage**. It could even be worthwhile renting one.

$ **Buy a dependable American-made car.** Foreign makes are more expensive to repair because of the cost of parts. A sporty number will also raise eyebrows and premiums at the insurance office

$ **Certain medical conditions will push up premiums** - particularly epilepsy and diabetes where there is a fear that a driver may become dangerously incapacitated at the wheel

$ **Annual mileage.** Some insurers offer discounts for low mileage. Insurance may be less for a family runabout than a car used for business

$ **Family membership** can bring discounts, but check with your agent whether one family member making a claim or being convicted of a driving offence will bump up the premiums for everyone else?

$ **A 'good driver discount'** (known in other countries as a 'no-claims bonus') can increase the size of your discount the longer you go without making a claim

$ **Staying sober.** Convicted drunk drivers will have their premiums doubled - if they are lucky

$ **Increasing the deductible will reduce premiums.** What is the maximum you could afford to pay out of your own pocket for repairs?

$ **Good safety records and lots of safety features** on a car are viewed positively by insurers: air bags, ABS braking and automatic seatbelts could all bring down the price you pay for coverage. The safety tests on a number of different types of car can be viewed on the Insurance Institute for Highway Safety's website at www.hwysafety.org/vehicle_ratings. Another useful website is **www.autosafety.org**

$ **Bundling your motor insurance** with your household insurance. You might be offered a discount

Making a Claim

The following steps should be followed:

↻ Make sure you get the **name, address and telephone** number of any person with whom you are involved in an accident.

↻ Keep your insurance **policy details in the glove compartment** so you have the relevant details to hand when you have to swap details with another driver.

↻ **Call your insurance company** as soon as possible and clarify the procedure for making a claim. Make a **note of the name, staff number** and direct phone number of the representative you speak to.

↻ **Get an estimate for any repairs before making a claim.** If your deductible, or excess, is $1,500 and the repairs will cost $1,600 it might be worth paying out of your own pocket to avoid the risk of increased premiums resulting from a claim.

↻ Check whether a claim will have any **affect on your premiums** and consider whether it is worth pursuing it.

↻ Ask your insurer whether repairs must be carried out by a **garage approved** by the company.

↻ If you have to send bills and receipts to the insurer do not send the originals, **send certified copies.** Keep a copy of all documents and send all letters by registered mail.

Where Can I Find Out More?

The Insurance Institute for Highway Safety: 1005 North Glebe Road, Arlington, Virginia 22201 (☎ 1-703-247-1600: www.hwysafety.org)

The Insurance Information Institute: 110 William Street, New York City, New York 10038. (☎ 1-800-221-4954; www.iii.org)

The Centre for Auto Safety: The Motorist Safety Information Bureau, 2007 Woodland Way, Deerfield Beach, Florida 33442-1219. (☎ 1-954-428-MSIB (6742); www.autosafety.org)

American Association of Retired Persons: 601 E St., NW, Washington DC 20049. (☎1-800-424-3410; www.aarp.org).

www.iDMV.com. This website will take you to the sites for the Departments or Divisions of Motor Vehicles for all 50 states. Department of Transportation. 400 Seventh Street SW, Washington DC 20590. (☎202-366-4000; www.dot.gov).

✦ High Point, North Carolina to Lowpoint, Illinois – 790 miles ✦

Driveaways

*'The car has become an article of dress without which
we feel uncertain, unclad and incomplete.'*
Marshall McLuhan, *Understanding Media,*1964

The Origins of the Driveaway

The massive expansion of the United States road system in the 1950s, coupled with the post-war economic boom, made America a much more mobile nation. People no longer lived and worked in the same towns they were born and brought up in - new communities sprang up and Americans followed the jobs around the country, possibly upping sticks and moving family and belongings three thousand miles to the other side of the continent.

Car delivery companies started appearing to meet the demand for vehicles which needed to be shipped across America and soon a mutually beneficial relationship evolved where the families travelled by air, sent their possessions by freight and the driveaway agents found foreign visitors eager to journey across mountains, prairies and deserts to deliver the car to its new home.

It seems a supreme act of trust for a car owner to lend his or her pride and joy to a complete stranger; how many of us would hand over the keys to someone who wanted to drive our car a few thousand miles on a sight-seeing trip? Americans will and us travellers and tourists benefit and that is all that matters.

Levels of Service

Driveaway companies offer four levels of service to people who want their car delivered.

- 🚗 **Standard Service.** The company assigns a qualified and contracted driver to deliver the car safely and on time
- 🚗 **Premium Package.** For more urgent deliveries the car is given priority dispatch to a specified destination
- 🚗 **Expedite Service.** A professional driver is assigned to the vehicle. The car will normally be on the road within 48 hours of its being handed over to the driveaway agent
- 🚗 **Truckaway Service.** The car is carried on the back of a truck

Why Do a Driveaway?

Who Does Driveaways?

The 'qualified and contracted driver' mentioned in the Standard Service is you. The car will be one for which the owner has chosen the most basic delivery package. The driveaway companies prefer to use casual drivers because they do not have to pay wages, or expenses. They only use professional drivers for the more expensive delivery packages where there is a bigger profit margin.

The driveaway companies particularly like backpackers but anyone whose itinerary is fairly flexible and who is less choosy about where they are going or how they get there is more than welcome. There is also a perception among agents that Europeans, especially the British, are better drivers than Americans - an important consideration when you are in charge of someone else's car.

The Pros and Cons

There are no hidden costs, no sudden shocks, no nasty surprises. What you see is pretty much what you get with a driveaway. As with all modes of transport there are pros and cons.

The Pros

- It is cheap
- You can find some pretty cool cars to deliver
- You can deliver a driveaway from the age of 21 without any additional charge
- No worries about insurance (see *Insurance* section further on for details)

The Cons

- Some of the cars can be a little thirsty
- Drivers are given a time limit in which to complete the delivery
- Drivers are limited in the number of miles they can travel and the route they can take
- They are not allowed to take the car in to National Parks or on certain roads such as the Pacific Highway
- The owner sometimes leaves luggage or other items in the trunk so space for your own belongings might be limited
- There may be a multitude of restrictions in the driveaway agreement. The more onerous and likely ones are detailed under the *En Route Restrictions* section further on

A Typical Driveaway

The author's trip from Washington DC to Los Angeles was fairly typical of the way a driveaway works.

Sarah Cohen lived in Maryland but she got a new job in London. Rather than leaving her Toyota Celica convertible in storage while she was in England, she offered to lend it to her daughter, Nicole, who lived in Los Angeles. The car was registered at the Auto Driveaway office in Arlington, Virginia, and that is where the author came in.

It is always worth calling local driveaway offices first thing in the morning - any time after 8.30 - to see if there are any new cars due in that day.

The author called at about 8.45am and was told the Celica was just being collected and after checking a few details over the phone - condition of the car, where exactly it was heading, mileage and time allowed for the delivery, stick or automatic - **the agent offered to hold the car for an initial deposit** of $100.

A quick trip to Arlington with the $100 secured the car with the author and the agent agreeing that the trip would start the following day on payment of the remaining $200 deposit and completion of the paperwork.

The following day the application forms were filled out, **a final condition check was completed** to avoid any misunderstandings on delivery (the author spotted a few nicks in the paintwork and cigarette burns in the upholstery which had not been listed on the condition check lists.

The delivery docket - or Bill of Lading - contained contact telephone numbers and details of the route the agent wanted the car to take. He had worked out the shortest possible route, in this case taking the I-81 south as far as Knoxville, Tennessee, and then turning west on to the I-40. However, this was not the most scenic route and **the author and the agent agreed on another route** - the I-70 - which would take in more of the Rockies in Colorado. The driveaway agent allowed a maximum of 3,250 miles for the trip - more than enough - and 10 days to complete delivery.

The journey allowed for visits to Arches, Bryce and Zion National Parks in Utah (although the author should point out that taking driveaways into national parks is against the rules) *and* Las Vegas.

On delivery, **the car's recipient called the LA driveaway office to confirm safe delivery so the author could reclaim his deposit.** She even provided a lift to the office where the local agent issued a cheque for the $300 deposit that was cashed at a bank just around the corner.

Driveaways are a great way to travel in America. They are cheap and flexible. A car comparable to that Toyota convertible would have cost anywhere between $50 and $75 a day to rent - and that would be *excluding* insurance. The author did not have to worry about rental charges or insurance, the only cost was gas which worked out at about $140 for the whole trip.

The Expected Costs

Driveaways are much cheaper than renting. Here is what a driver can expect to pay:

$ A deposit of $300-350. This will be returned upon safe delivery of the car. Many driveaway companies insist on a cash deposit

$ Gas. Some cars might come with a gas allowance, meaning the driver will get the deposit returned plus $50-100 for the gas on delivery of the vehicle

$ Sometimes applicants may be asked to pay a registration fee of about $10

What is Expected of the Driver

For the privilege of driving a car across the States for free, relatively little is required of the driveaway driver:

Drivers will be expected to cover about **300 miles a day** - about six hours driving. Obviously the more drivers there are, the less tiring it will be. The driveaway companies stipulate that no one driver must drive more than 500 miles in any 24 hour period and no more than 700 miles if there is more than one driver

Typically for a coast-to-coast trip drivers will be given eight to ten days. If the agent is especially keen to get a car delivered he **may allow more time**. It is always worth asking

The car must usually be **delivered by 3pm** on the scheduled day of arrival, but this rule is rarely enforced

Drivers are **responsible for any speeding fines** or jail sentences picked up on the way

The car must be **delivered in the same condition** as it was received - i.e. not a mangled wreck on the back of a tow truck

Formalities and Documents

Before heading out on the highway in someone else's car there will be a couple of formalities to sort out. First, there is the application form to fill out.

Photos and Fingerprints. Do not be surprised if the agent takes a mugshot with a Polaroid and asks for a set of dabs. This is just to help the FBI recognise drivers who do disappear with the car. Not all companies insist on this.

Licence. As with rental cars applicants will have to produce a valid driving licence for their own country, coupled with an International Driving Permit and/or passport.

References. Potential drivers might be asked for a couple of referees but most driveaway agents know that foreign drivers do not have an address book packed with local contacts. In the past the author has given the names of American friends of friends he has never met and the agents were happy with something to fill in the box on the form.

✉The Big Brown Envelope✉

When a driver takes the car out of the depot he will be carrying a big brown envelope full of documents. It will contain **insurance certificates,** the **delivery docket** (called the Bill of Lading), **delivery addresses**, **contact telephone numbers**, **contract agreements** between the driver and the agent *and* an **accident report form**. If involved in a collision, follow the instructions on the accident form and mail it to the address given.

The Bill of Lading

This document is proof that the driver is in legal possession of the car and it is the one that should be produced, along with a driving licence when pulled over by the police. On the reverse it also lists all the rules and regulations the driver has agreed to.

Insurance

The driveaway agent handles all insurance. However, the Driveaway Company's insurance *only* covers the car and other vehicles involved in an accident. Applicants will have to rely on their own travel insurance for medical and personal effects coverage. Anyone planning to deliver a car while on holiday in the United States should check with their insurers that they will be covered as drivers of a vehicle rather than simply as passengers.

Finding the Driveaway for You

Driveaway companies are listed in the Yellow Pages, under Automobile Transportation or Driveaway, or you can check out **www.movecars.com** that offers a list of hundreds of agents across the country. (There is also a list of driveaway companies at the end of this chapter).

Many agents will fax a list of available cars to backpackers' hostels every week so check the noticeboards. Other backpackers, who have already booked cars, might also put up notices looking for people to share the driving or expenses. Flexibility will be a big plus in the backpacker or tourist's favour, as agents do not know what cars are available until the day of their departures.

Choosing the Right Car

As with renting, choose the car most suitable for the journey and you can shop around other companies to see what they have. However, travellers are limited to what is available and if the only car to be delivered across the country is an Ego Metro, then tough.

The cars tend to be quite new - usually only a couple of years old and rarely more than five or six. This is because the types of people who use the services of driveaway agents tend to earn enough to drive decent cars. Some of the vehicles that need delivering are repossessions (see below) and these tend to be newer, top of the range models.

They say that to really know a man you should drive 200 miles in his car

Every Car Tells a Story

'I miss DC, but I can't go back yet. It's too soon.'

They say that to know a man you should walk a mile in his shoes. To really know him, drive a couple of hundred miles in his car. I had only met Troy Reynolds 10 minutes previously, even though I had 'borrowed' his car a week before. I had delivered Troy's Jetta from Washington DC to Oklahoma City. I had chosen his car because the route would take me through Memphis, allowing me to drop in on Elvis in Graceland and then on through the prairies of Oklahoma. The five or six days I spent in his car gave me time to imagine what sort of person he might be and why he had left D.C.

The trunk contained a cardboard box and inside that was a Washington Redskins football shirt, a Georgetown University baseball cap, a football helmet and a small set of dumb bells. The memorabilia of a man with a strong attachment to D.C.? And why move to Oklahoma City? It is a fairly nondescript place - only famous as the scene of Timothy McVeigh's bombing in 1996. Other peoples' cars take on the smells of the owners and the Jetta held a faint staleness of sweat. Was this a car regularly driven home from some kind of training? You cannot help but be intrigued by the stories of the owners and you fill in the gaps *en route*.

When I finally arrived in Oklahoma City Troy turned out to be black, in his mid-twenties and about 6' 4". He had been a footballer and had the build of a Block Tackle - in other words, very big. For a man so attached to football, why move to a part of the country not known for its NFL achievements? The final pieces of the story fell into place when Troy gave me a lift to the local Best Western Motel and I asked him what had brought him to Oklahoma City. Eight months previously he had witnessed the death of his best friend in a backstreet fight in DC and he'd left the city to escape the painful memories. He'd got a job cleaning bed linen in a local hospital in Oklahoma City - it was way below his qualifications and experience and he hated the job and the town. But he couldn't go home; 'It's too soon.'

Repos

Occasionally, you might be asked to deliver a car that has been repossessed by the finance company. (Do not worry, you will not get involved in repossessing the car. Someone else will already have done the dirty work).

A few words of caution on delivering repos, though. When returning a non-repo car to its owner you will drive it directly to their home. They are usually over-joyed to get their wheels back and you will get a warm welcome. The staff at finance companies, on the other hand, could not care less. Do not expect tea and biscuits and a roaring log fire upon arrival with a repo. Repossessed vehicles have to be taken to the finance company's pound and these are often in the middle of nowhere. Sometimes they are in a business park away from town and you will then face the hassle of getting back to civilisation.

Delivering a Repo

Andrew Vincent had to take a repossessed car to a finance company in Florida. It was returned at about 4.45pm on a Friday, about 15 minutes before the office closed for the weekend. The guy who took delivery of the car looked like he had fallen out of the miserable tree and hit every branch on the way down. He refused to call the driveaway company to confirm the car's safe arrival, thus preventing the author from getting the deposit back. He also would not allow the use of a phone to call a taxi. All because he wanted to go home. Fortunately, the driveaway agent accepted the author's word that the car had been delivered and gave permission for the local office to return the deposit. **So if delivering a repo, try and avoid returning it near closing time.**

Choosing Your Route

It is not always possible to find a driveaway that is heading *exactly* to where you want to go. For example, if a driver wants to travel from New York to Los Angeles he might find a car which needs delivering to somewhere like Twenty-nine Palms or San Diego, in which case he will have to complete the last short leg of the journey on a bus or a train; but having the free use of a car for 2,900 miles out of a 3,000 mile journey is nothing to complain about. This is where the driveaway companies websites come in handy. Taking Auto Driveaway as just one example, you can access all 60 of the company's offices through **www.autodriveaway.com.** Even if there is no car going directly to the desired destination it might be possible to get there via a couple of shorter deliveries. If there is nothing heading out of New York for L.A., try something going to Salt Lake City, for instance. Then check out Salt Lake City and see if that agent has anything going to Los Angeles.

Monitoring the agent's websites also gives you some bargaining power. It is worth monitoring driveaway agents' websites for a couple of weeks before flying out because it might be possible to spot some vehicles that have been awaiting delivery for a while. It could be because they are bound for less popular destinations. Knowing an agent has had trouble finding a driver gives a traveller a bit more to negotiate with; you could say you will take the car in return for a generous gas allowance or a little extra time to complete the delivery.

Regular Routes. There seem to be regular routes for driveaways, almost like the migration of buffalo. At Christmas there are a lot of cars, known as 'snowbirds', heading from the north-eastern United States down to Florida: they all head in the opposite direction in the Spring. Texas seems to draw in a lot of driveaways from the Midwest. Coast-to-Coast runs, in either direction, are also common. There will obviously be a big demand for driveaways during the peak summer months so it may be harder to get a car heading exactly for the chosen destination.

As mentioned in the previous chapter, a lot of rental cars - the 'deadheads' - need to be returned to their original depots from offices in popular tourist destinations so it may be worth giving the rental companies a call if travelling from the popular tourist destinations.

Multiple Driveaways

Sonia Boyle was able to piece together a trip around the Midwest and the South from one office.

'I wanted to visit Graceland from Washington D.C. Auto Driveaway's office in Arlington had a Volkswagen which needed to be delivered to Little Rock, Arkansas, which would take me through Memphis. Little Rock had a Lexus which needed to be delivered to Dallas. Dallas had a Toyota Pick-Up bound for Jacksonville, Florida. In Jacksonville there was a Grand Am waiting to go to Roanoke, Virginia. From Roanoke I caught the Greyhound back to D.C. in time for my flight. *All of these deliveries were arranged from the Arlington office; the other agents held the cars for me until I got there. And all four driveaways were completed on one £300 deposit that was transferred to each new delivery.* I picked up my deposit in cash, at the Arlington office, before heading to for the airport.'

On The Road

Collecting the Car

Most of the time the car will be collected from the driveaway office, although sometimes it might be from a private address in which case the driver will have to make their own way there after filling out all the paperwork. Similarly, the car will probably be delivered to a private address, a finance company or a driveaway agent.

⤷ **Check the car over.** The driver will be given a form on which to note any damage or wear and tear to the vehicle. **Be thorough** and note every little scratch and dent. Miss something now and it could result in a lost deposit on delivery of the car

⤷ Drivers must also **make a note of the mileage**. It *might* be possible to get away with adding 500 miles or so from the car's mileage to give a bit of leeway for sightseeing en route

⤷ The car should have **a full tank of gas** when it is collected

Once the driver and the agent are both satisfied with the condition of the car they both sign the form and from that moment the car becomes the driver's responsibility.

En Route Restrictions

When the car is collected the driver is given a written list of dos and don'ts - actually, it is mostly don'ts. The driveaway agents have it sewn up pretty tight as to what a driver can and cannot do whilst in possession of the car. **It is the condition in which you deliver the car, which matters most.** So long as it is presentable, safe and sound who is going to know what drivers get up to between A and B?

Typically, driveaway drivers are not allowed to carry:
- Pets
- Liquor
- Narcotics
- Any other passengers or drivers not named on the Bill of Lading. That includes hitchhikers

Other restrictions may include:
- The car must not be driven between 10pm and 5am
- A driver must not drive for more than 10 hours at a stretch
- Drivers must not to stray more than 50 miles from the shortest route
- The car must not be taken into national parks
- Often smoking and eating in the car is prohibited, although drivers can probably get away with the latter so long as the car is not delivered with a melted Twinkie encrusted in the velour seats
- The delivery will have to be completed via the shortest possible route and that usually means sticking to the freeways and interstates. The companies do allow some leeway, though, to allow for minor detours, looking for fuel and accommodation and getting lost
- The conditions state that about 25 cents must be paid for every mile over the mileage limit but the author has never experienced mileage checks

Delivering the Car

○ **Call the owner the day before** arrival to arrange a delivery time and to get directions

○ **Take the car to a car wash**, especially if it is has been driven through some pretty challenging weather and terrain. You have had the free use of his car, so a $5 car wash is not much to give back

○ **Have the owner call the driveaway office** to confirm safe delivery. Agents will not accept the signed receipt as sufficient proof.

○ **Get the owner to sign the receipt** and then …

○ **Pick up the deposit** from the local agent

Often owners will sign for their cars without checking them over because they are just pleased to get them back. It is worth trying to sweet-talk them into giving you a lift to somewhere you can catch a bus or a train.

Whilst it may be possible to get away with exceeding the mileage limit, **exceeding the time limit is a much more serious matter.** If delivery will be late, call the owner and let him know. (And you had better have a good reason). The Interstate Commerce Commission governs Driveaways and the enforcement agency is the FBI. If the driver goes AWOL with the car he will be treated as a federal felon.

Repairs

Unlike a rented car a driveaway may not be as well maintained so breakdowns are more likely. If the repair is going to cost up to $100 it is considered a reasonable sum for the driver to pay and to claim back from the owner on delivery. Get a receipt from the garage and a detailed account of the work carried out. $100 should be enough to cover running repairs like tyres, lights and basic engine problems. If the work is likely to cost more than $100 call the owner for authorisation and get them to pay either by credit card over the phone or by wiring the money to the garage.

Auto Driveway's Bernie Wright advises drivers not to get involved with more complicated repairs; 'If it's likely to cost more than $100, call the owner and put them on to the mechanic. Don't get involved; get out of that loop. It's their problem.' Again, get a list of the work done. Negotiate an extension to the delivery deadline to allow for the repairs.

Remember on a long journey to check the **oil** and **water** regularly and if driving in winter, particularly in the northern United States, make sure the car has **anti-freeze**.

Accidents

The driveaway agent takes care of all the insurance with coverage of up to $3 million. The big brown envelope will contain an accident report form for the delivery driver to fill out. The form asks the driver to explain what happened and there are simple diagrams of road layouts to mark the positions of the vehicles involved in the accident. That form will have to be sent to the driveaway office from which the car originated.

The driver will not have to worry about all those Collision Damage Waivers and Supplementary Liability Insurances involved in renting a car but he is not absolved of all responsibility; **if the car is involved in an accident whilst breaking the restrictions imposed in the driveaway agreement, the driveaway company and/or the owner and/or anyone else involved in the accident will come after the driver for money.** The American civil courts do not take prisoners.

Bernie Wright, who runs Auto Driveaway's office in Arlington, Virginia, is unequivocal in his advice about what to do in the event of an accident:

'No matter how minor it is, call the police. If they tell you to just swap insurance details and sort it out between yourselves tell them there are injuries so they have to come out. You can always say you've suffered whiplash.' However, Bernie says this because his company rather than you, the driver, would be liable to being sued in the event of an accident. Nevertheless, it is better to be safe than sorry and to heed his advice.

Professional Drivers

Driveaway agents do employ teams of full-time drivers but travellers can forget any dreams of delivering hot-rods across America and getting paid for it. True, applicants might get to drive some flashy cars but they will also get their fair share of mundane deliveries. If illusions are not already shattered - the pay is awful. The basic fee for a delivery is low enough to start with and it will also have to cover accommodation, food and possibly even gas.

Where Can I Find Out More

Driveaway Companies

American Auto Transporters; 1033 Turnpike St, Route 138, Canton, Massachusetts 02021. (☎1-800-800-2580; www.shipcar.com)

AmeriFleet; 1360 Union Hill Rd, Bldg One, Suite E, Alpharetta, Georgia 30004. (☎1-800-728-9235; www.amerifleet.com)

Auto Driveaway; 310 S Michigan Av, Suite 1401, Chicago, Illinois 60604. (☎1-800-346-2277; www.autodriveaway.com)

Schultz International; 936 Hermosa Av, Suite 109, Hermosa Beach, California 90254. (☎1-800-677-6686; www.transportautos.com)

For Links to Other Transport companies **www.movecars.com**

www.movingindex.com

The Ferrari Myth

When you enter the world of driveaways you will inevitably hear a story about a friend of a friend who knew a guy who once went out with someone whose brother once met a man in a bar who - God's-honest-truth - once got to deliver a Ferrari. Maybe, once in a blue moon, someone finds a Ferrari that needs to be delivered coast to coast. Generally, though, these stories are urban myths. Anyone who owns a Ferrari is probably *not* going to pass up the opportunity to drive it across country themself. If they do entrust it to a driveaway company they are likely to pay for it to be loaded on to a truck and delivered that way. And if they do allow it to be delivered by a driver they will probably insist it be done by one of the company's pool of professional drivers.

In other words, you are unlikely to get your mitts on a Ferrari, a Porsche, a Bugatti, a Lotus or any other kind of sports car. So accept your Ford Focus and be grateful.

✦ Boring, Oregon to Bummerville, California - 582 miles ✦

The American Road System

'Our national flower is the concrete cloverleaf.'
Lewis Mumford, Quote, 1961.

Getting Around the Cities

The layout of American cities makes navigation easy. All but the oldest and the most hilly cities are laid out in a grid pattern (hence the term, 'gridlock'); the streets cross at right angles to form squares or 'blocks'. There are between ten and twenty blocks to a mile and it is relatively easy to locate an address.

Taking New York as an example, avenues run north to south while streets run east to west. The Empire State Building is on the corner of 34th Street and 5th Avenue and when speaking Americans tend to drop 'street' or 'avenue' so the its location would be given as '34th and 5th'. Other cities, like Washington DC, assign letters of the alphabet to streets or avenues. So in the nation's capital, the lettered streets run east-west while the numbered streets run north to south. For instance, the youth hostel is on the corner of 11th and K.

Broadly, American cities follow a fairly standard pattern; they comprise a Central Business District, which is sometimes sign posted as 'CBD', an inner city of low-rent housing and small businesses and then sprawling suburbs. Smaller towns are often no more than a huddle of businesses and houses on either side of a main road.

As always, though, there are exceptions to the rule. Boston is laid out in a European style with a seemingly random muddle of roads and streets. San Francisco is laid out in a grid pattern - until you get to the Corona Heights district, where the straight streets and avenues give way to a tangle of curving roads. For the most part, though, American cities are neatly laid out and follow a logical pattern.

Addresses

The street numbers in American addresses can be very high - '2091 Ninth Street', for example. This does not mean there are more than 2,000 buildings on the street. The first block on a street may be numbered 0-100, the second block 101-200 and so on. Sometimes, however, there may be random gaps in a sequence, so 102 might be next door to 148. The numbering system does give an indication of which block a building is on, however. Look for signs on street corners that point to the block numbers - 201-300 to the left, 301-400 to the right, for example.

If a new building is constructed between two existing ones it will be allocated a half number. Short streets follow the numbering of the parallel main street so a road running next to the 201-300 block of 2nd Street, for example, would start at 201 rather than 1. This is a handy way of locating those smaller streets that are not immediately obvious on the map.

Many cities, such as Washington DC, are divided into quadrants - North-East (NE), North-West (NW), South-East (SE) and South-West (SW) and, again, this helps locate an address in the general area of a city. So an address might be given as 809 10th Street NW. Roads that run east to west will be split by an imaginary line through the centre of a city - hence East 33rd and West 33rd. In DC the quadrants meet at the Capitol Building on Capitol Hill.

Planning a Trip Downtown

The area of a town or city where you can find all the action is known as 'downtown'. This is where all the best shops, restaurants and entertainment tend to be concentrated. Downtown will often be sign-posted as such in other parts of the city and from the freeways. The area often seems to attract the city's most aggressive drivers and traffic is frequently clogged.

Driving is probably the least efficient way to get around downtown areas of cities, especially when there are cheaper alternatives. Why rack up a huge parking bill when you can explore all a city has to offer on foot, on the bus, underground or on a bike? A car might be great for getting you across the Great Plains of Kansas but it is not so good in downtown New York.

Los Angeles

Los Angeles has been called 'six suburbs in search of a city'. There is no distinct downtown LA, although each district will have a centre. The city is criss-crossed with freeways and negotiating them can be a test of will, resolve and nerves for the out-of-town driver. The highways fan out into six lanes, in places, with exit lanes on both the right and the left. Driving in LA can be a multi-dimensional experience with flyovers, underpasses, bridges and tunnels all intersecting above, below you and to your right and left.

Everyone knows the rules except you – an unnerving experience. The signing does not help either; road signs are designed with the assumption that everyone is a local and knows what they mean and they can be baffling to the visitor.

When you are heading into unfamiliar urban territory, plan, plan, plan:
- Work out your route on the map before you get behind the wheel.
- Write down the directions in simple, instructions, including street names.
- Downtown streets are often one-way so make a point of looking which way the little arrows on the map point before you leave.
- Do not let yourself be rushed and if your slowness does cause a chorus of car horns try not to be intimidated.

Public transport is usually the best way to get around downtown areas, although the quality and efficiency will vary enormously across the country. Some cities have developed public transport to a fine art, integrating the needs of both the pedestrian and the cyclist. In Seattle, for example, buses are free within the central zone of the city and they are fitted with bicycle racks.

Some cities also have very good underground systems. Washington DC's is clean, efficient and easy to understand. There are even lights set in the platform, which flash to tell passengers when a train is approaching. Los Angeles also has a good underground network, although it is much more extensive and, as result, a little harder to decipher. New York's network will not win any prizes for cleanliness but it is relatively safe.

Road Numbering

orth

0
8
6
4
2

All interstates carry the prefix 'I' and they are sign posted with a red, white and blue shield.

- Interstates that run *east to west are even* numbered.

- Interstates that run *north to south are odd* numbered.

- Interstates number upwards starting in the south west.

1   3   5   7   9   e t c East

So the I-5, for example, runs inland of the West Coast from San Diego right up to Vancouver. The I-95 runs from Houlton on the Maine-Canada border down to Miami.

All of the major interstates have one or two digits. Smaller spur roads, off the main interstates have three numbers, for example the I-225, which splits off from the I-25 running north to south through Denver. The last two of those digits, I-**225**, will be the same as the interstate it joins.

Even-numbered prefixes indicate that the road goes *around* the city

Odd-numbered prefixes show that the road goes *into* the city

---

For instance, the **2**70 splits off the east-west I-70 and takes traffic *around* the city while the **1**70 goes *into* St Louis, Missouri.

This numbering system does mean the same road numbers crop up in different parts of the country. So, for example, there is an I-270 around St Louis and another one around Denver.

Occasionally roads are given names as well as numbers; part of the I-70 is known as the Dwight D Eisenhower Memorial Highway because it was the first interstate to be built as part of his massive road-building programme in the 1950s. It is usually less confusing to navigate by the road numbers rather than their names.

Round or through town? How will you know whether you need to stay on the main interstate or to take the spur road? Look at the map; if you are just passing through a city look for the road that goes around it - do not assume it will be quicker to stay on the main interstate. The I-70, for example, passes through the heart of St Louis, which is completely gridlocked in the rush hour. The 270 follows a much quicker route – around it.

Watch out, also, for the signs indicating 'Thru', 'Business' or 'Downtown'. If you do not want to stop, take the 'Thru' route, otherwise you will find yourself being steered away from where you want to go and caught up in the urban congestion.

Junctions are numbered in a way which Europeans may find curious, but which has some logic: starting at the state line, junctions take their numbers from the distance from the border. Therefore, the first junction on the I-5 in southern California is numbered 1, but the next is 7.

Types of Road

Freeways and Interstates

America's freeways and interstates can seem intimidating to the foreign visitor, especially where they split into multiple lanes with everyone travelling at high speeds and switching lanes without signalling.

Getting On and Off Freeways and Interstates

Freeways and interstates are accessed via one-way ramps - or slip roads. The entrance may sometimes be next to an exit which will be clearly marked 'DO NOT ENTER - WRONG WAY'.

As soon as you are on the ramp, begin checking your rear view mirror, for any traffic which might also be entering the freeway behind you, and your left wing mirror for traffic on the freeway itself. Also check your blind spot over your left shoulder. Indicate and join the freeway at the same speed as the rest of the traffic.

On some ramps you will come up against a 'YIELD' sign. As soon as you get on to the entry ramp look ahead to see if vehicles are stopping before going on to the highway. Wait for a suitable gap in the traffic before joining. Hopefully vehicles already on the freeway or the interstate will move over to let you in. On busy stretches, entry may be controlled by a traffic light that only allows one car on at a time. A sign will tell drivers 'One car per green' which shows red as you approach it. You should only enter the freeway when it turns green. If you are behind another car do not follow it, even if the light is still green; you must stop, wait for it to turn red and then green again before joining the highway.

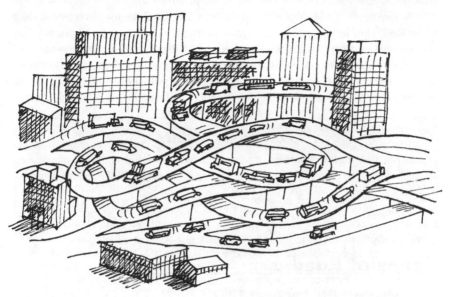

America's freeways and interstates can be intimidating for the foreign visitor

To leave the freeway or interstate, signal your intention to move right into the deceleration lane. Remember, once you are in an exit lane you must exit - do not try and rejoin the freeway. There will usually be an on-ramp close to the off-ramp, anyway, so it is easier to leave the freeway and rejoin straight away if you make a mistake.

Just to confuse matters, some exit lanes are on the left - ie, from the outside lane. These often appear on the approaches to big cities where the freeways split into lots of smaller roads. The safest course is to stay in the middle lane in built-up areas should you not wish to exit.

Federal Highways

Federal Highways are the most important roads after the interstates and pre-date the interstate network. Many have now declined in significance. They carry the prefix 'US' and they are marked by black numbers inside a white shield. *The numbering system is based on the same principle as for interstates with odd numbers running north to south and even numbers east to west.* They range in size from multi-lane routes to relatively small, suburban streets.

Where the federal highways beat the interstates is in kudos; no interstate has embedded itself in the American psyche as much as some of the highways. No one has written a song called 'Get Your Kicks on the I-96'. Route 66 has become America's 'Mother Road', while Highway 50 is known as 'America's Loneliest Road'. Highway 101, which follows the pacific coast from southern California to Oregon, is recognised as one of the most beautiful routes in America.

Confused Cowboy

Richard Milward remembers a fraught drive through Dallas:
'You can't afford to relax for a second driving into Dallas. The freeways split, converge, fan out into multiple lanes, exits veer off from the nearside and outside lanes and it all seems to be happening at 200 miles an hour. Even staying in the second lane didn't help because sometimes that became an exit lane. Coming from the north the I-35 splits into the I-35 West, which takes you to Fort Worth, and the I-35 East which goes through Dallas. The 35 East intersects with the 635, after that it meets the 354, the 348, the 183, the 482 and the 356. You've got six or seven lanes and cars are cutting in front of you, tailgating you and all the time you're trying to read the road signs while avoiding hitting anything. It's places like Dallas where you really need someone next to you - an extra pair of eyes'.

State Highways

State highways are funded by the states rather than the federal government and their quality can be even more varied than that of the federal highways - from glass-smooth asphalt freeways to dirt tracks. There is no nationally agreed numbering system and so they often change number at state borders. They are usually marked as black numbers inside a white oval, square or rectangle.

Turnpikes

Turnpikes are toll roads and they are marked in green on maps so mistaking them for scenic routes could be an expensive mistake. They often have names rather than route numbers, such as the *Ohio Turnpike* or the *New York State Thruway*. Tolls range from a quarter to a couple of dollars. Ask at a local gas station before deciding whether it is worth finding an alternative route.

It is also useful to keep a handful of coins ready when approaching a turnpike. There is nothing more irritating for the cashier or the drivers behind than someone fumbling for money. There are five ways of paying:

- Pay the cashier at the booth.
- Simply throw the money into the huge scoop at the tollbooth. The machine

will register whether you have thrown in enough money and, if not, a barrier will come up to stop you going any further.

- Collect a ticket from the machine, rather like in a parking lot, and pay when you exit the turnpike according to how far you have driven on it.
- Get yourself a token or pass and pay in advance. You just show the token or pass whenever you go on to the turnpike.
- Pay for a device in your car, which is automatically scanned when you enter the toll road. You pay your fees up front, use a designated lane at the turnpike and a scanner at the entrance registers that you have already paid and lets you through. (There have been a number of cases where the equipment has failed to recognise the car and drivers who have already paid their tolls have been summonsed for non-payment or found their way blocked by automatic barriers. The companies that make the scanners are working to improve the technology).

Turnpikes are more common in the north-east but there are toll bridges and tunnels across the country. Toll roads tend to be better maintained than federal or state-funded roads and they usually have good quality service stations and rest areas.

Sometimes the road widens, rather than narrows, as it approaches the toll booths and you could find the lane markers have disappeared and you are driving across a wide apron of asphalt with hundreds of other cars all jostling for the fastest moving queues. The signs over the booths should be large enough to tell you which one you need, whether you are paying by cash, token or your car is fitted with a smart card.

The other side of the tollbooths can sometimes seem like the start of a Formula One Grand Prix as vehicles either fan out or converge, depending on whether the turnpike widens or narrows. Try and pick out the lane markers and head for the lane that is straight ahead.

Signs, Lights and Lanes

Signs

The two most important to look out for are 'STOP' and 'YIELD'.

Regulatory Signs

Regulatory signs tend to give the warning in words as well as symbol form and their design is similar to European signs.

STOP is written in white lettering inside a red octagon. The sign means what it says so drivers must come to a halt even if their path is clear. A lot of drivers like to do what is known as a 'rolling stop' - in other words slowing right down before pulling out of the intersection. If a cop is watching it will earn the driver a ticket - stop means stop.

Four-way STOP signs can sometimes be found at crossroads that are not controlled by lights. There will be a small plaque with '4-way' at the bottom of the red octagon. The rule is that the first vehicle to the crossroads has right of way.

An intersection that catches a lot of people out is a '3-way' junction; traffic approaching from three directions must give priority to traffic coming from the fourth direction. Although the stop sign may say '3-way', it is not always clear who has right of way.

YIELD is written in red lettering on a white background inside an inverted triangle with a red border. Drivers are not required to come to a stop at a yield sign but they must give way to other traffic approaching the intersection.

Speed limits are written in black lettering inside a white rectangle and will indicate either **SPEED LIMIT** or **MINIMUM SPEED**. A variation is where there is a different speed limit at night and this will have white lettering inside a black rectangle - 'NIGHT 35', for example.

Warning Signs

Warning signs are yellow diamonds and many will be familiar to European drivers - the signs for animal hazard, slippery surface and narrowing road, for instance, are the same as in Europe.

Others will be less familiar. For example, the word **DIP** inside a yellow diamond is not an instruction to dip headlights but a warning that there is a dip in the road surface which may be flooded or which may obscure oncoming traffic. Another variation is a sign warning of roadworks - or a 'work zone' - ahead. This is written inside an orange diamond and may have orange flags attached to it. It will say **ROAD CONSTRUCTION** and give the distance to the roadworks ahead. A pictogram of a man holding a flag inside the diamond indicates that traffic is being manually controlled.

Mom's At Work

Look out for a construction worker in a fluorescent bib, a hard hat and carrying either a flag or a lollipop sign with the words **STOP** or **SLOW**. Remember that speeding fines are doubled inside work zones. The workers who hold the Stop or Slow signs are frequently women and there are often additional notices along the stretch of roadworks saying, 'Slow down. My Mommy works here.'

Schools are indicated by a yellow arrow shape with a pictogram of two children crossing the road. Speed limits around schools are lower than for the surrounding area - often around 20 mph - with higher penalties for breaking the limit.

The **school bus** should be treated like a moving roadsign. They are painted bright yellow (known as school bus chrome) and it is illegal to pass a school bus when it is stationary with its red lights flashing or it has its 'stop arms' sticking out (rather like the indicators on old cars). In some states school buses display flashing yellow lights when they are about to stop followed by red lights when they come to a halt. Vehicles coming in the opposite direction must also stop and wait while children disembark in case they run across the road. Drivers must not stop within 20 to 25 feet (6 to 7.6 metres) of a bus while it is loading or unloading.

Penalties for passing a stopped school bus could be a fine of up to £1,000, imprisonment or community service.

A large black 'X' inside a yellow circle, with the letters **RR** on either side indicates a railroad crossing ahead. It may also be accompanied by a flashing red light, which means you MUST stop. Crossings in some rural areas have no warning signs at all. Train drivers usually sound their horn when approaching a crossing but it is up to the motorist to look out for an approaching engine.

If a train is passing drivers must wait either for the signal to tell them to move off, or until they have a clear view of the line.

Marker Signs

Marker signs provide information such as the name or number of the road or the direction to a rest area.

Interstate signs consist of a blue shield with a red strip across the top. The word **INTERSTATE** will be written on the red strip and the number of the Interstate will be on the blue shield.

US Highways will be on a white shield with the number of the route inside the shield. Signs that tell drivers which lane they need to be in to reach their destination on interstates and freeways are on green boards, either suspended over or on the side of the highway.

Markers for facilities such as rest areas, camp sites or hospitals are written in white inside a blue rectangle.

Many road signs use words rather than symbols and in areas with large Hispanic populations, such as Southern California or Florida, they will be in both English and Spanish. Some parts of the United States are also beginning to adopt signs that give distances and speed in both miles and kilometres.

Traffic Lights

Fact; we spend two years of our lives waiting at red traffic lights.

The sequence of traffic lights in the United States is usually:

Red - - Green - - Yellow - - Red

Always be prepared to stop on approaching a green light with the assumption that it is about to change.

Right Turns

There is one rule that confuses most foreign visitors to the United States.
You can turn right on a red light.

You must come to a halt before making the turn and only make the manoeuvre when it is safe to do so. If you are turning right across a pedestrian crossing then you must give pedestrians a right of way. Watch out for signs warning of an exemption to the right turn rule - they will be clearly marked 'NO TURN ON RED'. New York City does not allow right turns at red lights but the rest of the state allows the manoeuvre.

Left Turns

There are a few states where it is also legal to turn left on a red light when turning from one one-way street into another one-way street. Such instances are rare but will be signed.

Some lights display filter arrows which indicate which way you can go even if the other lights are red. If a green arrow is pointing left *and* flashing that means oncoming traffic has the right of way. If a green arrow is pointing right and flashing that means pedestrians may be crossing and that they have right of way.

The positioning of traffic lights in the United States can also be confusing for foreign visitors. They are often positioned on the far rather than the near side of the junction and sometimes suspended on cables over the intersection rather than on posts at the roadside. So drivers must get into the habit of looking for lights straight ahead and above the road rather than to the side.

Crossroads Confusion

Dave Brierley brought the traffic to a stop when he came up to traffic lights in a mid-west town:
'I saw a red light on a cluster of lights suspended on a cable over an intersection so I stopped right underneath it. I thought it was an odd place for a stop light because it left me blocking the crossroads, but maybe that was the way they did things in America. Suddenly I was being beeped at from both sides as cars coming from my left and right found their way blocked by my car. Fortunately, or unfortunately, the car behind me was a cop who explained very forcefully where I was supposed to stop.'

Helpfully, there are often flashing amber lights to warn that there are stop lights about a hundred yards or so ahead. Alternatively, there may be a sign displaying a set of traffic lights inside a yellow diamond warning of stop lights ahead – so not noticing the lights is no excuse for jumping a red.

The flashing amber lights may also serve as a means of controlling traffic in their own right and not as a warning of stop lights ahead. These flashing lights may be switched on during busy periods with the sign 'Proceed with caution.'

Roundabouts

Roundabouts are called **rotaries or traffic circles** in the United States. The difficulty for foreign visitors not used to driving on the right is in having to drive *anti-clockwise* around the roundabout. On arriving at a roundabout remember to give way to traffic coming from the left – stopping at the 'YIELD' sign. Roundabouts are few and far between in America and most of them, like turnpikes, are concentrated in the northeast. Their rarity is a mixed blessing; it means you will rarely have to deal with one but it also means you never quite get used to them.

Overtaking

It is legal to pass on the inside (the right) on American roads, although the law is a little confusing.

It is illegal to move to an inside lane specifically to overtake a slower vehicle. However, if you are already in the inside lane and there is a slower vehicle on the outside, it is legal to pass. In practice drivers often move to the inside to overtake, especially if they come up behind someone that has obviously set their cruise control and will not budge. Because cars may be passing on the inside it is essential to check your right blind spot before moving back into an inside lane. The only states where overtaking on the right is illegal in all circumstances are Connecticut, Maryland and Nebraska.

Take particular care with overtaking manoeuvres in the Mid-West where crosswinds can whip up across the plains and the prairies. Trucks can be especially unstable and at risk of being blown out of their lane. Furthermore, huge American trucks can throw out tremendous turbulence, destabilising passing cars.

If someone is trying to overtake you, especially on a two-way road, maintain your speed. If you slow down the other driver may run into the back of you. You should only slow down if the overtaking driver has obviously misjudged; decelerate if the front of the other car is ahead of yours.

There are some drivers who like to set their cruise control and who will refuse to brake or accelerate, no matter what the situation demands. It is most irritating when they are overtaking a vehicle that is travelling just half a mile an hour or one mile an hour more slowly than they are. They will take forever to pass the slower vehicle, oblivious to the queue of traffic building up behind them.

Truckers are the worst offenders. Profit margins are tight so fuel consumption is critical and they are keen to avoid any unnecessary braking or accelerating. So the cruise control is king in the trucker's cab and he would rather crawl past a slower truck than put his foot down to get by more quickly. The other trucker, meanwhile, will also be on cruise control and equally reluctant to slow down to let the other vehicle pass. This slow motion overtaking can sometimes last for miles, especially on long inclines, with tailbacks building up behind. There is little you can do other than be patient or seethe - whichever offers more comfort.

Lanes

American road lanes are delineated as follows:

- Broken yellow lines, in the middle of the road, separate traffic travelling in opposite directions
- An unbroken yellow line to the right of the centre line, on your side, means no passing in your lane
- Two unbroken lines means no passing in either direction
- Broken white lines separate lanes travelling in the same direction
- Solid white lines also mark the inside edge of the road along the kerb
- Yellow lines also mark the outside edge of one-way roads or divided highways
- Sometimes a centre lane may be used for turning by traffic from both directions. The centre lane will be marked on each side by an unbroken white line with arrows indicating which direction vehicles are allowed to turn.

In Los Angeles lane discipline is a case of 'Dodge eat Dodge' and if you do not take a gap as soon as you see it someone else will. The sunshine states, particularly Florida, have a high concentration of retirees, whose reactions and awareness are not what they were. It pays to be watchful.

A common practice in America is lane hogging, where drivers (or 'Cruisers' as they are known) set their cruise control to a steady 60 or 65 and let other vehicles pass either side of them.

Carpool Lanes

Carpool lanes are for cars carrying two or more occupants. They are designed to encourage ride sharing and so reduce the number of vehicles on the road. Depending on which part of the country you are in you might also see them sign-posted as HOV for High Occupancy Vehicles or MOV for Multiple Occupancy Vehicles.

The carpool lane is usually the outside lane on a freeway and during the rush hour the cars in it are zipping by while the lone drivers crawl along in the jam. Do not be tempted to move into the carpool lane if you are the sole occupant of your vehicle because the police are always on the look out for cheats.

Carpool lanes are marked by a white diamond on the road surface or a white diamond against a black background on the signposts.

Where Can I Find Out More?

511

In July 2000 the Federal Communications Commission allocated the telephone number **511** as the single number for all travel information. However,

the implementation of that service will be a local decision and at the time of writing only a few pilot schemes were operating around the country.

The 511 initiative will be reviewed in 2005 before

a decision is made on whether to continue offering federal grants to help local jurisdictions adopt the system.

The Federal Highway Agency; FHWA, 400 7th Street SW, Washington DC 20590. ☎ 202-366-0537; www.fhwa.dot.gov

U.S. Department of Transportation, 400 7th Street SW, Washington D.C. 20590 ☎202-366-4000; www.dot.gov

State Departments of Transport

Alabama; ☎334-242-6358; www.dot.state.al.us; Road conditions 334-242-4378

Arizona; ☎602-712-7766; www.dot.state.az.us ;Road conditions 602-651-2400

Arkansas; ☎501-569-2000. Toll Free: 1-800-245-1672; www.dot.state.ar.us; Road Conditions 501-569-2374

California; ☎1-800-427-7623; www.dot.state.ca.us; Road conditions 916-445-7623

Colorado; ☎1-800-925-3427; www.dot.state.co.us; Road conditions 303-639-1234

Connecticut; ☎860-594-2000; www.state.ct.us/dot; Road conditions 860-594-2650

Delaware; ☎ 302-760-2080 or 800-652-5600 *Instate Only;* ; www.deldot.net; Road conditions 302-739-4313

Florida; ☎850-414-4100 or Toll Free at 866-374-FDOT 3368; ; www.myflorida.com; Road conditions North 904-752-3300. Middle 954-777-4090. South 305-470-5349

Georgia; ☎404-635-8027; www.dot.state.ga.us; Road conditions 404-624-7890

Hawaii; ☎ Construction Hotline 808-536-6566. Pothole Patrol 808-536-PUKA 7852; www.dot.state.hi.us

Idaho; ☎208-334-8000; www.dot.state.id.us; Road conditions 208-336-6600

Illinois; ☎217-782-6953; www.dot.state.il.us; Road conditions 1-800-452-4368

Indiana; ☎317-232-5533; www.ai.org/dot; Road conditions 317-232-8300

Iowa; ☎515-239-1101; www.dot.state.ia.us; Road conditions 515-288-1047

Kansas; ☎785-296-3585; www.ink.org/public/kdot; Road conditions 785-291-3000

Kentucky; ☎502-564-4890; www.kytc.state.ky.us; Road conditions 1-800-459-7623

Louisiania; ☎225 379-1100; www.dot.state.la.us;

Road conditions 504-295-8500

Maine; ☎207-287-2551; www.dot.state.me.us; Road conditions 207-287-3427

Maryland; ☎ 888-713-1414;www.mdot.state.md.us; Road conditions 410-545-8489

Massachusetts; ☎617-973-7800; www.magnet.state.ma.us; Road conditions 617-374-1234

Michigan; ☎517-373-2090; www.mdot.state.mi.us; Road conditions 1-800-337-1334

Minnesota; ☎651-296-3000. Toll-free from Greater Minnesota: 800-657-3774; www.dot.state.mn.us; Road conditions 612-374-1234 or 1-800-542-0220

Mississippi; 39215-1850. ☎601-359-7001; www.dot.state.ms.us; Road conditions 601-987-1212

Missouri; ☎1-888-ASK-MODOT 275-6636; www.dot.state.mo.us; Road conditions West 816-524-1407. East 314-340-4000. Central 573-751-1000

Montana; ☎ 406-444-6200; www.mdt.state.mt.us; Road conditions 406-444-6339 or 1-800-332-6171

Nebraska; ☎ 402-471-4567; www.dor.state.ne.us; Road conditions 402-471-4533

Nevada; ☎775-888-7000; www.nevadedot.com; Road conditions North 775-793-1313. South 702-486–3116

New Hampshire; ☎603-271-3734; www.dot.state.nh.us; Road conditions 603-271-6900

New Jersey; ☎609-530-2000; www.state.nj.us/transportation; Road conditions 908-727-5929

New Mexico; ☎505-827-5100. www.nmshtd.state.nm.us; Road Conditions 1-800-432-4269

New York; ☎518-457-6195; www.dot.state.ny.us; Road conditions 1-800-847-8929

North Carolina; ☎1-877-DOT4-YOU 368-4968; ; www.dot.state.nc.us; Road conditions 919-549-5100

North Dakota; ☎701-328-ROAD 7623; ; www.dot.state.nd.us; Road Conditions 701-328-7623

Ohio; ☎614-466-7170; www.dot.state.oh.us; Road Conditions 614-466-2660

Oklahoma; ☎405- 522-8000 Informational Recording; www.okladot.state.ok.us; Road Conditions 405-425-2385

Oregon; ☎1-888-ASK-ODOT 275-6368; www.odot.state.or.us; Road Conditions 541-889-3999

Pennsylvania; ☎717-787-2838;www.dot.state.pa.us; **Road Conditions 814-335-6044**

Rhode Island; ☎ 401 222-2481; www.dot.state.ri.us; Road Conditions 401-222-2545

South Carolina; ☎ 803-737-2314; www.dot.state.sc.us; Road Conditions 803-737-1030

South Dakota; ☎ 605-773-3265; www.sddot.com; Road Conditions 605-367-5707

Tennessee; ☎ 615-741-1751; www.tdot.state.tn.us; Road conditions 1-800-858-6349

Texas; ☎ 512; 463-8588; www.dot.state.tx.us; Road Conditions 1-800-452-9292

Utah; ☎ 801-965-4000; www.dot.state.ut.us; Road conditions 1-800-492-2400

Vermont; ☎ www.aot.state.vt.us ; Road conditions 802-828-2468

Virginia; ☎ 804-786-2801. Road conditions 1-800-367-ROAD 7623; www.dot.state.va.us; Road conditions 1-800-367-7623

Washington state; ☎ 360-705-7000; www.wsdot.wa.gov; Road conditions 1-800-695-ROAD 7623;

West Virginia; ☎ 304-558-3456; www.wvdot.com; Road conditions 304-558-2889

Wisconsin; ☎ 608-266-2211; www.dot.state.wi.us; Road conditions 1-800-762-3947

Wyoming; ☎ 307-777-4375; www.wydotweb.state.wy.us; Road conditions 307-635-9966

✦ Straight, Oklahoma, to Curve, Tennessee, 862 miles ✦

The Routes of a Nation

'The World is a book and those who do not travel read only a page.'

St Augustine

America awaits and it is time to hit the road. The United States contains four million miles (nearly 6.5 million kilometres) of paved roads. Its territory extends into the Arctic Circle, down to the Gulf of Mexico and from the Atlantic to the Pacific. So there is *bound* to be something for everyone: when it comes to driving, the country offers challenges and pleasures to meet every taste - whether it is mountain passes, desert highways, prairie roads, endless stretches of two-lane blacktop or dusty back roads. Here are some of the most glorious routes in America including stretches where they become Highways to Heaven.

(The Estimated Driving Times are based on a consistent, high mileage every day. Similarly the Total Distances are by the most direct route and without any detours along the way. Wherever possible, the tolls for turnpikes are quoted for cars - heavier vehicles will be charged more. All tolls are subject to change).

Route 66 - The Mother Road

No road has captured the imagination as much as Route 66, between Chicago and Los Angeles. The road symbolises the roving spirit of America and has been called the 'Mother Road', 'Glory Road,' 'Road of Second Chance' and 'America's Main Street.' It opened in 1926 and was always more of a chain of roads rather than a single highway. Steinbeck immortalised Route 66 in *The Grapes of Wrath*, his novel of Depression-era migrants escaping the dustbowls of the East and heading for California where work was supposedly plentiful and grapes grew the size of apples. Bobby Troup's song *Route 66* was released in 1946 and Nat King Cole was the first of many to have a hit with it. In the early 1960s the TV series *Route 66* (always with a lower case 'r' for some reason) followed the adventures of Buz and Tod as they travelled the highway in their Corvette.

The old Route 66 was 2,500 miles long. Anyone who wants to drive Route 66 today will have to look hard to find it. There was no place in modern America for a winding route over road surfaces of often dubious quality and it has been replaced by interstates and highways. Williams, Arizona, was the last town to say goodbye to a stretch of the original Route 66 when it was replaced by the I-40 in 1984. Overall, Route 66 has been gradually replaced by the I-55 between Chicago and St Louis, the I-44 from St Louis to Oklahoma City, the I-40 from Oklahoma City to Barstow, the I-15 between Barstow and San Bernardino and the I-10 from there to Santa Monica and Los Angeles.

The old Mother Road now only exists in memories, history books and old maps. Souvenir hunters have stolen the few Route 66 signs which remained. To travel the Glory Road today takes time and patience to negotiate the numerous highways which now trace its length but the route remains a classic and to follow it is to study an intricate part America's history and culture.

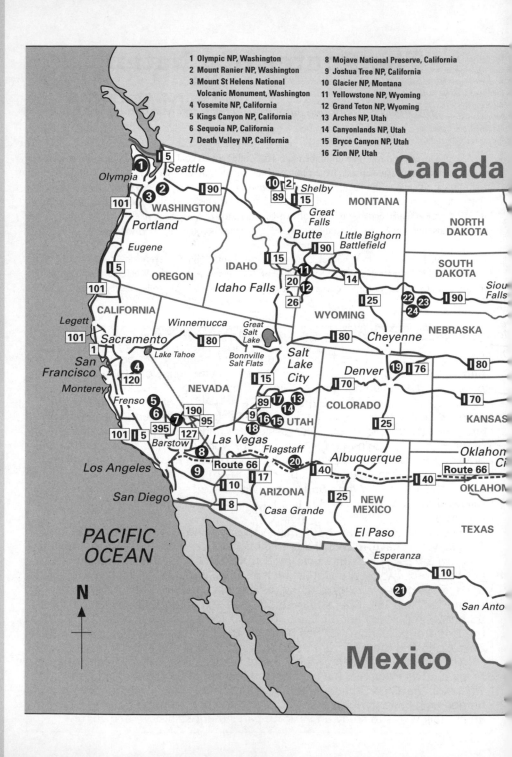

1 Olympic NP, Washington
2 Mount Ranier NP, Washington
3 Mount St Helens National
  Volcanic Monument, Washington
4 Yosemite NP, California
5 Kings Canyon NP, California
6 Sequoia NP, California
7 Death Valley NP, California

8 Mojave National Preserve, California
9 Joshua Tree NP, California
10 Glacier NP, Montana
11 Yellowstone NP, Wyoming
12 Grand Teton NP, Wyoming
13 Arches NP, Utah
14 Canyonlands NP, Utah
15 Bryce Canyon NP, Utah
16 Zion NP, Utah

Canada

Seattle
Olympia
WASHINGTON
Shelby
MONTANA
Great
Falls
NORTH
DAKOTA
Butte
Little Bighorn
Battlefield
SOUTH
DAKOTA
Portland
Eugene
OREGON
IDAHO
Idaho Falls
Siou
Falls
WYOMING
NEBRASKA
CALIFORNIA
Legett
Winnemucca
Great
Salt
Lake
Cheyenne
Sacramento
Lake Tahoe
Bonnville
Salt Flats
Salt
Lake
City
Denver
San
Francisco
Monterey
NEVADA
COLORADO
KANSAS
Frenso
UTAH
Barstow
Las Vegas
Flagstaff
Albuquerque
Oklahom
Ci
Los Angeles
Route 66
Route 66
OKLAHOM
San Diego
ARIZONA
NEW
MEXICO
TEXAS
Casa Grande
El Paso
PACIFIC
OCEAN
Esperanza
San Anto
N
Mexico

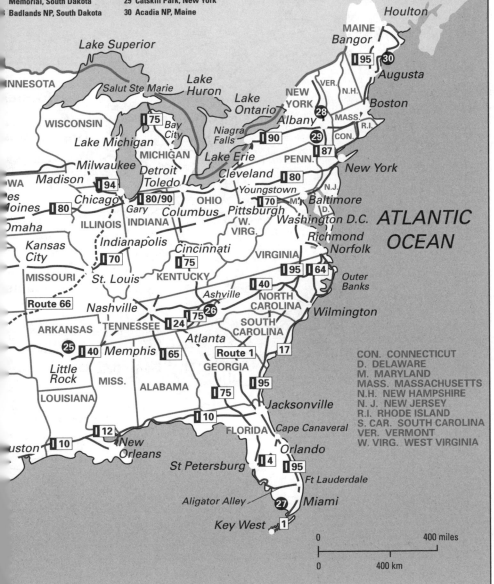

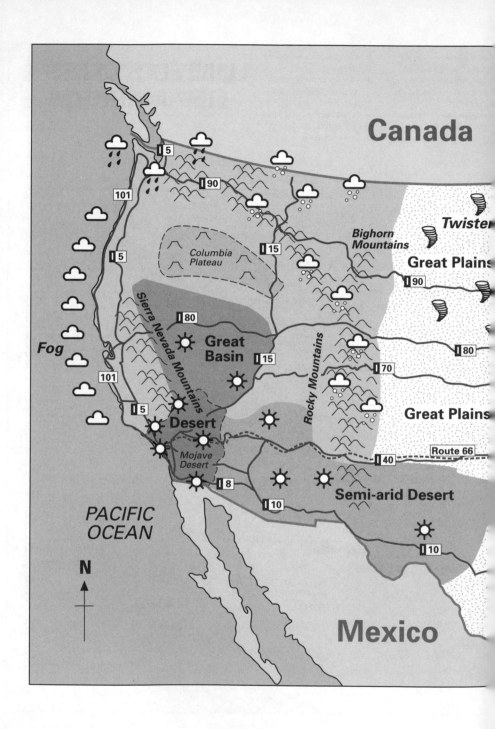

Canada

Twister

Bighorn
Mountains

Great Plains

Columbia
Plateau

Sierra Nevada Mountains

Fog

Great
Basin

Rocky Mountains

Great Plains

Desert

Route 66

Mojave
Desert

Semi-arid Desert

PACIFIC
OCEAN

N

Mexico

101

5

90

5

15

80

15

101

5

8

10

70

40

10

90

80

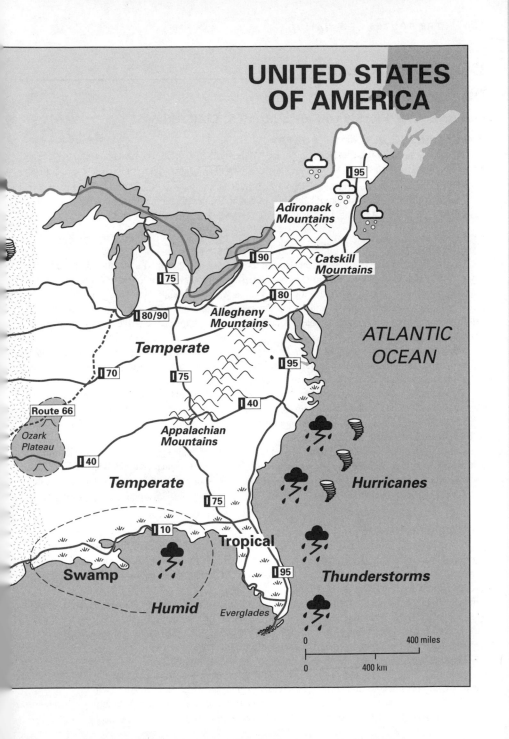

UNITED STATES OF AMERICA

Adironack
Mountains

Catskill
Mountains

Allegheny
Mountains

Temperate

Route 66

Ozark
Plateau

Appalachian
Mountains

Temperate

*ATLANTIC
OCEAN*

Hurricanes

Tropical

Swamp

Humid

Everglades

Thunderstorms

I 95
I 90
I 75
I 80
I 80/90
I 70
I 75
I 95
I 40
I 40
I 75
I 10
I 95

0   400 miles

0   400 km

East-West Routes

Interstate-10

(Jacksonville, Florida to Santa Monica, California – 2,441 miles/3,906 km - 9 days)

For anyone wanting to explore the Deep South, the I-10 is *the* route to drive. The road plugs into the jazz and blues of New Orleans and sweeps through the Cajun country of Louisiana with its French culture and cuisine. Further west lie the wide open spaces of Texas and its huge skies which seem to stretch away forever.

Starts in Jacksonville, Florida and **finishes** in Santa Monica, California, just west of Los Angeles. **Passes through** Florida, Alabama, Louisiana, Texas, New Mexico, Arizona and California.

The Journey

To drive the I-10 and *not* visit New Orleans would to miss one of the most vibrant cities in America. The city is rich in jazz and blues music and Bourbon Street is the rhythm section of the state. So take time to visit its bars and clubs and try and make a date in February for the annual Mardi Gras when New Orleans revels in excess, decadence, carnival and colour. The event started out in 1837 as an orgy of self-indulgence before Lent. Further afield, Louisiana boasts America's largest swamp and the I-10 crosses it on a series of causeways, well worth a look.

The 10 passes through semi-arid terrain between San Antonio, Texas, and Phoenix, Arizona. There is plenty of opportunity for some good open road driving. The flat landscape makes the sky seem huge and it is along this section of the I-10 that the traveller will appreciate the scale of the country.

The interstate hugs the border with Mexico between Esperanza and El Paso as it runs alongside the Rio Grande. Even if you do not plan to visit Mexico you can gaze across the border into America's neighbour.

If you like what you see, you can turn on to the I-8 at Casa Grande, Arizona, and head for San Diego before turning south to the border and Tijuana.

One of the highlights of the trip through southern California is the groves of Joshua trees, shimmering in the heat haze and stretching away on either side to the road. Joshua Tree National Park offers an unconventional beauty with its stark landscape and spikey trees - something different from the usual gushing waterfalls, towering mountains and lush forests.

Driving Conditions

Pace. You can notch up hundreds of miles a day across the open countryside of the south-western states.
Terrain. Florida, Alabama and Louisiana are level and the roads are relatively well maintained. Louisiana is crossed on causeways over swampland. Texas opens out into flat, sandy plains. The I-10 crosses desert through New Mexico, Arizona and California.
Climate. Florida's climate is subtropical which means long, hot summers but also a lot of rain, especially from May to October. Humidity rises to an uncomfortable 76% in June. August temperatures top 90F (32C) with January highs of 76F (23C) and lows of around 59F (15C). The state's wettest months are June, September and October. Winter and Spring are the most comfortable months to visit.

The high humidity is also a feature of the summer climates through Alabama, Mississippi and Louisiana. September to the Spring is probably the most comfortable time of year for visitors used to more temperate weather. During Mardi Gras, in February, New Orleans' temperatures can reach 64F (18C).

The states along the Gulf of Mexico are also prone to hurricanes, especially in August and September. Fierce thunder storms are also frequent visitors to the region in the summer.

The summer heat in Texas can be sapping. July temperatures rise to around 93F (34C). The best times to visit are March to May and mid-September to mid-November. Further west into New Mexico, Arizona and southern California the summer temperatures can soar as the terrain turns to desert. Rainfall in Arizona, for example, is negligible in May and June with temperatures becoming uncomfortably hot in July and August. **The Knowledge.** Drivers who want to by-pass New Orleans should take the I-12 around the northern shore of Lake Pontchartrain, rejoining at Baton Rouge. The 10 also serves as New Orleans' main street so the I-12 is a shorter and less stressful alternative for travellers who do not want to visit the city.

Houston, Texas, is surrounded by one of the most complicated networks of freeways in America. Avoid the area in the rush-hour and take the I-610 or Beltway 8 toll road around the north of Houston. As with Houston, the stretch of the I-10 which passes through Los Angeles requires concentration.

Do not to be surprised to be stopped by immigration patrols along the route as they check for 'wetbacks' from across the Mexican border.

Highway Highlights starting from Jacksonville
Louisiana

🚗 556 miles/890 km. **Lake Pontchartrain** and the **Pontchartrain Causeway**, north of New Orleans. The Causeway is the world's longest over-water bridge: ruler-straight and 24 miles (38 km) long. Round-trip toll for a car - $6 (**www.thecauseway.com**)

🚗 **The swamps** - S of I-10 across the state. Best explored on one of the many boat tours - around $20

Texas

🚗 884 miles/1,414 km. **Houston Space Centre.** 25 miles (40 km) south-east of the I-10, along the I-45

🚗 1,233 miles/1,973 km. **Amistad National Recreation Area** and the **Rio Grande River.** 91 miles (146 km) south of the I-10 on Highway 227

🚗 1,523 miles/2,437 km. **Big Bend National Park** - 98 miles (157 km) from the I-10. Highway 385 from Fort Stockton, the park is tucked up against the Mexican border

🚗 1,558 miles/2,493 km. **Carlsbad Caverns National Park,** New Mexico. 99 miles (158 km) north of the Van Horn, Texas, exit

🚗 **New Mexico**

🚗 1,820 miles/2,912 km. **White Sands National Monument.** 49 miles (78 km) from the I-10 at Las Cruces.

🚗 1,892 miles/3,027 km. **Shakespeare Ghost Town.** Just a couple of miles south of the interstate exit for Lordsburg

Arizona

🚗 1,945 miles/3,112 km. **Tombstone.** Site of the shoot-out at the OK Corral. 25 miles south of Exit 306 for Benson

🚗 1,969 miles/3,150 km. **Ironwood Forest National Monument.** 2 miles from the interstate at Exit 242

🚗 2,069 miles/3,310 km. **Organ Pipe Cactus National Monument.** 115 miles (184 km) from South Tucson Exit 260. Take US 86 and turn south at Why. To rejoin the I-10, head back to Why and turn west on to the US 85 to meet the interstate 85 miles (136 km) away at Buckeye

California

🚗 2,336 miles/3,738 km. **Joshua Tree National Park.** The I-10 skirts the southern edge of the Park

Highway to Heaven. The route through Alabama and Louisiana through the swamplands.

Interstate-40

(Wilmington, North Carolina to Barstow, Southern California – 2,715 miles/4,344 km - 9 days)

This interstate takes in some classic Americana - the Appalachian Mountains, the capital of Country music - Nashville, Tennessee - Elvis Presley's home in Memphis, and even a piece of the Mother Road - Route 66.

Starts in Wilmington, North Carolina and **finishes** in Barstow, southern California, where it meets the I-15. **Passes through** North Carolina, Tennessee, Arkansas, Oklahoma, Texas, New Mexico, Arizona, and southern California.

The Journey

The interstate starts out from Wilmington by heading north-west to North Carolina's state capital, Raleigh, before turning west towards Winston-Salem at the foot of the Appalachian Mountains. The 634 miles between Winston-Salem and Nashville, Tennessee, offer some challenging mountain driving through one of the country's most beautiful ranges. Asheville, North Carolina, is a good point to decide whether you want to stay on the I-40 as it bisects Cherokee National Forest to its north and Great Smoky Mountains National Park to its south or make a diversion on Highway 23, US 74 or US 19 to explore the length of the Appalachians.

The highpoint of the Appalachians is Clingman's Dome which straddles the state line. Its peak is 6,642 feet high (2,025 metres), although access roads are closed in the winter.

Nashville is the meeting point for three interstates so after soaking up the atmosphere of the 'Country Music Capital of the World' you can choose to head south to Alabama on the I-65 or the I-24. The I-24, south, will also take you to Georgia. The I-65 and the I-24, north, head into the Bluegrass State - Kentucky.

The I-40 passes through a part of the United States which is best served by local radio stations - and not just country music. The whole trip, from North Carolina to California can be driven to the soundtrack of your choice as you skip between radio stations.

215 miles (344 km) west of Nashville lies Memphis where the must-visit attraction is the home of Elvis - Graceland - on Elvis Presley Boulevard. The I-40 then crosses the Mississippi which marks the state lane between Tennessee and Arkansas. The journey through Oklahoma, Texas and New Mexico gives an idea of the wide open spaces of south-western USA. At Flagstaff, Arizona, there is the opportunity to turn north on to Highway 89 to visit the Grand Canyon before rejoining I-40 via Highway 189. An alternative road to Grand Canyon is to drive further on to Williams and turn north there.

Another detour worth taking is between Needles and Ludlow, in southern California, where it is possible to follow part of Route 66. Take Highway 95, north, turn right at the sign-post for Goffs, drive through Fenner (crossing the I-40 again) and pick up the Old National Trail Highway for about 74 miles to Ludlow where the road rejoins I-40. The stretch between Needles and Barstow provides some real desert driving.

An alternative desert drive would be through Mojave National Preserve. Midway between Ludlow and Goffs, on the I-40, there is a small road sign-posted to Kelso. This cuts through the middle of the National Preserve and meets the I-15 where it will be possible to turn west back towards Los Angeles or carry on north on US 127 to Death Valley.

Driving Conditions

Pace. Do not expect to cover vast numbers of miles through the mountains and prepare for congestion around Nashville and Memphis.

Terrain. Be prepared for some of the smaller roads through the Appalachians to be closed during the winter months and carry the appropriate supplies for the conditions. The terrain for this route is broadly similar to that of the I-10.

Climate. The eastern part of the route will enjoy a similar climate to Florida's, although the weather becomes less settled through the Appalachians with cold winters and heavy snow fall. The summers through Tennessee, Arkansas and Oklahoma tend to be long, warm and comfortable. Memphis, for example, enjoys top temperatures of 93F (34C) in July with an average 11 hours of sunshine. Further west, the I-40 passes through climate very similar to that of the I-10.

The Knowledge. The quality of the road surface in Arkansas is poor and provides an uncomfortable ride through the state. Watch for potholes and crumbling tarmac. Once into Oklahoma, however, it should be relatively easy driving all the way to California.

Highway Highlights starting from Wilmington

North Carolina/Tennessee

- 413 miles/661 km. **Great Smoky Mountains National Park.** 30 miles (48 km) from I-40. Take Exit 27, Highway 23/74, Highway 19 to Cherokee. Highway 441, the Newfound Gap Road, winds through the mountain range. Stay on the 441 to rejoin I-40

Tennessee

- 876 miles/1,402 km. **Graceland, Memphis.** About 16 miles from I-40. Leave the I-40 at Exit 12B-C, I-240 around the south of Memphis, turn south on to I-55 for about a mile, turn on to Elvis Presley Boulevard at Exit 5B.

Arkansas

- 1,081 miles/1,730 km. **Hot Springs National Park.** 65 miles north of the I-40 from Little Rock.

Oklahoma

- 1,451 miles/2,322 km. **The Oklahoma Route 66 Museum** at Clinton. The town is just a few minutes drive from the interstate.

Arizona

- 2,119 miles/3,390 km. **Petrified Forest National Park.** Take Exit 311, passing through the Painted Desert Visitor Centre which is next to the interstate. The Park straddles the I-40 and the round trip to the Rainbow Forest Museum at the other end is 42 miles (67 km)

- 2,314 miles/3,702 km. **Grand Canyon.** 58 miles (93 km) north, from the I-40 at Williams to the South Rim Visitor Centre

- 2,485 miles/3,976 km. **London Bridge**: Lake Havasu City. 19 miles south of the I-40, from Exit 9, on US 95

California

- 2,602 miles/4,163 km. **Mojave National Preserve.** The I-40 forms the southern border of the preserve. There are three ways into Mojave National Preserve from the I-40. 30 miles (48 km) after crossing the state line from Nevada, take Goffs Road north into the Preserve. About 17 miles (27 km) after that there is Essex Road. Finally, a further 50 or so miles (80 km) there is Kelbaker Road. All of these are sign-posted from the I-40.

Highway to Heaven. The Old National Trail Highway, southern California

Interstate-70
(Baltimore, Maryland to Utah - 2,184 miles/3,494 km - 7 days)

Travellers looking for room to breathe, open spaces, big skies and unclogged roads should take the I-70 across the American Mid-West, where farming communities lie scattered around the plains. The interstate rolls through the foothills of the Appalachians, the farmlands of Missouri and Nebraska before twisting and turning through the mountain passes of the Rockies.

Starts just west of Baltimore, Maryland and **finishes** on the western edge of Fishlake National Forest in Utah, where it meets the I-15 just south of Cave Fort. **Passes through** Maryland, Pennsylvania, West Virginia, Ohio, Indiana, Illinois, Missouri, Kansas, Colorado and Utah.

The Journey

The I-70 winds its way gently through the wooded valleys of the Allegheny Mountains, at the northern end of the Appalachians, in Pennsylvania. Hagerstown, Maryland, offers the opportunity to turn south on to the I-81 into West Virginia for travellers wanting to drive along the spine of the Appalachians.

The I-70 leaves the mountains behind just south of Pittsburgh and heads on through Columbus in Ohio, Indianapolis in Indiana and St Louis, Missouri. Kansas presents the most relaxing driving of the whole trip with long straights and fields of cereals stretching away to the horizon on either side of the road.

After negotiating Denver, the reward is the Rockies which offer the challenge of real mountain driving up steep climbs, down fast descents and around sweeping curves. Crags and rock faces huddle close to the interstate, in places, providing a stunning backdrop to your road trip. The I-70 sweeps by some of Colorado's most exclusive ski resorts like Breckenridge and Vail.

After the challenges of the Rockies, Utah offers much easier driving conditions before the I-70 meets the I-15 which runs north and south across the state. Utah is, in many places, a geological freak show and the I-15 passes many of the most unusual features.

To the north lies Salt Lake City, the home of the Mormons. Brigham Young led church members there to flee persecution at their first home in Illinois. It is claimed he chose Utah because no one would want to follow them there.

Driving Conditions

Pace. The sections between the big cities can be covered quite quickly. The slower sections will be through the urban congestion and through the Rocky Mountains.

Terrain. The route over the Appalachian Mountains is not too demanding. There are four big cities to get through - Indianapolis, St Louis, Kansas City and Denver. From Denver to the end of the I-70 is mountain terrain which can be particularly challenging in the winter.

Climate. The weather in Maryland and Pennsylvania is changeable because of the Gulf Stream which can bring rain at short notice. Washington DC is best visited in the spring (hot in the summer, cold in winter, wet in the autumn). Ohio and Indiana are also prone to frequent rainfall but mostly sunny in the summer.

April to June is 'twister' season as tornadoes whip up across the Great Plains of the Mid-West. Here the weather is at its most predictable in the Autumn when the tornado threat has receded and the rainfall is tailing off.

The rain is less of a problem through Colorado. Denver boasts more hours of sunshine than Florida and Texas. The snow starts falling heavily between November and March. Winter temperatures can fall as low as -12F (-25C) and rising to 100F (38C) in the summer. Sudden lightning storms are not uncommon between May and September. Wind chill is another factor so guard against it in the mountains.

The altitude in Denver and the Rockies cannot be ignored. It can take a few days to adjust to the thinner air, especially for children and smokers. Denver has a serious smog problem.

The Knowledge. There is an 86 mile stretch of toll road in Pennsylvania between Breezewood and New Stanton. The total charge for that section of turnpike will be $3.60 for a car (**www.paturnpike.com**).

The route around Columbus, Indianapolis and St Louis can be intimidating for the inexperienced driver - especially St Louis. The 70 cuts right through the middle of St Louis and is grid-locked in the rush hour. Instead, take the 270 around the city and rejoin the I-70 on the other side.

If you do not like driving in heavy snow, avoid the I-70 through the Rockies between October and March. You can by-pass the most challenging parts of the Rockies by turning north on to the I-25 at Denver and joining the I-80 West at Cheyenne in Wyoming, then later meeting the I-15 in Salt Lake City.

Highway Highlights starting from Baltimore

🚗   38 miles/61 km. **Washington DC**

Pennsylvania

🚗   246 miles/394 km. **Pittsburgh** - 26 miles (42 km) from I-70 on I-76 north or 33 miles on I-79.

Ohio

🚗   350 miles/560 km. **Salt Fork State Par**k - 60 miles (96 km) from I-70 on I-77/Highway 22 north.

🚗   490 miles/784 km. **Dayton.** (Dayton Speedway - 15 miles (13 km) south on I-75/Route 4

🚗   543 miles/867 km. **Cincinnati** - 53 miles (85 km) south of Dayton on I-75

Indiana

🚗   600 miles/960 km. **Indianapolis.** (Indianapolis Speedway - I-465 north from I-70)

🚗   663 miles/1,061 km. **Hoosier National Forest** - South on US 37 from Indianapolis

Illinois

🚗   783 miles/1,253 km. **Carlyle Lake** - 19 miles south of I-70 on US 127

Missouri

🚗   841 miles/1,347 km. **St Louis.**

🚗   **Mark Twain National Forest.** Stretching across Missouri, south of I-70

🚗   964 miles/1,542 km. **Jefferson City** (State capital) - 32 miles south of I-70

Kansas

🚗   1,087 miles/1,793 km. **Kansas City;** 1,148 miles/1,837 km. **Topeka (State capital)**

Colorado

🚗   1,690 miles/2,704 km. **Denver (State capital)**

🚗   1,717 miles/2,747 km. **Boulder** - 27 miles (43 km) north of Denver on Highway 36.

🚗   1,761 miles/2,818 km. **Rocky Mountain Nat. Park** - 71 miles north of Denver on US 19, 72 and 7.

🚗   1,760 miles/2,816 km. **Colorado Springs** - 70 miles south of Denver on I-25

🚗   1,781 miles/2,850 km. **Vail;** 1,886 miles/3,018 km. **Aspen**

🚗   **White River National Forest** - either side of the I-70 between Denver and the Utah state line

Utah

🚗   2,047 miles/3,275 km. **Arches National Park** - 29 miles (46 km) south of I-70 on Highway 191

🚗   2, 057 miles/3, 291 km. **Canyonlands Nat. Park** - 39 miles south of I-70 on Highway 191/US 313

🚗   2,124 miles/3,398 km. **Capitol Reef National Park** - 84 miles (134 m) south of I-70 on US 24

🚗   2,246 miles3,594 km. **Bryce Canyon Nat. Park** - 80 miles south of I-70 on Highway 89/US 12.

🚗   2,303 miles/3,685 km. **Zion National Park** - 137 miles (219 km) south of I-70 on Highway 89/US 9.

Highway to Heaven. Where the I-70 crosses the Rockies.

Interstate-80

(Ridgefield Park, New Jersey to San Francisco, California – 2,900 miles/4,640 km - 10 days)

This interstate offers an alternative coast-to-coast route through the mid-west, running roughly parallel to the I-70 but further north. Travellers who want to visit the rolling prairies should take the 80 because it passes through Wyoming. Although the interstate misses the most spectacular parts of the Rocky Mountains, it more than makes up for this with its route over the Sierra Nevada Mountains into California.

Starts in Ridgefield Park, New Jersey just west of New York City and **finishes** in San Francisco, California. **Passes through** New Jersey, Pennsylvania, Ohio, Indiana, Illinois, Iowa, Nebraska, Wyoming, Utah, Nevada and northern California.

The Journey

The I-80 is the best route for anyone planning a coast-to-coast road trip ending in San Francisco. The interstate follows the shoreline of Lake Erie, though Ohio, and briefly skirts Lake Michigan before striking out over Iowa's farmlands and the Mid-west.

Nebraska's long straights allow drivers to turn on the cruise control and let the car do the work. At the state line with Colorado there is the opportunity to take the I-76 to Denver and the Rockies.

The interstate passes north of the highest Rockies, crossing the Wyoming prairies, before heading out across the salt lakes of Utah and the Great Basin of Nevada. Utah boasts some strange topography, ranging from lunar landscapes to rock towers of red and orange stone.

At Wendover, the Bonneville Salt Flats make the trip worthwhile: a vast expanse of water, just a few inches deep, rests on a bed of white salt to create a giant mirror lake. The area is a popular location for filming car commercials and a favourite shot is of the car apparently driving on water. The three-inch-deep lake is the perfect set. This is also the area where land speed records are attempted.

After the moonscape of Nevada, the I-80 winds its way up and over the Sierra Nevada Mountains into California. The Sierras seem to go on forever, which just prolongs the enjoyment of the scenery.

Driving Conditions

Pace. From Indiana to the foot of the Sierra Nevada it is easy to cover the ground fairly quickly - 300 miles (480 km) a day is achievable. The Sierra Nevada will slow progress, especially in winter.

Terrain. Probably the most consistent terrain of all the east-west routes, because it avoids the most mountainous areas until reaching California and the Sierra Nevada.

Climate. The north-eastern states are wettest in the winter The southern states are prone to summer rain. New York, New Jersey, Maryland and W'ton DC all experience summer heatspells but very cold winters.

The route through Ohio, Illinois, Iowa, Nebraska and Wyoming is characterised by hot summers and severe winters. The section of the I-80 through Nevada and California illustrates the extremes of driving across the United States; within a few hours the terrain and climate passes from barren, flat and baking to lush, mountainous and cold. The Rockies and the Sierra Nevada mountains are subject to sudden changes in weather so check forecasts regularly and pack clothing for all conditions.

The Knowledge. From 6 miles west of Youngstown, Ohio, to Gary, Indiana there is over 300 miles of toll road. This entire toll section of the I-80 will cost just under $13 for a car. (**www.ohioturnpike.org/class1 and www.state.in/us/dot/tollroads/schedules**).

Between Elyria, Ohio, and Gary the I-80 shares the route of the I-90.

Highway Highlights starting from Ridgefield Park

New Jersey

🚗 58 miles/93 km. **Kittatinny Mountain/Delaware Water Gap Nat. Rec'n Area** - Route 615 north

Pennsylvania

🚗 140 miles/224 km. **Moshannon, Sproul and Susquehannock National Forests** - 20 miles (32 km) north on US 144

🚗 200 miles/320 km. **Allegheny National Forest** - 26 miles (42 km) north on Highway 219 or US 66

Ohio

🚗 300 miles/480 km. **Youngstown**

🚗 375 miles/600 km. **Cleveland/Lake Erie**

🚗 494 miles/790 km. **Toledo**

Indiana

🚗 664 miles/1,062 km. **Gary/Lake Michigan/Indiana Dunes National Lakeshore**

Illinois

🚗 684 miles/1,094 km. **Chicago** – the *Windy City*

Iowa

🚗 884 miles/1,414 km. **Iowa City** - 20 miles (32 km) south on Highway 218, **Riverside and Captain James T. Kirk's future birthplace**

🚗 1,015 miles/1,624 km. **Des Moines**, state capital

Nebraska

🚗 1,065 miles/1,704 km. **Omaha**

🚗 1,123 miles/1,797 km. **Lincoln**, state capital

Wyoming

🚗 1,561 miles/2,498 km. **Cheyenne**, state capital

🚗 1,613 miles/2,581 km. **Laramie**

🚗 1,643 miles/2,629 km. **Medicine Bow National Forest** - 30 miles (48 km) south on US 130

🚗 1,821 miles/2,629 km. **Rock Springs - Grand Teton National Park,** 179 miles (286 km), Highway 191 north. **Yellowstone National Park,** 259 miles (414 km) Highway 191 north. **Flaming Gorge National Recreation Area** - 20 miles south of I-70 on US 530

🚗 1,988 miles/3,181 km. **Wind River mountain range** - 167 miles (267 km) north on Highway 191

Utah

🚗 1,997 miles/3,195 km. **Salt Lake City/Great Salt Lake**

🚗 2,119 miles/3,390 km. **Bonneville Salt Flats** and **Bonneville Speedway**

Nevada

🚗 2,173 miles/3,467 km. **Humboldt-Toiyabe National Forest/Ruby Mountains** - 28 miles south on Highway 93

🚗 2,550 miles/4080 km. **Carson City**, state capital

California

🚗 2,595 miles/4,152 km. **Lake Tahoe** - 12 miles south of I-70 on US 89

🚗 2,695 miles/4,312 km. **Sacramento**, state capital

🚗 2,775 miles/4,440 km. **Yosemite Nat. Park** - 180 miles south of Lake Tahoe on US 89/Highway 395

Highway to Heaven. Crossing the Sierra Nevada into California.

Interstate-90

(Boston, Massachusetts to Seattle, Washington –
3,070 miles/4,912 km - 15 days)

The best word to describe the scenery for most of this route is 'rugged'. The I-90 takes in some of America's best natural attractions, crossing the northern states and terrain covered by the early pioneers.

Starts in Boston, Massachusetts and **finishes** in Seattle, Washington. **Passes through** Massachusetts, New York state, Pennsylvania, Ohio, Indiana, Illinois, Wisconsin, Minnesota, South Dakota, Wyoming, Montana, Idaho and Washington.

The Journey

When the I-90 reaches Albany, the state capital of New York, the traveller can choose to take the I-87 north to the Adirondack Mountains or south to the Catskills. Staying on the 90 takes you to Buffalo where it is a short hop to Niagara Falls.

Then the interstate runs along the shoreline of Lake Erie before joining the I-80 at Cleveland. The interstates go their separate ways at Gary, Indiana, although the 90 then shares the route of the I-94 for a short distance.

From South Dakota, onwards, it is worth taking time to explore the sights off the I-90. There are Badlands National Park and Mount Rushmore (where the heads of four American Presidents are carved into the rock), in South Dakota, Bighorn National Recreation Area in Montana (and, along US 212, the site of the Battle of Little Bighorn) and Yellowstone and Grand Teton National Parks to the south, in Wyoming.

There is one detour worth taking in Montana and that is to Glacier National Park. At Missoula, 100 miles west of Butte, take US 200 and Highway 93 the 157 miles (253 km) north to the National Park. Once in the Park take time to drive the 52 miles (83 km) of the Going-to-the-Sun Road. It has been called the most beautiful road in the world. It crosses the Continental Divide and includes 17 scenic viewpoints with snow melt cascading over sheer cliffs among its twisting hairpin bends.

The approach to Seattle could bring more unusual sights; 'UFOs' might be seen in the sky. These will be the strangely-shaped Stealth bombers operating out of the nearby Tacoma airbase.

Driving Conditions

Pace. With so much to see and savour, the I-90 is a road which should be taken at a leisurely pace, especially through Montana so 150-200 miles (240-300 km) a day should be expected at most.

Terrain. Probably one of the most rewarding routes in terms of terrain: it crosses mountains, passes lakes, negotiates big cities (Cleveland and Chicago), traverses plains and prairies and passes through forests.

Climate. Massachusetts can be surprisingly muggy in the summer with temperatures in Boston reaching 95F/35C. In winter, however, the route will test the cold weather driving skills. Make sure the car is up to the journey and all necessary provisions are on board before tackling the route.

Despite the cold, the northern states of Wisonsin, Minnesota, South Dakota, Montana and Idaho enjoy much sunshine. Great Falls, Montana, has January lows of 12F(-11C) and August highs of 84F(29C). Icy roads are a big danger. Snow closes some sections of the Going-to-the-Sun Road October-May.

The Pacific north-west is particularly prone to rain all year round, especially around Seattle. Fog is another element to challenge drivers in winter. Seattle's rainfall averages 6 inches (152 mm) in December. July temperatures in the city can reach a comfortable 84F (29C) with an average 10 hours a day sunshine.

The Knowledge. The I-90 starts out as the Massachusetts Turnpike, in downtown Boston. (By late 2002 the I-90 will be extended to Logan Airport). The Masspike runs 135 miles to the border with New York and will cost less than $4 (**www.massturnpike.com/toll_mileage/class_1**) for a car. The Masspike then becomes the New York State Thruway toll road until reaching Pennsylvania. These 387 miles through New York will cost

$12.15 (**www.thruway.state.ny.us/tolls/calc/index**).

After Elyria, in Ohio, there are a few more sections of toll road up to the Illinois/Wisconsin state line for which the tolls come to $4.85 (**www.illinoistollway.com/trates1**). So the total cost of tolls on the I-90 from downtown Boston to the Wisconsin state line will be about $21.

Highway Highlights starting from Boston

Massachusetts
- 95 miles/152 km. **Springfield**

New York
- 172 miles/275 km. **Albany**, state capital - **Adirondack Mountains**, 53 miles north on I-87. Catskill Mountains, 52 miles south on I-87
- 318 miles/509 km. **Syracuse**
- 470 miles/752 km. **Bufallo - Niagara Falls/Lake Erie,** 24 miles north-west on I-190

Pennsylvania
- **Allegheny Mountains -** 73 miles (117 km) south from I-90 on Highway 219

Ohio
- 654 miles/1,046 km. **Cleveland**
- 773 miles/1,237 km. **Toledo**

Indiana
- 953 miles/1,525 km. **Gary/Lake Michigan/Indiana Dunes National Lakeshore**
- 973 miles/1,557 km. **Chicago**

Wisconsin
- 1,129 miles/1,806 km. **Madison - Milwaukee/Lake Michigan** 78 miles (125 km) on I-94

Minnesota
- 1,270 miles/2032 km. **Hardwood State Forest**

South Dakota
- 1,583 miles/2,533 km. **Sioux Falls**
- 1,863 miles/2,981 km. **Badlands National Park**
- 1,929 miles/3,086 km. **Rapid City - Hot Springs** and **Wind Cave National Park**, 61 miles (98 km) south on US 79. **Mount Rushmore** 29 miles (46 km) south on Highway 16. **Geographical Centre of the United States,** 25 miles north on Highway 85

Wyoming
- 2,141 miles/3,426 km. **Bufallo/Bighorn Mountains**
- 2,176 miles/3,482 km. **Sheridan**. **Yellowstone National Park,** 337 miles, Highway 14 and 20

Montana
- 2,206 miles/3,530 km. **Battle of Little Big Horn** battlefield site
- 2,307 miles/3,691 km. **Billings**. 2,530 miles/4,048 km. Butte
- 2,648 miles. **Missoula - Glacier Nat. Park**, 140 miles north on US 200, Highway 93 and US 93

Washington
- 2,793 miles/4,467 km. **Spokane**
- 2,964 miles/4,742 km. **Ellensburg - Mount Rainier National Park**, 119 miles, Highway 12

Highway to Heaven. Going-to-the-Sun Road, Montana.

North-South Routes

The Pacific Coast Highway - Highways 1, 101 & the I-5
(San Diego to US/Canada border - 1,371 miles/2,194 km - 5 days)

Highways 1 and 101 run from Los Angeles all the way up to Washington state. The roads cling to the Pacific coastline - waves crash against the shore just a few yards from the car in some places - as they wind around bays, coves, fishing villages and towns populated by artists, writers, and assorted bohemians.

Starts: Highway 1 in Dana Point, south of Los Angeles; Highway 101 in Glendale, north of Los Angeles; I-5 in San Diego, southern California. **Finishes:** Highway 1 in Leggett, northern California; Highway 101 - Olympia, Washington; I-5 - Blaine, Washington, on the US/Canada border. **Passes through** California, Oregon and Washington.

The Journey

The three roads need to be considered together because they are so entwined on their route along the Pacific coast. The route starts in the birthplace of California, San Diego, where the Mission San Diego de Alcala was established in 1769. The I-5, also known as the San Diego Freeway, covers the 96 miles between San Diego and the starting point of Highway 1 at Dana Point, south of Los Angeles. (Anyone wanting a quick drive up to Seattle should stay on the I-5 at this point).

The 1 and the 101 meet at Oxnard and go their separate ways 35 miles (56 km) later at La Cruces. At this point the 101 goes further inland. Highway 1 meanders slightly inland, passing Los Padres National Forest, before returning to the coast and continuing on to Big Sur, Carmel, Monterey, Half Moon Bay and hundreds of other stopping off points to kick back and relax and watch the Pacific.

Highway 1 crosses the Golden Gate Bridge in San Francisco, travels through the wine country of Marin County and follows the coast until turning inland and meeting Highway 101 at Leggett. From Santa Barbara until being reunited with Highway 1 at Leggett, the 101 runs roughly parallel with the coast road but about 30 miles (48 km) inland.

Highway 1 ends at Leggett and Highway 101 takes up the baton, returning to the coast just south of Eureka about 100 miles (160 km) from the Oregon state line. Any road atlas will show the Oregon coast line with a long, closely-typed list of scenic areas, recreation sites, heritage sites and memorial parks - starting with Winchuk Recreation Site at the California state line and ending with Fort Stevens Scenic Park at the Washington line. The National Geographic Road Atlas, alone, shows 77 parks and scenic viewpoints along the 400 or so miles (640 km) of Pacific coast through Oregon – a most scenic route.

The route along the Washington coast is even more winding as the 101 works its way around Willapa Bay and Grays Harbor. The Highway then circles Olympic National Park, turning south towards Olympia where it meets the I-5 which carries on north to Seattle and eventually Canada.

Driving Conditions

Pace. The Pacific Coast Highway is *not* a road to be rushed. It is not just its winding nature which makes it a slow route to travel; there is so much to see. Pick a shorter stretch and explore it in more depth if this suits.

Climate. Much of California has a Mediterranean climate, although the deep south of the state is desert. The weather for most of the Pacific Coast Highway's route through California is fairly consistent. The summers are comfortable and the winters are mild, if wet. The year-round average temperature for Los Angeles' beaches is 68F/20C and can rise to 84F (29C) in August. 385 miles (616 km) further north, San Francisco's August highs average 66F (19C).

Mark Twain once wrote, 'the worst winter I ever spent was summer in San Francisco.' Although famous for its Pacific mists, San Francisco averages 162 clear days a year, compared with 93 in New York and 57 in Seattle. The city often enjoys an Indian summer - so September is a good time to visit. Smog can be a problem.

The weather in Oregon and Washington is generally wetter and the coastal areas are more prone to storms whipped up off the Pacific. Fog is another regular feature along the route, but particularly in and around San Francisco.

Terrain. Most of the route is winding and twisting as it rises up and over sea cliffs or sweeps down into bays and beaches. This makes driving at night or in poor visibility difficult but given the scenery, the road should be driven in daylight anyway. Coastal erosion means that the road surface has crumbled in places: frequent roadworks and temporary traffic lights are common where the Highway passes close to the sea.

The Knowledge.

The only toll is for $3 per car to cross Golden Gate Bridge. Cars carrying three or more people and motorbikes can cross free between 5am and 9am and 4pm and 6pm weekdays, excluding holidays.

Highway Highlights starting from San Diego
California

- 104 miles/166 km. **Disneyland** - Exit off the I-5 for Anaheim
- 140 miles/224 km. **Santa Monica/Venice Beach - John Paul Getty Museum** - Highway 1
- 154 miles/264 km. **Hollywood** - intersection of I-5 and Highway 101
- 238 miles/381 km. **Santa Barbara** – a beautiful small town- Highway 101
- 342 miles/547 km. **Fresno** - US 99 (splits from I-5 at Mettler). **Kings Canyon** and **Sequoia National Parks**, 53 miles (85 km), US 180 from Fresno
- 383 miles/620 km. **Big Sur Village**; 450 miles/720 km. **Monterey** - Highway 1
- 508 miles/813 km. **San Francisco** - Highway 1. **Yosemite National Park,** 183 miles (293 km), I-580, I-205, US 120. **Lake Tahoe,** 185 miles, I-80
- 812 miles/1,299 km. **Redwood National Park** - Highway 101

Oregon

- 877 miles/1,403 km. **Brookings** - Highway 101
- 975 miles/1,560 km. **Coos Bay** - Highway 101
- 1,023 m/1,637 km. **Florence** - Highway 101. Eugene, 61 miles (98 km), on US 126 from Florence.
- 1,073 miles/1,717 km. **Newport** - Highway 101
- 1,100 miles/1,760 km. **Lincoln City** - Highway 101. **Portland** 81 miles on US 18 from Lincoln City

Washington

- 1,213 miles/1,941 km. **Olympia**, state capital - from I-5
- 1,228 miles1,965. **Mount Ranier National Park**. 31 miles (50 km) from I-5 at Exit 68
- 1,233 miles/1,973 km. **Pacific Pines Scenic Park** and **Willapa Bay** - US 103 from Highway 101
- 1,424 miles/2,278 km. **Olympic National Park (Visitor Centre)** - Highway 101
- 1,271 miles/2,034 km. **Seattle** - I-5

Highway to Heaven. The whole route.

Interstate-15

(San Diego, southern California to Sweet Grass, Montana, on the Canadian border – 1,440 miles/2,304 km - 5 days)

I-15 takes in Los Angeles, the Californian desert and the mountains of Montana, via the Utah salt lakes. The interstate offers the contrast of flat and arid desert and rich and rolling landscape - all within a five-day trip.

Starts in San Diego, southern California and **finishes** in Sweet Grass, Montana, on the Canadian border.
Passes through California, Nevada, Arizona (very briefly), Utah, Idaho and Montana.

The Journey

The I-15 sets out from San Diego and heads north-east into the desert towards Mojave. The interstate offers a number of jumping off points to explore other parts of southern California; there is Los Angeles or travellers can turn west onto the I-10. Further north the I-15 meets the I-40 at Barstow where, again, there is the opportunity to head west and travel part of Route 66 on the Old National Trail Highway, starting at Ludlow.

At Baker US 127 heads north to Death Valley National Park. Between Baker and Mountain Pass the I-15 forms the northern perimeter of the Mojave National Preserve. To reach the preserve, take the Kelbaker Road south at Baker or drive another 30 miles (48 km) on to the junction with Cima Road. A third alternative is to leave the I-15 at Nipton Road and then enter the Preserve via the Morning Star Mine Road.

Las Vegas lies another 40 miles (64 km) beyond the National Preserve where there is the chance to win back - or lose - your expenses.

After clipping the north-west corner of Arizona for about 35 miles (56 km), I-15 enters Utah. US 17 takes visitors to Zion National Park, named by the Mormons after the Heavenly City of God. The sculpted, multi-coloured rocks are in complete contrast to the plan arid desert which the I-15 passes through. About an hour's drive further on from Zion is Bryce Canyon National Park with its orange-red rock formations: take the US 9 out of Zion, then Highway 89 north and then the US 12 east. Bryce Canyon itself is a natural bowl of red-orange spikes, pinnacles and towers of rock called 'hoodoos'. One of the founders of the Church of Jesus Christ and Latter Day Saints (the Mormons), Brigham Young, described Bryce as, 'a Helluva place to lose a cow.'

There are two ways to get back on to the I-15 after visiting Bryce Canyon. Either head back on US 12, taking Highway 89 north and then US 20 west. Or stay on Highway 89 north to join the I-70 at Sevier and drive 22 miles (35 km) west to meet the 15 near Cave Fort.

The Great Salt Lake lies north of Salt Lake City. The I-80 heads east and west across the I-15. The 15 heads due north into Idaho and Idaho Falls provides a good link with Highway 26 to Grand Teton National Park and Highway 20 to Yellowstone National Park, both in neighbouring Wyoming.

Finally there are the mountains and forests of Montana. The interstate meanders through Beaverhead Deerlodge, Lolo, Helena, Flathead and Lewis and Clark National Forests. Highway 2 crosses I-15 at Shelby and takes visitors into Glacier National Park via the eastern entrance.

Driving Conditions

Pace. There will be some congestion around San Diego and Los Angeles but it will be easy to cover the ground quickly through the desert; 300-400 miles (480-640 km) a day should be manageable. However, allow *at least* a day for each of the national parks. To rush through them is to miss out on some of America's greatest landscape.

Terrain. From San Diego right up into Idaho the terrain is relatively gentle. Some of the roads in the parks offer more challenging driving; in Zion, for example, there are a number of hairpin bends and one very long winding tunnel through a mountain. The route through the forest and mountains are also more demanding with wildlife presenting a risk of collision.

Climate. Prepare for extremely hot conditions for much of the trip, but especially through southern California, Nevada, Arizona and Utah. Take plenty of water, both for occupants and the car. With temperatures up in the 90s (30sC) in the summer, the air conditioning will be working hard and that will affect fuel consumption. Maximum July temperatures in Las Vegas can reach 106F (41C). The extreme summer temperatures of Death Valley and the Mojave desert mean that they are heavily visited in winter and spring, particularly late March and early April when the wild flowers briefly bloom.

However, Zion, Bryce, Grand Teton, Yellowstone and Glacier National Parks are *all* prone to extremely cold weather. The Utah parks are in the path of Alaskan cold fronts which can send temperatures plummeting and cause heavy snow falls.

The Knowledge. A toll-free route and, perhaps, under-rated as a journey in its own right. Because it meets the I-10, I-40, I-70, I-80, I-84, I-86 and the I-90, it offers access to almost anywhere in the Western US.

Highway Highlights starting from San Diego

California

- 130 miles/208 km. **Disneyland** at Anaheim - 30 miles west of I-15, along US 91

- 181 miles/290 km. **Barstow. Sequoia National Park**, 149 miles (238 km) from Barstow - US 58 west, Highway 395 north at Four Corners. **Death Valley National Park western entrance**, same route but take US 190 at Olancha

- 327 miles/523 km. **Death Valley National Park eastern entrance**. 84 miles (134 km) from Baker, US 127 to Death Valley Junction. To get back on to the I-15 from Death Valley, one can double back on to the 127. Or if driving right through the National Park towards the Western exit, take state highway 178 South to Ridgecrest and then Highway 395 South until it rejoins the I-15 just West of Hesperia. Total distance 153 miles (245 km)

Nevada

- 337 miles/539 km. **Las Vegas. Hoover Dam**, 23 miles , from Las Vegas along Boulder Highway

Utah

- 503 miles/805 km. **Zion National Park**. 25 miles from I-15 on US 17

- 586 miles/938 km. **Bryce Canyon National Park**. 108 miles from I-15 on US 17, Highway 89 north and US 12 east. 754 miles/1,206 km. **Lake Salt City/Great Salt Lake**.

- **Crand Canyon NP.** To get to the Northern Rim of the Grand Canyon from I-15, leave the interstate at Exit 16, Utah, and take US 9 to Hurricane before turning on to US 59 into Arizona. US 59 becomes US 389. Take Alt 89 at Fredonia and then US 67 at Jacob Lake. The 67 takes you to Grand Canyon Lodge on the Northern Rim. However, the best views are from the Southern Rim. To get there from I-15, take I-515 from Las Vegas and join Route 93 (which crosses Hoover Dam). Route 93 joins I-40 at Kingman, Arizona, and the Southern Rim can be reached via US 64 from Williams or Route 89 from Flagstaff. To rejoin I-15 from the Southern Rim, either retrace your route or take Route 89 and Alt 89 north to Fredonia.

Idaho

- 952 miles/1,532 km. **Idaho Falls. Yellowstone Nat. Park** (Wyoming) 109 miles along Highway 20

Montana

- 1,395 miles/2,232 km. **Shelby. Glacier Nat. Park** 88 miles to east entrance on Highway 2 or 89 north

Highway to Heaven. Access to so much else, especially the National Parks.

Interstate-75

(Sault Ste. Marie, Michigan to Fort Lauderdale, Florida – 1,699 miles/2,718 km - 6 days)

This interstate plunges south from the northern tip of Michigan, at the Canadian border, to southern Florida. It serves as a spine road to explore two of the Great Lakes, cross the Appalachians *and* the Everglades.

Starts in Sault Ste. Marie, (pronounced Soo San Marie) Michigan and **finishes** just west of Fort Lauderdale, Florida. **Passes through** Michigan, Ohio, Kentucky, Tennessee, Georgia and Florida.

The Journey

Starting out from Sault Ste. Marie, which straddles the border with Canada, the I-75 passes east of the conifers of Hiawatha National Forest. The interstate state leaves the Upper Michigan peninsula and crosses to Lower Michigan via the Mackinac Bridge (known locally as the Big Mack) over the Straits of Mackinac ($1.50 for passenger cars - **www.mackinacbridge.org**).

At Mackinaw City, travellers can either turn east on to Highway 23 and follow the shoreline of Lake Huron or drive a couple of miles further to Exit 336, where Highway 31 heads towards Lake Michigan. Those following Lake Huron can rejoin the 75 at Bay City or stay on US 13 and 25 and rejoin it at Detroit. Visitors to Lake Michigan can rejoin I-75 by cutting across the state on the I-94 from Benton Harbor or by driving on into Indiana and picking up the Indiana East-West Toll Road at Michigan City and meeting the 75 south of Toledo, Ohio.

The I-75 crosses the I-70 just north of Dayton, Ohio, offering the choice of heading for the Mid-West or the Eastern Seaboard. The Bluegrass State of Kentucky and the southern hills of the Appalachians lie further south. Then the interstate passes through Atlanta, Georgia, before crossing into Florida and turning towards the state's west coast along the Gulf of Mexico.

At Naples the I-75 turns due east and becomes Everglades Parkway, otherwise known as Alligator Alley, and crosses Big Cypress National Preserve and the Everglades before meeting the I-595 just outside Fort Lauderdale.

Driving Conditions

Pace. The Great Lakes should be explored at leisure. Expect a lot of congestion around Detroit but further south the driving should be fairly smooth. The I-75 does pass through a lot of built up areas in Florida so, once again, congestion will slow progress.

Terrain. A relatively undemanding route, even over the southern end of the Appalachians.

Climate. Michigan, Ohio and Kentucky are prone to higher rainfall than other Mid-West states but the weather is generally milder around the Great Lakes. Further south into Tennessee and Kentucky the summers are comfortably warm - Memphis averages 10-11 hours of sun a day between May and August.

Georgia is prone to high humidity, especially in Atlanta where there are no sea breezes to cool the air and the tall, glass and steel skyscrapers absorb and release the heat.

Not for nothing is Florida known as the Sunshine State, boasting an average 10 hours a day in Miami in June. January temperatures top 76F (23C). Northern Florida is more changeable. June, September and October are the wettest months when it is prone to fierce thunder. Winter and Spring are the most comfortable seasons to visit but be prepared to share the state with hundreds of thousands of other tourists.

Highway Highlights starting from Sault Ste. Marie
Michigan
- 🚗 86 miles/138 km. **Mackinaw** and **Huron State Forests** either side of I-75
- 🚗 182 miles/291 km. **Lake Michigan** and **Sleeping Dunes National Lakeshore** via Highway 31
- 🚗 346 miles/554 km. **Detroit**

Ohio
- 🚗 590 miles/944 km. **Cincinnati**

Kentucky
- 🚗 675 miles/1,080 km. **Lexington**
- 🚗 752 miles/1,203 km. **London - Daniel Boone National Forest**

Tennessee
- 🚗 847 miles/1,355 km. **Knoxville**. **Great Smoky Mountains NP**, 53 miles (85 km) east, Highway 129

Georgia
- 🚗 1,057 miles/1,691 km. **Atlanta**

Florida
- 🚗 1,336 miles/2,138 km. **Intersection** with I-10. **Jacksonville** and I-95, 59 miles (94 km) west
- 🚗 1,516 miles/2,426 km. **Tampa/St Petersburg**. **Orlando** and **Walt Disney World** 82 miles (131 km) east on I-4
- 🚗 1,678 miles/2,685 km. **Naples** and **Everglades National Park** along Everglades Parkway to **Fort Lauderdale** or via Highway 41 to Miami

Highway to Heaven. The Everglades.

Border Crossings

Border crossings between the United States and Canada and the United States and Mexico are relatively trouble-free. People travelling into Canada will need their passports and/or proof of citizenship. US citizens who are planning to stay in Canada for less than six months do not need visas.

American drivers' licences are valid north of the border but it is always worth taking an International Driver's Permit as a precaution. Foreign drivers' licences are accepted in Mexico and the US. American motor insurance is valid in Canada but visitors have to carry proof that they are insured.

For drivers crossing from Canada to the United States, Canadian licences are valid for one year and proof of vehicle registration, ownership and insurance must be presented to customs officials. There are no duties or fees to pay.

Visitors travelling to Mexico must obtain a tourist card from a Mexican consulate, tourist office or border office if they are planning to stay between 72 hours and six months. American driver's licences are valid in Mexico but visitors must obtain a temporary import permit for their vehicles. Permits are available from a Mexican Customs Office at the border.

American motor insurance policies are not valid in Mexico but it is possible to buy short-term policies at border crossings. Sanborn's Mexico Insurance has offices at most crossing points. Alternatively, most American insurance companies also offer coverage for Mexico.

The Eastern Seaboard - Interstate-95 and Route 1
(Houlton, Maine to Key West, Florida - 2,100 miles/3,360 km - 9 days)

From the Canadian border to within 90 miles (144 km) of Cuba, the Eastern Seaboard route takes in the forests of New England, the buzz of New York, the rugged coasts of the Carolinas, the chic resorts of Florida and, finally, the southern-most point of the United States mainland - Key West.

Starts: I-95 - Houlton, Maine, on the Canadian border; Route 1 Fort Kent, Maine, on the Canadian border. **Finishes:** I-95 - Miami, Florida; Route 1 - Key West Florida. **Passes through** Maine, New Hampshire, Massachusetts, Rhode Island, Connecticut, New York, New Jersey, Pennsylvania, Delaware, Maryland, Virginia, North Carolina, South Carolina, Georgia and Florida.

The Journey

Without doubt the best time of the year to visit the New England states of Maine, New Hampshire and Vermont is in the Autumn when the trees turn a hundred shades of red and gold. New England in the Fall is a sight *everyone* should see at least once.

As with the I-5 on the West Coast, the I-95 enables travellers to move at speed down the East Coast and make diversions to explore places of special interest in New England and along the Eastern Seaboard. For example, at Bangor, Maine, it is worth taking a detour off the I-95 and heading east on Route 1 (or its sister road, Alt 1) to Acadia National Park on Mount Desert Island. The Park contains thousands of acres of evergreen forest, granite cliffs and crashing surf against rock faces dotted with lighthouses.

Further south there is the chance to visit some of the places where the Union of States was first forged. There is Boston, which has a distinctly European feel and then the tranquil Rhode Island, America's smallest state. New York City offers a complete contrast – fast and furious – the City that never sleeps.

The I-95 circles the east of Washington DC - jump off point to explore the nation's capital. Further south into Virginia, turn towards the coast at Richmond and take the I-64 out to Newport News.

To get really close to the ocean, follow US-168, Highway-158 and US-12 to the Outer Banks of N.Carolina's Cape Hatteras and Cape Lookout - a strand of islands running up to 30 miles off the mainland at some points. The route passes through Kitty Hawk, where the Wright brothers made the first powered flight in 1903. At Ocracoke you face the choice of either doubling back the 79 miles (126 km) to the mainland or taking the ferry to Cedar Island where US-12 and Highway-17 carry on south along the coast.

The coastal route through South Carolina and Georgia passes hundreds of bluffs, coves and inlets before arriving in the more tropical climate of Florida. Again, Route 1 offers the more scenic but slower alternative to I-95. The 95 comes to an end at North Miami Beach but Route 1 presses on south and heads out to sea at Florida City, island hopping along the Keys on a chain of causeways, before arriving at Key West - just 90 miles from Cuba.

After nearly 2,000 miles of driving, ensure you have time to watch the sunset over the Gulf of Mexico - one of the most beautiful in the world.

Driving Conditions

Pace. From New England to Maryland it will be slower away from the I-95 but around 200 miles a day should be manageable. Following the coast through North Carolina, South Carolina and Georgia will be a very 'out-of-the-way' route and take time. Florida can be covered fairly quickly – if necessary.

Terrain. Away from the I-95 the roads are winding but on the coastal routes the weather will provide the main challenge. The roads are mostly well-maintained and easy to drive. Florida is very flat and the roads are straight: any delays will come from urban congestion rather than weather or road conditions.

Climate. New England winters are long and snowy with falls often reaching 100 inches (2.5m). Spring is short and muddy as the snow turns to slush with the odd blizzard - sometimes as late as May. Autumn is mild and the best time to see the forests. Rain and fog are two regular visitors to New England.

South into Massachusetts and New York, expect heavy snow in winter. The highest August temperatures in Boston can reach 82F (28C) and drop to 21F (-6C) in January. Washington's weather is extremely varied but can be very hot in the summer.

Out on the coastal roads storms coming in off the Atlantic are the biggest problem with the occasional hurricane between July and October. Florida's is a tropical climate and extremely humid in the summer but it is prone to fierce thunder storms which can make driving hazardous.

The Knowledge. The Maine Turnpike costs $3.25 (**www.maineturnpike.com**). From Ridgefield Park, the 118 mile New Jersey Turnpike costs $5.50 (**www.state.nj.us/turnpike/tollcalc**). After a short distance comes the Delaware Turnpike. The 11 mile (17.5 km) stretch will cost $2 .

Highway Highlights starting from Houlton

Maine

🚗 40 miles/64 km. **Baxter State Park** - US 159 from I-95

🚗 163 miles/261 km. **Acadia National Park** - 41 miles (66 km) from **Bangor** (state capital) along Alt 1
Massachusetts

🚗 409 miles/645 km. **Boston**, state capital. **Cape Cod** 72 miles (115 km) from Boston along US 3
New York

🚗 624 miles/998 km. **New York City**
Maryland

🚗 814 miles/1,302 km. **Baltimore**. Washington DC, 38 miles (61 km) from Baltimore
Virginia

🚗 960 miles/1,536 km. **Richmond**, state capital. **Virginia Beach** 107 miles east of Richmond, via I-64
North Carolina

🚗 1,076 miles/1,722 km. **Rocky Mount. Pocosin Lakes Nat. Wildlife Reserve/Nags Head**, 147 miles
(235 km) along Highway 64. Nags Head to **Ocracoke**, along the Outer Banks, 79 miles (126 km)
South Carolina

🚗 1,363 miles/2,181 km. **Charleston** - 40 miles (64 km) along I-26 from I-95
Georgia

🚗 1,412 miles/2,259 km. **Savannah**
Florida

🚗 1,547 miles/2,475 km. **Jacksonville**

🚗 1,638 miles/2,621 km. **Daytona Beach**

🚗 1,680 miles/2,688 km. **Kennedy Space Centre** on Route 1 and NASA Parkway from Titusville

🚗 1,694 miles/2,710 km. **Orlando**, via I-4, to **Walt Disney World**

🚗 1,892 miles/3,027 km. **Miami. Everglades National Park** west on Highway 41

🚗 2,071 miles/3, 312 km. **Key West**

Highway to Heaven. New England in the Fall.

Where Can I Find Out More?

Routes

Route 66: National Historic Route 66 Federation, PO Box 423, Tujunga, California 91043-0423. (☎ 818-352-7232: www.national66.com). The website provides links to all of the Route 66 museums and organisations along the highway.

National Scenic Byways Program: PO Box 4059, Logan, Utah 84323-4059. (☎ 435-797-8787: www.byways.org). This organisation is dedicated to the promotion and preservation of America's smaller scenic routes and is a great source of information for places to visit off the beaten track.

Tourist Information

Alabama: *The Heart of Dixie*
Alabama Bureau of Tourism and Travel, 401 Adams Ave., PO Box 4927, Montgomery, Alabama 36103. (☎ 1-800-252-2262. 333-242-4169: www.touralabama.org).

Alaska: *The Great Land*
Alaska Division of Tourism, PO Box 110801, Juneau, Alaska 99811-0801. (☎ 907-465-2010: www.dced.state.ak.us/tourism)

Arizona: *The Grand Canyon State*
Arizona Office of Tourism, 2702 N. Third St., Suite 4015, Phoenix, Arizona 85004. (☎ 1-800-842-8257. 602-230-7733: www.arizonaguide.org)

Arkansas: *The Natural State*
Arkansas Department of Parks and Tourism, One Capitol Mall, Little Rock, Arkansas 72201. (☎ 1-800-628-8725. 501-682-7777: www.1800natural.com)

California: *The Golden State*
California Division of Tourism, PO Box 1499, Department TIA, Sacramento, California 95812. (☎ 1-800-862-2543. 916-322-2881: www.gocalif.ca.gov)

Colorado: *The Centennial State*
Colorado Travel and Tourism Authority, PO Box 3524, Englewood, Colorado 80155. (☎ 1-800-265-7623: www.colorado.com)

Connecticut: *The Constitution State*
Connecticut Office of Tourism, 505 Hudson St, Hartford, Connecticut 06106. (☎ 1-800-282-6863. 860-270-8080: www.ctbound.org)

Delaware: *The First State*
Delaware Tourism Office, 99 Kings Highway, Dover, Delaware 19901. (☎ 1-800-441-8846. 302-739-4271: www.state.de.us/tourism)

Florida: *The Sunshine State*
Florida Tourism Industry Marketing Corporation, PO Box 1100, Tallahassee, Florida 32302. (☎ 1-888-735-2822. 850-488-5607: www.flausa.com)

Georgia: *The Empire State of the South*
Georgia Department of Industry, Trade and Tourism, PO Box 1776, Atlanta, Georgia 30303. (☎ 1-800-847-4842. 404-656-3590: www.georgia.org)

Hawaii: *The Aloha State*
Visitors Bureau, 2270 Kalakaua Ave, Honolulu, (☎ 1-800-464-2924. 808-923-1811: www.gohawaii.com)

Idaho: *The Gem State*
Idaho Department of Commerce, PO Box 83720, Boise, Idaho 83720-0093. (☎ 1-800-635-7820: www.visitid.org)

Illinois: *The Land of Lincoln*
Illinois Bureau of Tourism, 100 W. Randolph St., Suite 3-400, Chicago, Illinois 60601. (☎1-800-226-6632. 312-814-4732: www.enjoyillinois.com)

Indiana: *The Hoosier State*
Indiana Tourism, 1 N. Capitol Ave., Indianapolis, Indiana 46024. (☎ 1-800-759-9191. 317-232-4685: www.enjoyindiana.com)

Iowa: *The Hawkeye State*
Iowa Division of Tourism, 200 E. Grand Ave., Des Moines, Iowa 50309. (☎ 1-800-345-4692. 515-242-4705: www.traveliowa.com)

Kansas: *The Sunflower State*
Kansas Travel and Tourism Development Division, 700 SW. Harrison, Suite 1300, Topeka, Kansas 66603. (☎ 1-800-252-6727. 785-296-2009: www.kansascommerce.com)

Kentucky: *The Bluegrass State*
Kentucky Department of Travel, Capital Plaza Tower, 500 Mero St., Suite 22, Frankfort, Kentucky 40601. (☎ 1-800-225-8747: www.kentuckytourism.com)

Louisiana: *The Pelican State*
Louisiana Office of Tourism, PO Box 94291, Baton Rouge, Louisiana 70804. (☎ 1-800-695-4064. 205-342-8100: www.louisianatravel.com)

Maine: *The Pine Tree State*
Maine Publicity Bureau, PO Box 2300, Hallowell, Maine 04347-2300. (☎ 1-888-624-6345. 207-287-8070)

Maryland: *The Old Line State*
Maryland Office of Tourism Development, 217 E.

Redwood St., Baltimore, Maryland 21202. (☎ 1-800-445-4558: www.mdisfun.org)

Massachusetts: *The Bay State*
Massachusetts Office of Travel and Tourism, 10 Park Plaza, Suite 4510, Boston, Massachusetts 02116. (☎ 1-800-447-6277. 617-727-3201: www.massvacation.com)

Michigan: *The Great Lakes State*
Michigan Travel Bureau, PO Box 3226, Lansing, Michigan 48909. (☎ 1-888-784-7328. 517-373-0670: www.michigan.org)

Minnesota: *The Gopher State*
Minnesota Office of Tourism, 500 Metro Square, 121 Seventh Place, St Paul, Minnesota 55101. (☎ 1-800-657-3700. 651-296-5029: www.exploreminnesota.com)

Mississippi: *The Magnolia State*
Mississippi Division of Tourism, PO Box 849, Jackson, Mississippi 39205. (☎ 1-800-927-6378. 601-359-3297: www.visitmississippi.com)

Missouri: *The Show Me State*
301 W. High St., PO Box 1055, Jefferon City, Missouri 65102. (☎ 1-800-877-1234.: www.missouritourism.org)

Montana: *The Treasure State*
Travel Montana, 1424 Ninth Ave., Helena, Montana 59620. (☎ 1-800-847-4868. 406-444-2654: www.visitmt.com)

Nebraska: *The Cornhusker State*
Nebraska Travel and Tourism, PO Box 94666, Lincoln, Nebraska 68509-4666. (☎ 1-800-228-4307. 402-471-3796: www.visitnebraska.org)

Nevada: *The Silver State*
Nevada Commission on Tourism, 401 N. Carson St., Carson City, Nevada 89701. (☎ 1-800-638-2328. 775-687-4322: www.travelnevada.com)

New Hampshire: *The Granite State*
New Hampshire Office of Travel and Tourism Development, 172 Pembroke Rd., PO Box 1856, Concord, New Hamphire 03302-1856. (☎ 1-800-386-4664 (Seasonal). 603-271-2666: www.visitnh.gov)

New Jersey: *The Garden State*
New Jersey Division of Travel and Tourism, 20 W. State St., PO Box 820, Trenton, New Jersey 08625-2470. (☎ 1-800-537-7397. 609-292-2470: www.visitnj.org)

New Mexico: *The Land of Enchantment*
New Mexico Department of Tourism, 491 Old Santa Fe Trail, Santa Fe, New Mexico 87503. (☎ 1-800-733-6396: www.newmexico.org)

New York: *The Empire State*

New York State Division of Tourism, PO Box 2603, Albany, New York 12220-0603. (☎ 1-800-225-5697. 518-474-4116: www.iloveny.state.ny.us)

North Carolina: *The Tar Heel State*
North Carolina Division of Tourism, Film and Sports Development, 301 N. Wilmington St., Raleigh, North Carolina 27601. (☎1-800-847-4862. 919-733-4171: www.visitnc.com)

North Dakota: *The Flickertail State*
North Dakota Tourism, 604 E. Boulevard Ave., Bismarck, North Dakota 58505-0825. (☎1-800-435-5663. 701-328-2525: www.ndtourism.com)

Ohio: *The Buckeye State*
Ohio Division of Travel and Tourism, 77 S. High St., 29th Floor, Columbus, Ohio 43215. (☎ 1-800-282-5393: www.ohiotourism.com)

Oklahoma: *The Sooner State*
Oklahoma Department of Tourism and Recreation, PO Box 60789, Oklahoma City, Oklahoma 73146. (☎ 1-800-652-6552. 405-521-2409: www.travelok.com)

Oregon: *The Beaver State*
Oregon Tourism Commission, 775 Summer St NE., Salem, Oregon 97301-1282. (☎ 1-800-547-7842. 503-986-0000: www.traveloregon.com)

Pennsylvania: *The Keystone State*
Pennsylvania Office of Travel, Tourism and Film Promotion, Room 404, Forum Building, Harrisburg, Pennsylvania 17120. (☎ 1-800-847-4872. 717-787-5453: www.state.pa.us)

Rhode Island: *The Ocean State*
Rhode Island Tourism, 1 W. Exchange St., Providence, Rhode Is 02903. (☎ 1-800-556-2484: www.visitrhodeisland.com)

South Carolina: *The Palmetto State*
South Carolina Department of Parks, Recreation and Tourism, PO Box 71, Columbia, South Carolina 29201. (☎ 1-888-727-6453: www.travelsc.com)

South Dakota: *The Mount Rushmore State*
South Dakota Department of Tourism, 711 E. Wells Ave., Pierre, South Dakota 57501-3369. (☎ 1-800-732-5682: www.travelsd.com)

Tennessee: *The Volunteer State*
Tennessee Department of Tourist Development, 320 Sixth Ave. N., Rachel Jackson Building, Nashville, Tennessee 37243. (☎ 1-800-491-8366: www.state.tn.us)

Texas: *The Lone Star State*

Texas Department of Economic Development, Tourism Division, PO Box 12728, Austin, Texas 78711-2728. (☎ 1-800-888-8839. 512-462-9191: www.traveltex.com)

Utah: *The Beehive State*
Utah Travel Council, Council Hall/Capitol Hill, Salt Lake City, Utah 84114. (☎ 1-800-200-1160. 801-538-1030: www.utah.com)

Vermont: *The Green Mountain State*
Vermont Department of Tourism and Marketing, 6 Baldwin St., Montpelier, Vermont 05633-1301. (☎ 1-800-837-6668. 802-828-3236: www.1-800-vermont.com)

Virginia: *Old Dominion*
Virginia Tourism Corporation, 901 E. Byrd St., Richmond, Virginia 23219. (☎ 1-800-847-4882. 804-786-4484: www.virginia.org)

Washington: *The Evergreen State*
Department of Community Trade and Economic Development, Washington State Tourism Division, PO Box 42500, Olympia, Washington 98504-2500. (☎ 1-800-544-1800: www.tourism.wa.gov)

Washington DC:
WCVA Visitors Services, 1212 New York Ave. NW., Suite 600, Washington DC 20005. (☎ 1-800-422-8644. 202-789-7000: www.washington.org)

West Virginia: *The Mountain State*
West Virginia Division of Tourism, 2101 Washington St. E., Charleston, West Virginia 25305. (☎ 1-800-225-5982. 304-558-2286: www.callwva.com)

Wisconsin: *The Badger State*
Wisconsin Department of Tourism, PO Box 7976, Madison, Wisconsin 53707. (☎1-800-432-8747: www.tourism.state.wi.us)

Wyoming: *The Equality State*
Wyoming Division of Tourism, I-25 at College Drive, Cheyenne, Wyoming 82002. (☎1-800-225-5996. 307-777-7777: www.wyomingtourism.org)

✢Grand Detour, Illinois, to Road's End, California, 1,849 miles (2,958 km)✢

Road Etiquette

'Manners maketh man.'

14th Century Adage, Anon

The pursuit of happiness is a right enshrined in the Declaration of Independence and a developed road network gave Americans the opportunity to hunt it down in every corner of their nation. Roads took them into places the pioneers had had to hack through, climb over and swim across.

In 1956 President Eisenhower was able to implement his vision of a web of interstates criss-crossing the country. He realised both the economic and military benefits for an interstate network; Americans would be able to move more freely and trade and commerce would grow. American troops would also be more mobile in the event of an emergency. It was ordered that every so often an interstate should be straight so that it could serve as a landing strip should the Cold War ever become hot. Today America has four million miles of paved roads and highways.

Driving Etiquette

Not all American drivers are bad, just as not all of them are good. Some cities have particularly bad reputations - New York drivers are portrayed as being particularly aggressive, while motorists in Boston are stereotyped as being reckless.

Generally though, two factors influence the quality of driving in the United States:

- **Congestion** breeds aggressive drivers. It is a simple case of adapt and survive.
- **Insurance.** In areas where the law only requires a minimum level of coverage, drivers do not have to worry about their premiums going up if they are involved in an accident so there is little incentive to drive cautiously.

Lights

There is one vital piece of driving etiquette which foreign visitors to the United States must remember; **flashing your headlights means you are claiming priority and not giving way to another vehicle.** The context in which headlights are flashed can mean different things, however:

- If a car is travelling in the opposite direction it could be to warn other drivers that there is a police speed trap ahead or that there is some obstruction, like an accident. (Warning other drivers of a speed trap by flashing your headlights is illegal in some states).
- If a vehicle has just overtaken you on a two-lane highway it is okay to flash your lights to let him know he has enough clearance to pull in.

- Generally, though, if two vehicles on a narrow street meet at an obstruction like a parked car, the first to flash its headlights goes first.

The rules for using headlights are broadly similar across all the states. Dipped headlights (or low beams) must be used between sunset and sunrise. They must also be on when visibility is less than 500 or 1,000 feet (150-300 metres). Full or high beams must be dipped within 500 feet of an oncoming vehicle or within 300 feet (90 metres) of a vehicle in front. Heat haze can impair visibility so much that headlights have to be switched on in the daytime in some parts of the south-west. As a rule of thumb, **be the first to switch on your lights - not the last.**

Helping Other Road Users

If you are passing a vehicle which has pulled on to the hard shoulder on a freeway it is usually a wise precaution to move into the outside lane to avoid any collision.

If you feel someone could do with some help think of how it might look if you pull up - especially if it is an isolated or dark road, the stranded driver is a woman and you are a man. The dilemma you face is that the driver could be at risk if you do not stop. If it is safe to do so, pull alongside and speak to the other driver without getting out of your own vehicle. Ask if you can call the police or a breakdown service if you have a phone. Then, if the stranded driver wants you to stay, pull in some distance away and stay in your own vehicle until help arrives.

If you are the stranded driver *never accept lifts from strangers*. Stay in your own car and lock yourself in if necessary. When a patrol officer or a mechanic does arrive, ask them to pass their identification through a crack in the window. Any bona fide official will not have a problem with identification being examined.

Parking

Parking is often known as 'standing' in America so signs will refer to 'No standing' or 'Standing restricted'. It is a movie cliché that characters always seem to find a space right outside the downtown building they are visiting. For ordinary mortals, however, the search is likely to be long and fruitless.

American cities are often divided into parking zones; suburban areas tend to be unrestricted, apart from the main highways passing through them. Downtown parking is usually metered or prohibited altogether. Parking fees vary according to the popularity of the locations and a meter may cost you anything from 25 cents to several dollars and be limited to a maximum period. Meter feeding is illegal. Vehicles must be parked facing the direction of the traffic flow on the nearside of the road.

Parking restrictions in America are marked by colour coded kerb stones:
- **Red** - no parking

- **Yellow** - stopping only allowed for the loading and unloading of freight or passengers and only for the length of time specified
- **White** - stopping only allowed to load or unload passengers during the time specified or to deposit mail in the adjacent mailbox
- **Green** - parking for limited time only
- **Blue** - disabled parking. There will sometimes be a painted area next to a disabled parking space to allow room for drivers and passengers with wheelchairs - do not park in the painted area. (Expect a fine of *at least* $500 for parking illegally in a disabled space)

Parking is also prohibited within ten feet (3 metres) of a fire hydrant. The law states that a fire hydrant must be both accessible *and* visible to fire crews from the street. Fire stations, ambulance stations, hospitals and schools will also have restricted parking zones outside. Similarly, parking on rural highways is illegal and vehicles must pull completely off the road. Signs stating 'No overnight parking' are common and these are to prevent people from camping cheaply.

Look out for signs indicating specific parking regulations and times; some areas may restrict parking during rush hours. Residential streets may prohibit parking for just two hours a week to allow street cleaning. In colder regions, parked cars have to make way for the snowplough when the snow reaches a certain level specified on the local signs.

Many commercial premises offer validated parking - your parking will be free if you spend so much in a shopping mall or a store and have your parking receipt stamped by the sales assistant. Other shops, stores and malls offer free parking for a limited period: vehicles are checked regularly or tokens are administered at the sales counter to catch out freeloaders.

Tickets

Parking regulations are strictly enforced, either by local police or by private company traffic wardens (often paid on a results basis and so particularly zealous). In time-restricted parking areas officers or wardens often chalk the time they checked your car on the sidewalk. It is an offence to change or rub out the chalk mark.

Clamping

This is a common practice in the United States. A wheel clamp is known as a Denver Shoe, after the city in which it was first used. If your vehicle is clamped you must go to the clamping station listed on the ticket, pay the unclamping fee and then return to the vehicle to wait for it to be released. Expect to wait a couple of hours during busy periods. If the clamp has been on a vehicle for a certain length of time - say 48 hours - and no one has paid a release fee then it will be towed away.

Towing

If your car is towed away you could face a bureaucratic nightmare getting it back. First you will have to find out where it has been taken and that could mean a long trip across town. Then there will be the fine to pay and then the storage fees. You will also need to produce all relevant documentation - such as proof of ownership, financial responsibility and a driving licence. So if you have been driving uninsured you will be found out and face an even bigger fine.

Towing and unclamping fees must usually be paid in cash because it is possible to stop cheque or credit card payments after the vehicle has been returned.

Pedestrians

Nearly 15% of road-deaths, every year, are pedestrians. Many more are injured. The surprising fact is that most of those fatalities occur at crossings rather than when people are jaywalking. The Los Angeles Police Department says this is because people using crossings are over-confident and they forget to look, so be especially vigilant when driving past crossings.

Pedestrians have a right of way where a side street meets a main road, even if no crossing is marked - and crossings are often unmarked in residential areas. The moment a person puts a foot on the road at a crossing, he has right of way even if it is not controlled by stop lights. Similarly, pedestrians have priority when a road crosses a public footpath such as an entrance or exit into a parking lot.

In Hartford, Connecticut, it is illegal to cross the street by walking on your hands.

The area where pedestrians walk is called the sidewalk in the US. Where there is no sidewalk pedestrians should walk in single file on the left-hand side of the road, facing the oncoming traffic, or on the outside of a sharp left-hand bend to give drivers a better chance to see people in the road.

Of course pedestrians should always make themselves as visible as possible, especially at night or in poor weather conditions, using reflective materials or bright colours.

The Law

'I fought the law and the law won.'
The Clash, second album, Give 'Em Enough Rope, 1978.

America has more than half a million police officers serving 40,000 forces. The system extends from the X-Files' Mulders and Scullys of the FBI down to the Dukes of Hazzards' Sheriff Roscoe P Coltrane at local level. An encounter with the forces of law and order in any country can be an unnerving experience for a foreign visitor. At least in America, with a few exceptions, the system is generally fair and honest. However, any institution is only as good as the sum of its parts and people are flawed so there will inevitably be a few prejudiced, corrupt or simply inefficient individuals wearing police badges or judge's robes.

Get Your Hair Cut!

The author was travelling with a long-haired, unkempt-looking friend in California when the pair pulled into a one-horse town looking for accommodation. The friend approached a cop resembling Police Chief Wiggum from the *Simpsons* who was sitting outside a doughnut shop and asked if he could suggest a good place to stay. The officer looked him up and down and said in a drawl only cops seem to speak in, 'Jail, boy!'

The Law in Order

The FBI. The Federal Bureau of Investigation deals with major crime such as murder, kidnapping and robbery and crimes that extend across state borders such as extortion and fraud. It employs 20,000 officers and most foreign visitors are unlikely to come into contact with the FBI.

The National Guard. The National Guard is called out when things get *really* bad, usually to quell civil unrest or to enforce law and order during or after a natural disaster. It is made up of civil reservists who are called up by the state governor. The Guard is concerned with enforcement and not investigation.

The State Police. That is 'state' as in the 50 states, not the federal government. The State Police provide the Highway Patrol Officers, also known as State Troopers. Whilst contact with the FBI and the National Guard is unlikely, you will see a lot of State Police Officers. They deal with driving offences and crimes across county lines.

The City or County Police. American states are broken down into administrative counties. These forces deal with law enforcement at a strictly local level.

These are the main levels of law enforcement but within each of these divisions there is often a baffling array of sub-divisions - for example, transport police, metro police, schools police. In addition, many local police stations also employ volunteer officers, part-timers and even sheriff's posses when the need arises. (Although pursuit will more likely be in a four-wheel drive rather than on a team of horses).

In Southern California, Arizona, New Mexico and Texas, the states which border Mexico, drivers might find themselves pulled over by **immigration officers** looking for 'wetbacks' - illegal immigrants. These patrols often range miles into the United States so do not be surprised to have your papers checked some distance from the border.

The basic 'off-the-shelf' police officer is called a patrolman or patrolwoman. The **patrolman's standard issue kit** will include:

- **A revolver** - a .38 special being the most commonly issued - and usually a shotgun in the car
- **A night-stick** - a type of truncheon
- Some forces issue officers with pepper spray or **CS spray** (*not* CS gas - a common misconception. CS gas is altogether more powerful and more useful for incapacitating whole armies, rather than individual criminals)
- **'Tazers'** which are devices which can administer a short electric shock to temporarily paralyse an offender

Dealing with the Police

Do not attempt to bribe a cop

By and large, most officers are honest so *do not consider bribing one if you are pulled over for a motoring offence.* The stories of drivers who hand over their licences with $50 bills inside are myths. It is true that corruption has been an on-going problem in many forces, especially New York. The widespread dishonesty depicted in the 1970 Al Pacino film *Serpico* continued to haunt the force despite several purges of the rotten apples. Where corruption does occur, however, officers will be targeting larger sources of income than squeezing hapless motorists for a few bucks here and there.

Most patrol officers are polite and courteous, using Sir and Ma'am, but they are also very firm when they want something. Do not annoy a police officer. The cliché that most Americans do not have a sense of irony seems particularly true of the police. If the defiance goes beyond the verbal to the physical then an officer is more than capable of dealing with it.

How To Avoid Being Stopped by the Highway Patrol

The key to avoiding the attentions of John Law, in America, is to be as inconspicuous as possible.

🚗 **Do not stand out from the crowd.** Keep to the speed of the rest of the traffic, do not change lanes too frequently and do not annoy other road users. There is safety in numbers on American roads - drivers generally stand a better chance of avoiding being pulled over when they are travelling in a line of vehicles. It is the car that behaves differently which interests the highway patrols, so beware of breaking the limit in light traffic or on quiet roads. Truckers are often a reliable measure of speed enforcement. Many are linked by Citizens Band radio and will get advanced warning of traps or patrols so a group of trucks all sticking to the speed limit is often a sign that the police are in the area somewhere

🚗 **Keep your eyes peeled**. On-coming cars might flash their lights to warn of speed traps (even though this is illegal), traffic ahead might start to bunch up behind a police car, look for vehicles on the hard shoulder where drivers might already be pulled over by the police

🚗 **Use your mirrors.** Look for police cars behind you. Be suspicious of cars that approach quickly and then slot in behind and match your speed - you might be being 'clocked' by an unmarked car. Generally, though, by the time you spot a patrol car if you are speeding - it is too late

🚗 **Lights.** A broken brake light, a faulty indicator or a missing licence plate bulb are just the transgressions the cops are looking for

🚗 **Cleanliness is next to lawfulness.** Make sure your car looks presentable. Cops will tend to assume a driver who takes care of his or her car will be a responsible citizen on the road

🚗 **Politically motivated car stickers** can sometimes start the blue lights flashing. America is a free country committed to freedom of speech - but not in every backwoods town

🚗 **The weather.** Police officers are only human and might be reluctant to get out of their warm patrol cars to book a speeder in the pouring rain or in the freezing cold so you *might* be given the benefit of the doubt on a lousy day. Bear in mind, however, that *you* are putting yourself and other road users at more risk when driving too fast in poor weather conditions

How to Behave if You Are Pulled Over

With a little courtesy and common sense the encounter should not be too daunting.

🚗 **If you are signalled to stop, pull over somewhere safe and convenient and switch off the ignition.** Patrol cars usually signal by flashing their roof lights. They do not usually sound their sirens unless they think a driver has not seen the blue light. Unmarked police cars have their blue lights fitted behind the radiator grills. Sometimes the officer in the passenger seat will hold a red torch out of his window. **Patrol officers do not signal motorists to pull over by flashing their headlights alone. If a car behind you does this, be suspicious**

🚗 **Do not get out of the car when you stop.** Staying in the car cannot be misinterpreted as a threatening move. Wait for the officer to come to you. He will park behind you, leaving his blue lights on to warn other drivers of the obstruction on the roadside

🚗 **Keep your hands visible on the steering wheel and do not make any sudden moves.** Try not to keep your driving licence in the glove compartment because that is a favourite place to keep guns so any move in that direction could be misinterpreted. Another favoured hiding place for a weapon in underneath the seat, so do not make any move in that direction, either. If your licence and papers *are* in the glove compartment then ask the officer if it is okay to open it before doing so

🚗 **Be polite and the officer should be polite in return.** Police officers are wise to what they call 'bootlicking', often showing itself as over-use of 'Sir' or 'Ma'am'. However it is considered respectful to refer to an officer by his or her rank - 'Sergeant' or 'Deputy'. Make sure you get their rank correct - inadvertently demoting an officer is not likely to win you any favours. If unsure, use the term 'officer'. It is always worth emphasising that you are a foreign visitor. It might explain your inadvertent transgression of the law

🚗 **Do not argue or plead your case.** The cop's job is to enforce the law; it is the court's to administer it. Any argument you come up with is only likely to be included in the cop's list of favourite excuses. If you do end up in court, remember how you behave at the roadside could come back to haunt you later

🚗 **Do not volunteer any self-incriminating information.** If you are asked if you know how fast you were travelling then just reply, 'yes' or 'at the speed of the traffic'

🚗 **If an officer asks for permission to search your car then you do not have**

to give it. Asking permission indicates he or she does not have **'probable cause'** - in other words a reasonable suspicion that you are committing a crime or carrying something illegal. If the officer does have probable cause a search will be carried out anyway, without your consent

🚗 **Finally, a useful psychological tip;** if you are asked to get out of the car, try and **make yourself shorter** than the officer - perhaps by perching on the hood - because it makes them feel superior and therefore more willing to show a little magnanimity

If You Are Arrested

You have certain constitutional rights and these **must** be made clear to you by the arresting officers. This is known as the Miranda Warning or being 'Mirandised'. In 1963 Ernesto Miranda was arrested in Arizona for rape and kidnapping and questioned for two hours before he signed a confession. He won his appeal three years later when he convinced the Supreme Court that he was not informed of his rights.

However, **an officer is not obliged to read you your rights on arrest.** The Miranda Warning need only be given when the suspect is about to be questioned. So it may not be given until you are in the interrogation room.

The Miranda Warning

The words of the Miranda Warning are:
'You have the right to remain silent. Do you understand?'
'Anything you say can and will be used against you in a court of law. Do you understand?'
'You have the right to speak to an attorney and to have an attorney present before and during any questioning. Do you understand?'
'If you cannot afford a lawyer, one will be provided for you at government expense. Do you understand?'

If an officer asks any further questions at this point and the suspect answers then the officer will be considered to have obtained an Implied Waiver. However, the officer must then ask the following question to obtain an Express Waiver:
'Do you want to talk to me/us now?'

There are two situations in which the police **do not** have to read you your rights: The police are allowed to ask routine booking questions such as your name, address, date of birth and social security number to establish your identity.
You can be asked to take a breathalyser test without being given the Miranda Warning.

The best way to protect your rights, however, is not to do anything that gets you arrested in the first place. A working knowledge of the rules of the road in America will keep you out of jail and stop you wasting your hard-earned spending money on parking and speeding fines.

Speed

The national speed limit of 55 mph, introduced in the wake of the 1973 oil crisis, was abolished in 1995, leaving states to set their own limits which now range from 75 mph in Wyoming to 40 mph in the American protectorate of Puerto Rico.

Speed limits can change with the driving and road conditions. For example, limits are lower near schools, through road repairs and at railroad junctions. Speed limits apply to railroad crossings and other blind intersections; if the driver is within one hundred feet of the crossing or the intersection and cannot see 100 feet to the right or left then he or she must slow to 15 mph. Where a speed limit is marked as 'posted', this means no maximum is laid down in state legislation and drivers should keep to the speeds posted on signs in the area they are driving through.

Below is a table that lays out the speed limits in all 50 states in miles per hour. The list is not exhaustive and only covers the four main types of road that most drivers will encounter:

State	School Zone	Urban	Freeway	Interstate
Alabama	Posted	30-35	55	65
Alaska	20	20-25	65	65
Arizona	15	25	65	60
Arkansas	25	30	60	60
California	25	25-35	55	65
Colorado	Posted	30	55	65
Connecticut	Posted	Posted	55	65
Delaware	20	25	50-55	Posted
District of Colombia	15	25	Posted	Posted
Florida	Posted	30	55	70
Georgia	Posted	30	65	70
Hawaii	Posted	Posted	Posted	Posted
Idaho	Posted	35	65	75
Illinois	Posted	30	55	65
Indiana	Posted	30	55	65
Iowa	25	Posted	55	65
Kansas	Posted	30	55-65	70
Kentucky	Posted	35	55	65
Louisiana	Posted	Posted	55-65	70
Maine	15	25	60	65
Maryland	Posted	30-35	55	65
Massachusetts	Posted	Posted	Posted	65
Michigan	25	25	55-65	70
Minnesota	Posted	25-30	55	65
Mississippi	Posted	Posted	65	70
Missouri	Posted	Posted	55-65	70

Montana	Posted	25	65	65 (d) 55 (n)
Nebraska	Posted	20-25	50-65	75
Nevada	15-25	Posted	Posted	75
New Hampshire	25-35	55	65	Posted
New Jersey	25	25-35	55	65
New Mexico	15	35	Posted	75
New York	Posted	Posted	Posted	65
North Carolina	Posted	35	55-65	70
North Dakota	20	25	55-65	70
Ohio	20	25	50-55	65
Oklahoma	25	Posted	65	75
Oregon	20	20-25	55	65
Pennsylvania	15	35	55	65
Rhode Island	20	25	50 (d) 45 (n)	Posted
South Carolina	Posted	35	55	Posted
South Dakota	15	25	55-65	75
Tennessee	15	Posted	65	70
Texas	Posted	30	60 (d) 55(n)	70 (d) 65 (n)
Utah	20	25	55	Posted
Vermont	Posted	Posted	50	Posted
Virginia	15-25	Posted	55	65
Washington	Posted	25	55-60	Posted
West Virginia	15	25	55	55
Wisconsin	15	25-35	55	65
Wyoming	20	30	65	75

Source: National Highway Traffic Safety Administration
1 January 1999

Speeding is known as a 'moving violation' in America and the degree of enforcement varies according to the excess over the limit and from state to state. The federal government offers a powerful incentive for local police forces to make sure drivers keep within the limit: if a certain proportion of vehicles, over 50 per cent for example, are detected breaking the local limits (using monitors embedded in the road surface) then states can lose their federal road grants.

At a local level, speeding fines may be a major source of income for the community and that can be reflected in the enthusiasm of the police. Raising local revenue is considered an acceptable reason for enthusiastic enforcement of speed limits in many southeastern states.

Enforcement will also vary according to the type of highway; the police tend to be more vigilant on urban and residential roads than on the interstates, although there is no room for complacency on *any* type of road.

American speed signs have black writing on a white rectangle. Some areas may display *minimum* speed limits - for example, in tunnels or other locations where traffic has a tendency to bunch up and cause congestion.

Whistling in The Wind

Whilst driving through the tunnel linking Norfolk and Hampton, beneath the James River in Virginia, Andrew Vincent once saw a man on a gantry blowing a whistle and waving at the traffic to keep it flowing. It was obvious what the man was trying to do but he made such an unusual sight that passing drivers slowed down to take a better look. The more people slowed down, the more he blew and waved his arms and the greater his efforts, the more people slowed down. At the time of passing the traffic was at a virtual standstill.

Some roads are subject to different speed limits at night and these are displayed in white writing on a black rectangle. **Advisory** speed limits are on a yellow background and these may be found posted on potentially dangerous sections of road such as bends. (Speed limits on bends are compulsory in the New England states).

It can seem as if speeding, and the catching of speeders, is a national sport in the United States. The police are far stricter in America than in many other countries, employing a range of tactics and technology to enforce the law including radar guns, speed cameras, marked and unmarked police cars, aircraft and helicopters.

Radar

Radar. The police use both hand-held radar guns, called Vascar, and systems fitted in police cars.

Radar from All Directions

Drivers from countries where the carriageways are separated by a crash barrier may be used to ignoring patrol cars travelling in the opposite direction. However, American interstates are divided by a wide strip of grass or scrub which police cars and other emergency service vehicles can cross as Michael Andrews found to his cost.

'I was delivering a Nissan Altima to San Francisco and I was travelling on the I-80 near Rawlins in Wyoming. The speed limit on the Interstates in Wyoming is 75 mph, but even that seems slow across the prairies. Traffic was light, it was a clear day and the road was straight so I set the cruise control at 85 mph. About ten minutes later I saw a patrol car travelling in the opposite direction and I didn't think anything of it. However, American highway patrols think nothing of U-turns on interstates. The next thing I saw in my rear view mirror was this police car bumping across the grass strip separating the two carriageways to slot in behind me with his lights flashing. His radar had been scanning the traffic in both directions and having set my cruise control on 85 I was asking for it. It cost me a $95 on-the-spot fine. Incidentally, the ticket says I 'did unlawfully commit the following offence against the peace and dignity of the state of Wyoming.' I'm rather proud to have offended Wyoming's peace and dignity within ten minutes of arriving in the state.'

Radar detectors are legal in all states except Connecticut, Michigan, Virginia and the District Of Columbia. Detectors can be bought in many car accessory stores and they operate by sounding an alarm inside the car when it is being tracked by police radar. The more sophisticated models can even tell from which direction the radar signal is coming.

Radar jammers are illegal everywhere in the United States. The law is clear; it is illegal to carry any device that transmits or initiates a signal that interferes with emergency service broadcasts. A radar beam sent out from a speed gun or a patrol car is considered a broadcast so it is illegal to jam it. You could be charged with 'malicious interference' or 'obstructing justice'. It is possible to buy radar jammers, often under the counter from less-than-honest retailers who will claim that the outlawing of the devices is an infringement of civil liberties.

Detection From the Air

There is no escape from the long arm of the law even on the most isolated highway. Even when it seems safe enough to put the pedal to the metal those flashing blue lights can appear in the rear view mirrors. Aircraft or helicopters can track speeding vehicles from some miles away and direct patrol cars to offenders. You might see white strips or chevrons painted across the road and these help the airborne patrols calculate your speed. There will also be signs warning that police aircraft operate in the area.

Speed Cameras

As In Britain, cameras are located on stretches of road known for speeding or where there have been a number of accidents. However, over the next few years a new type of camera will be appearing in America; several states have started using cameras concealed inside cats' eyes in the middle of the road. Another development, on both sides of the Atlantic, is cameras that measure a vehicle's speed between two points, making it impossible to 'camera surf' - i.e., slowing down for cameras before accelerating away.

Speed Traps

It is impossible to track the location of all the speed traps on America's roads but help is available on the web. The **Speed Trap Exchange on www.speedtrap.org** invites drivers to submit details of speed traps, including their location, frequency and the times of day the police like to set them up. For example, at the time of writing the page for Maine listed speed traps submitted by drivers along with some helpful observations:

'Durham - Route 136. Beware of a trap beyond the Durham Variety Store. Just around the 50 mph sign is a large cornfield where John Law likes to hide. This is a long straight and speeds of 60 mph are not unusual. On many occasions I have seen a State Police Car among the stalks of corn late at night.'

A particularly unnerving sight in America is a road sign that flashes up an approaching vehicle's speed. These signs are fitted with radar and will display something like, 'The speed limit is 45mph. Your speed is…54mph…slow down.' This personal touch certainly pricks the conscience and makes a driver comply.

The best way to avoid a speeding ticket, however, is to obey the speed limit.

Penalties

It is impossible to provide a comprehensive list of penalties for all 50 states because there is such a range of sanctions. The severity of any punishment will depend upon the circumstances of the offence and the minimum and maximum penalties laid down in state legislation. For example, speeding in a school zone is likely to be treated more severely than travelling 10 mph above the limit on an interstate and fines are usually doubled for speeding through 'work zones' (roadworks).

Generally, there are four options open to the courts:

Fines

Speeding motorists will be fined a base amount for the offence - say, $50 or $60 - plus so much for every mile per hour, around $10, over the limit. This may vary according to the circumstances and the road and weather conditions. In some jurisdictions, police officers are empowered to collect on-the-spot fines, actually called 'bonds', for clear-cut offences, which is a big relief for those who have an itinerary to keep to and cannot wait for a court appearance. Read the back of the ticket for an explanation of the local procedure but these notes from a Wyoming speeding ticket are fairly typical:

'Disposition Procedure.'

Except for offences requiring your personal appearance, you may avoid court appearance if you deposit bond and costs fixed by the Wyoming Supreme Court or the municipal court for the offence for which you are charged. You may post this bond with the officer who has issued this citation (if authorised by law), with the court or by mail. If you wish to pay by mail, please do so by money order or cashier's check (no cash). The payment must be for the exact amount and must be received before the court date.

Failure to comply with one of the above procedures may result in the issuance of an arrest warrant for you with the possible additional charge of failure to appear.'

Officers empowered to accept on-the-spot fines will usually accept cash, cheques or travellers' cheques but they are not equipped to take credit cards. They can give change if you do not have the exact amount. If the officer offers you the option of paying your fine by mail, do not think you can forget about it once you are out of the state. Most states are signed up to the Non-resident Violator Compact - an agreement allowing members to pursue offenders and impose penalties, such as suspension of a licence, on each other's behalf.

Prison

Imprisonment is usually reserved for the more serious offenders, such as those caught doing 75 mph in a school zone. Sentences can range from one day to several months at a state penitentiary for repeat offenders. Prison is an option open to the courts for *all* motoring offences so it is a sobering thought when setting the cruise control above the local speed limit.

Licence Suspension or Revocation

A licence can be suspended for as little as a month or as much as a couple of years. The revocation of a licence is an even more serious matter - it means a driver will have to re-take a test to get it back.

Traffic School or Driver Improvement Interviews

Serious offenders may be required to re-take their driving tests (both theoretical and practical), to attend refresher courses or to face an interview where they have to address the problematic areas of their driving. Driver Improvement Interviews are not an easy option - they are usually imposed in conjunction with a licence suspension and the interviewer has to be convinced lessons have been learned before it is restored.

Traffic School may sometimes be offered as an alternative to incurring penalty points on a licence, which is worth considering if the tally is bringing a driver close to suspension. However, if the total number of points is close to the maximum the court may decide a licence suspension is in order rather than offering the Traffic School option.

The law is the law, no matter where you are - whether it is in a school zone or a traffic-free stretch of desert road. In fact it is those desert roads where drivers need to watch their speed as Gerry Brown found to her cost:

Nearly Charmed by an English Gerry

'I was on Highway 190, one of the main routes into Death Valley National Park. I was driving a rented Pontiac Grand Prix - six cylinders and a lot of engine. It was also a smooth ride, with comfortable seats and a soundproofed interior - so it was easy to forget what speed you were doing. The car felt as smooth at 80 as it did at 30. That was the problem. I hadn't realised I was doing more than 90 in a 65-mph zone. There were no bends, it was a clear day and there were no other cars on the road. Apart from the police car, that is. It was travelling in the opposite direction but he still registered my speed on the radar. He immediately turned on his lights and too late I looked at my speedo. I was booked for doing 92mph.'

Sometimes an English accent and charm will be enough to persuade a police officer to give a motorist the benefit of the doubt. However, *even Gerry* admits that 27mph over the speed limit did not give the officer much leeway. The officer who booked Gerry was Robert McCulloch, from the

---

California Highway Patrol.

'We've all done it,' he admitted, 'I've got a ticket before I became a police officer. Do you know the worst offenders? The Germans. I stop more Germans for speeding than any other nationality. Maybe its because they don't have speed limits on their autobahns. But the English come a close second. Germans and English - the two biggest speeding offenders. What's the English excuse? You have speed limits and it's only 5mph faster than here in California.'

Gerry was not offered the option of an on-the-spot fine and had to wait to be notified by post how much she would have to pay. It came to a hefty $270.

The prospect of being fined *after* you have left the country sounds like an easy get out for foreign visitors but Patrolman Robert McCulloch has a word of warning; 'You could just tear up the ticket and throw it away when you get home and there's not a lot we can do about it. But it will be there on the computer the next time you come back to the States and it will show up either at immigration or if you get pulled over again. We'll be waiting for you!'

Drinking and Driving

Nearly two million Americans are arrested for drunk driving every year and assuming that far more people get away with it, then the actual number driving must be horrifying. More than 15,000 road deaths a year are attributed to alcohol and many of those are innocent, sober victims. There are 2.6 million drunk-driving crashes in America every year affecting 4 million people who are either injured or have property damaged. It is estimated that every year about 16 billion miles are driven while drunk.

The States have tackled the drunk-driving problem with mixed success; for example, in 1999 Texas reported the lowest percentage of alcohol-related road deaths at 21%. The District of Columbia and Alaska tied for the dubious honour of first place - 53% of their fatalities on the roads were linked to alcohol.

The Drink-Drive Limits

The amount of alcohol in a person's body is measured by the weight of the alcohol in a certain volume of blood. This is known as the **Blood Alcohol Concentration or BAC.** Measuring in this way allows for different body sizes and gives a reasonably consistent result. It is calculated on grams per decilitre, or g/dl, so in most American states a driver is considered over the limit if their blood test shows a reading of BAC 0.10 g/dl - in other words, alcohol makes up 1% of their blood.

In some states, the limit is BAC 0.08 and in October 2000 Congress set 0.08 as the national standard. This does not mean states *have* to adopt the lower limit but those that have not done so by 2004 will face pressure from Washington; they will have 2% cut from their highway construction funds. States that are still refusing to reduce their limit to 0.08 by 2007 will suffer an 8% cut in grants.

Those states that have already cut the drink-drive limit to 0.08 have reported a significant drop in the number of alcohol-related fatalities.

How Much Can You Drink?

It is impossible to give a definitive answer to how much alcohol is safe when driving a car because different people react in different ways; body size, gender, medication and the amount of food consumed can all influence blood alcohol levels. Therefore, the following can only be a very general guide:

Ⴧ One drink equals 0.54 ounces or 15.3 grams of alcohol
Ⴧ That is approximately one shot of spirits, one 12-oz (340g) can of beer or one 6-8 oz (170-227g) glass of wine.
Ⴧ One drink will give the average person a BAC of .02.
Ⴧ A 12 stone (76kg) man would have a BAC of .076 after five drinks taken over three hours.
Ⴧ A 10 stone woman (64kg) woman would have a BAC of .08 after four drinks taken over three hours.

The table below, taken from the Wyoming Driver's Manual offers a very rough guide to how much people can drink in a one-hour period. Approximately, the body will break down one drink of alcohol after every subsequent hour.

WEIGHT (lbs/kgs)	DRINKS (ONE HOUR PERIOD)							
100/45.4	1	2	3	4	5	6	7	8
120/54.5	1	2	3	4	5	6	7	8
140/63.6	1	2	3	4	5	6	7	8
160/72.7	1	2	3	4	5	6	7	8
180/81.8	1	2	3	4	5	6	7	8
200/90.9	1	2	3	4	5	6	7	8
220/100	1	2	3	4	5	6	7	8
240/109	1	2	3	4	5	6	7	8
	Prudent				Best Not		Do Not Drive	
BAC	Up to 0.05				0.05 - 0.09		0.10 and over	

How Alcohol Can Affect Performance

- **BAC .02** Light to moderate drinkers begin to feel some effects
- **BAC .04** A feeling of relaxation begins to set in
- **BAC .06** Judgement and the ability to make rational decisions are impaired Drivers may begin to feel over-confident about their driving abilities
- **BAC .08** The drink-drive limit in 25 states. Muscle co-ordination becomes impaired and driving skills deteriorate. Research by the National Highway Traffic Safety Administration suggests that between the levels .08 and .10 the risk of a fatal accident increases by 11% for driver aged 35 and over. For drivers aged between 16 and 20 the risk jumps by 52%
- **BAC .10** Reaction time and control deteriorates rapidly
- **BAC .12** Vomiting usually occurs
- **BAC .15** Balance and movement are impaired. At this level there is the equivalent of half a pint of whiskey in the blood stream
- **BAC .30** Loss of consciousness
- **BAC .40** Risk of death
- **BAC .45** Breathing stops - fatal dose for most people

What Makes a Police Officer Suspect a Drunk Driver?

The reasons for suspicion are sufficiently broad as to give a police officer 'probable cause' to pull over most motorists. Some of the causes may seem obvious - striking another vehicle, for example- but they are all defined by law as legitimate reasons to allow an officer to ask for a breath test - so beware!

- Making wide turns
- Illegal turns
- Sudden turns
- Almost striking another vehicle, particularly if it is stopped or parked
- Following another vehicle too closely
- Erratic braking
- Sudden acceleration or deceleration
- Driving very slowly
- Inappropriate stopping - even on the hard shoulder
- Straddling the centre line
- Swerving, weaving or drifting
- Driving off the road
- Driving without headlights
- Slow response to traffic signals
- Failing to stop for traffic signals
- Driving the wrong way along the carriageway

Roadside Tests

One of the defining characteristics of drunkenness is the inability to perform two tasks at the same time so the police have developed a number of 'challenges' to test a suspect's co-ordination. A police officer will first sniff your breath and any hint of alcohol could provide 'probable cause', in other words a reason to demand a test. Any other unusual behaviour could also give cause for suspicion - slurring words or slow response to questioning.

All states have 'implied chemical consent laws' meaning that by driving a car you are automatically giving your consent to be tested for alcohol. An officer can demand that you take a test but he must, by law, explain what that test involves. He does not have to read you your Miranda Rights.

Field Sobriety Tests (FSTs). A driver may be asked to stand on one leg or walk along an imaginary line to test balance. Co-ordination will also be tested by getting a suspect to lean back with his eyes closed whilst touching the tip of his nose with his finger. Sometimes officers like to throw in a little extra challenge such as alternating the nose touching with clapping the hands or patting the stomach. Mental skills are also put to the test by reciting the alphabet (remembering the letter 'Z' is pronounced 'zee' in America) or by counting backwards from a random number.

The Horizontal Gaze Nystagmus or HGN Test. The officer will ask the driver to follow his pen with the eyes without moving the head. He will be watching for an inability to follow the movement smoothly.

The Breathalyser or Datamaster. The breathalyser is a fairly standard piece of kit across the world. Most of those used in America come with a needle display and that can give borderline readings, with a margin of error of plus or minus .005. The Datamaster - a more sophisticated breathalyser - gives a print out of the exact breath test reading.

If the roadside test proves a driver is over the limit then he will be arrested and taken to the police station where a further blood or urine test will be taken. There is a time lag for alcohol to enter the urine so there is a possibility that it will give a lower reading. A blood test gives a far more accurate reading of the alcohol level in the system at the time of testing (which may be some time after drinking).

If A Driver is Over the Limit

Drunk drivers will invariably face charges of Driving While Intoxicated (DWI), Driving Under the Influence (DUI - which also applies when drug use is alleged) or Driving While Ability Impaired (DWAI). The police will charge the driver twice - with DWI or DUI and DWAI *per se*.

This gives them a second chance to make a conviction stick: if they cannot prove that the defendant's driving abilities were impaired or dangerous, the fact that the BAC reading was over the legal limit is enough, *per se*, to secure a conviction. Although a driver will face two charges, he will only be convicted on one of them.

Only in Massachusetts is a reading over the drink-drive limit evidence of alcohol-related impairment but not illegal *per se* (impairment must be proven).

Penalties

The severity of the penalties varies from state to state with fines for a first offence ranging from a couple of hundred dollars to a couple of thousand and prison sentences from a few days to a year. Some states impose a mandatory 48-hour prison term for first-time offenders. Community service orders are another option open to the courts. A driving licence can be suspended or revoked.

The American legal system wastes no time in seizing the licences of drunk-drivers - even before they have been proven guilty. Officers have the power to take a driver's licence at the roadside from the moment they make an arrest. What is known as an *administrative suspension* may also be imposed from the moment that a driver fails a blood or urine test. This remains in force for anything up to six months (in Florida's case) and will be in addition to any penalty later imposed by a court.

In some cases a driver may be issued with a temporary permit while the case is being processed. The permit might just as well have 'SUSPECTED DRUNK DRIVER' printed on it because any police officer who pulls the motorist over again will know that it means. A driver may be able to get a permanent licence returned by appealing to the local licensing agency - but do not count on it.

Another option open to the court might be ordering a convicted drunk driver to have an Interlock device fitted to the car. This is a breathalyser that the driver must blow into before the ignition will work. More than half the states will order repeat offenders to forfeit their vehicles (not just impounded - but seized and sold with the proceeds going to the state).

Limits and Penalties

Here are examples of the alcohol limits and the penalties for breaching them in five different states (the limits for all the states are given at the very end of the chapter; source; www.NHTSA/Insurance.com):

State	BAC Limit per se	Administrative License Suspension	Interlock	Forfeit	Percent of alcohol related accidents in 1999
Alabama	0.08	90 days	No	No	38
Maine	0.08	90 days	Yes	Yes	32
New York	0.10	Prosecution completion	Yes	Yes	22
Nevada	0.10	90 days	Yes	No	45
California	0.08	120 days	Yes	Yes	38

Defences against Drunk Driving Charges

A drunk driving charge is very hard to defend because the evidence tends to be irrefutable. The reading from the breathalyser or Datamaster will be accurate and the results of a blood or urine test will remove any doubt. It does not really matter if the defendant's driving skills were not impaired because their BAC will be an offence *per se*.

However, attorneys have had some success with the following arguments:

Υ **The Sobriety Test was unfair.** For example, the defendant had trouble counting backwards from 100 in multiples of seven because he was nervous. A woman wearing heels could not be expected to walk an imaginary line. It was hard to stand on one leg because the sidewalk was icy. The officer failed to explain the test clearly. (Although the Sobriety Test is supposed to be standardised across the country, officers like to introduce their own variations).

Υ **The Eye Nystagmus Test (or HGN) was unreliable.** An eye condition made it impossible for the defendant to follow the moving object. It was hard to see because it was dark.

Υ **The Breathalyser or Datamaster reading was misleading.** The defendant had recently vomited so there was alcohol present in the mouth. Even hiccuping or burping can bring some alcohol back up. A brace on the teeth, a dental plate, or even a cap trapped some alcohol in the mouth. Some medications - for ulcers or asthma, for example - can distort readings. Mouth ulcers, sores, or other wounds in the mouth can also produce inaccurate readings. However, the police are wise to these excuses. A suspect will be expected to inform the officer of any medical conditions or medications that might affect the reading. A patrolman might wait anything up to 15 minutes after stopping a driver before administering a breath test to make sure a suspect has not vomited, hiccuped or put anything into his mouth which might give a distorted reading.

Υ **The Blood Test was inaccurate**. The way blood is tested may vary. Police crime labs will test the 'whole blood' which tends to give an accurate blood alcohol count. However, some hospital labs only test the 'blood serum' that can produce a BAC up to one third higher than from a whole blood test. A swab used on the skin where the syringe is inserted may contain alcohol. Again, the police will be aware of this although it could be a factor if the sample is taken at a hospital - after an accident, for example.

Simply *carrying* alcohol in the passenger area of a car can be an offence in some states, even if the can or bottle has not been opened. If the liquor is visible inside the car, the driver could be breaking the 'container laws' which state that alcohol must be kept out of sight. Beer, wines, or spirits should be carried in a bag or stowed in the trunk to comply with the laws.

Horns

The horn is becoming increasingly redundant in America; air conditioning means most drivers cannot hear a horn because they have their windows up. Even if they do have their windows down they may be too far away or their own stereo may drown it out. More and more cities are clamping down on the use of the horn as an expression of anger - in New York the offence carries a $300 fine.

Seatbelts

The use of seat belts is mandatory in *all* states except New Hampshire. Where the laws differ is over which occupants of a vehicle have to wear them and how seriously the offence is treated by the police.

In 18 states failure to wear a seat belt is only a secondary offence, meaning the police cannot stop a car for violation of that law - the driver can only be pulled over for some other offence, for example speeding or a faulty light, and then ticketed for failure to wear a belt.

In 17 states damages collected by someone injured in a crash may be reduced if they were not wearing a seat belt. Two states, Arkansas and Wyoming, actually offer some financial incentive for wearing a belt; drivers fined for another traffic violation will get a $10 reduction if they were belted up.

There are also differences of opinion between the states over who is responsible for ensuring children are safely restrained in vehicles. Most place the onus on the driver while six states insist only the parent or guardian is responsible. Children under 5, weighing less than 40 lbs (18.2kg), or less than 40 inches (101.6cm) tall *must* sit in an approved safety seat. Failure to carry a child in a safety seat can incur a $500 fine.

Summary of United States Seat Belt Laws

Here are examples of the seatbelt laws and the penalties for breaking them in four different states; variations for the other states are generally no greater than for these:

State	Primary Offence	Maximum Fine for First Offence	Occupants	Responsibility for Children	Damages Reduced for Non-Use
Alaska	No	$15	All seats	Driver	Yes
District of Columbia	Yes	$50	All seats	Driver	No
Idaho	No	$5	Front	Driver	No
Texas	Yes	$200	All	Driver	No

Mobile (or Cellular) Phones

At the time of writing only New York State had banned outright the use of hand-held mobile telephones whilst driving. The offence carries a $100 fine although their use is permitted in an emergency.

A few other states - Arizona, California and Massachusetts - will only prosecute if the police believe use of the mobile phone caused a hazard. A handful of towns and cities have also adopted outright bans but so far New York's is the only state-wide legislation. That is likely to change, however. Forty-one states are considering banning the use of hand-held phones whilst driving and it seems likely legislation will eventually go through.

A study by the University of Utah on behalf of the National Safety Council found that hands-free phones in cars were just as distracting as hand-held sets. The researchers tested drivers in car simulators and asked them to carry out a number of tasks such as changing radio stations, listening to audio books and talking on both hands-free and hand-held telephones. Drivers missed twice as many stoplights whilst talking on either type of telephone than they did performing any other activity. The study found no significant difference in reaction times between drivers talking on hands-free phones and those using hand-held sets.

Most of those 41 states considering banning the use of mobile phones in cars said more research was needed before any legislation could be formulated. The University of Utah study looks like just the research they were looking for so expect states to start adopting tougher laws over the next few years.

The Mann Act

No Women, Booze or Cigarettes across the State Line

In 1910 Senator James Mann sponsored a bill which made it illegal to transport women from one state to another for immoral purposes. The aim of the law was to stamp out child prostitution, which was rife in many parts of America. The law is still on the statute books today and has been used as a 'catch-all' law to give police officers a reason to arrest someone. It was also used as a tool by parents to stop their daughters seeing someone they thought was unsuitable. They would report that their daughter was being taken out of state for immoral purposes and that would give the police probable cause to arrest the boyfriend and return the daughter to her parents.

There are also similar laws prohibiting the transportation of alcohol and tobacco across state lines. The legislation was designed to stop people avoiding taxes. In Ohio, for example, the police have the power to confiscate cars used in the illegal transportation of alcohol and tobacco.

People living close to borders where states have differing Sunday trading laws are particularly vulnerable to arrest. For instance, Missouri allows liquor stores to open on Sundays whilst neighbouring Kansas does not. So, while Kansans could hop across the state line to buy a few beers at a store, they would be guilty of a misdemeanour in Missouri as soon as they tried to take it back to Kansas with fines of up to $500 and a possible jail term.

Where Can I Find Out More?

Protecting The Rights of The Motorist

There are hundreds of organisations across America dedicated to protecting the rights of the motorist. Some are local pressure groups, while others represent members on a national basis. This is a list of the major organisations offering help and advice to America's road users.

The American Automobile Association (Triple A); 1000 AAA Drive, Heathrow, Florida, 32746-5063 (☎ 1-800-874-7532; www.aaa.com).

The American Driver and Traffic Safety Education Association (ADTSEA); Highway Safety Center, Indiana University of Pennsylvania, R & P Building, Indiana, Pennsylvania 15705 (☎ 724-357-4051; www.adtsea.iup.org).

The American Highways Users Alliance; 1776 Massachusetts Avenue NW, Suite 500, Washington DC 20036 (☎ 202-857-1200; www.highways.org).

The National Motorists Association; 402 W. 2nd Street, Waunakee, Wisconsin 53597 (☎ 608-849-6000; www.motorists.org).

The NMA also runs the Speed Trap Exchange at www.speedtrap.org.

Protecting The Rights of The Motorcyclist

There is also a host of groups representing motorcyclists' interests. The Big Three are:

American Brotherhood Aimed Toward Education (ABATE); 158 South Fir Street, Ventura, California 9300 (☎ 805-641-2334; www.abate.org).

American Motorcyclist Association; AMA Membership Services, 13515 Yarmouth Drive, Pickerington, Ohio 43147 (☎ 1-800-AMA-JOIN (262-5646); www.ama-cycle.org).

Motorcycle Riders Foundation; PO Box 1808, Washington DC 20013-1808 (☎ 202-546-0983; www.mrf.org).

A comprehensive listing of motorcyclist lobby groups across the US can be found at **www.weaselusa.org.**

A Note of Caution

There has always been a strong tradition of fighting authority in America. It started with the War of Independence and now extends to the internet. There are thousands of websites aimed at motorists angered by some perceived infringement of their rights - the compulsory use of seatbelts, toll roads, speed limits, bans on radar jammers, etc. Many of these single-issue sites may well offer sound advice but they are also campaigners with an axe to grind and their objectivity and reliability may be dubious. Readers are advised to exercise careful judgement when searching for legal advice on the net.

State Drink-Drive limits in BAC

Alabama-0.08; Alaska-0.10; Arizona-0.10; Arkansas-0.08; California-0.08; Colorado-0.10; Connecticut-0.10; Delaware-0.10; District of Columbia-0.08; Florida-0.08; Georgia-0.10; Hawaii-0.08; Idaho-0.08; Illinois-0.08; Indiana-0.10; Iowa-0.10; Kansas-0.08; Kentucky-0.08; Louisiana-0.10; Maine-0.08; Maryland-0.08; Massachusetts-0.08; Michigan-0.10; Minnesota-0.10; Mississippi-0.10; Missouri-0.10; Montana-0.10; Nebraska-0.08; Nevada-0.10; NewHamshire-0.08; New Jersey-0.10; New Mexico-0.08; New York-0.10; Carolina-0.08; North Dakota-0.10; Ohio-0.10; Oklahoma-0.10; Oregon-0.08; Pennsylvania-0.10; Rhode Island-0.08; South Carolina-0.10; South Dakota-0.10; Tennessee-0.10; Texas-0.08; Utah-0.08; Vermont-0.08; Virginia-0.08; Washington-0.08; West Virginia-0.10; Wisconsin-0.10; Wyoming-0.10.

Strange Laws

Until recently, drivers in Minnesota had to sound their car horn every 50 feet while travelling along country roads

Until the 1980s a law in Memphis, Tennessee, stated that a woman could not drive a car unless a man walked in front of it with a red flag

In Alabama it is illegal to operate a vehicle while blindfolded. (It is illegal everywhere, but Alabama's legislators felt the need to write a law to be absolutely sure everyone knew)

In Baldwin Park, California, it is illegal to ride a bicycle into a swimming pool

Further afield, in Uruguay, being drunk is an acceptable defence for having an accident while driving

✦ Judge, Missouri, to Justice, Illinois - 400 miles ✦

Personal Safety and Security

'Crime will be considered a disease after 1985 and will cease to exist by AD 2000.'
John Langdon-Davis, A Short History of the Future, 1936.

America's detractors might portray the country as a lawless ghetto of murderers, gangsters and drug pushers but it is, in fact, a very safe place to visit. Gangs do not prowl every street, serial killers do not lurk in every garden and muggers do not pounce from every alley. This chapter explores the risks that exist and the precautions that can be taken to ensure a trip to the United States is memorable for all the right reasons. **Do not be scared - be careful.**

Protecting Your Car

A car is stolen every 23 seconds in America. Make sure it is not yours. The advice for making a car secure in America is the same as for any country.

- **Keep it locked,** even outside your own house or hotel, **park it in a well-lit area**.
- **Do not leave valuables** on the seats and try and get **a car stereo which is removable**.
- **Hide removable stereos.** However every thief knows the glove compartment is the most obvious hiding place. Lock it in the trunk.
- **Steering locks** are useful deterrents, because they are so visible. If the car has custom wheels or an external spare tyre, as on many four-wheel drives, buy some **locking lug nuts** to hold them in place.
- **Do not keep the car's registration documents or your driving licence in the glove compartment** because it makes it easier for the thieves to sell the vehicle or commit a fraud.
- **Keep an eye out for anyone who might be watching your car** when parking up at stores or banks
- **Disconnect the battery** if the car is going to be parked up any length of time. A thief may give up rather than waste precious time trying to figure out why the car will not start. Thieves can also use the number etched on the ignition key to order a duplicate set so make a note of it somewhere safe and get a locksmith or key cutter to remove it.

Protecting Yourself

It is not just your car that could be at risk. You could be, too.

- 🚗 **Make sure the car is well maintained** to avoid breakdowns in isolated areas.
- 🚗 **Keep the gas tank at least half-full** to be sure of not running out of gas
- 🚗 **Stick to the main roads** until you are familiar with a city's layout - many cities have no-go areas

---

The best way to ensure you do not become a victim of crime is to avoid looking like a tourist. Rental cars do not carry any markings to indicate they are hired but those efforts by the agent will be undone if the driver plainly looks like he has just stepped off the banana boat. **Buy a local newspaper** or magazine and keep the map wrapped inside it. Try and **avoid looking at a map in public** and if asking for directions do not broadcast the fact. **Wearing expensive jewellery** or flashing cash are other give-aways for a tourist as is **clearly visible luggage**.

- 🚗 **Be vigilant** from the moment of arrival and keep an eye on belongings at the car rental counter and the airport shuttle
- 🚗 **Check out the car** from a safe distance when returning to it and look for anything that might delay your departure, such as a flat tyre

A long road trip is likely to involve **overnight stays in motels.** Try and get a room that can only be accessed through the lobby rather than a door opening directly on to the parking lot or balcony. Be suspicious of any unexpected knocks on the door, especially from people claiming to be room service. Call the lobby to verify whether anyone has been sent to the room.

Self Defence

If the attacker's aim is robbery then **do not resist** - give him what he wants and let him go and claim on your holiday insurance later. However, if you are the target of a violent or sexual attack then you will have to make a snap judgement based on which is going to cause you least harm.

The advice from Sergeant Pam Marshack, from Delaware State Police, is never carry a lethal weapon. A gun or a knife will up the stakes and it is unlikely you would have time to get to it anyway. It is illegal to carry a gun in a glove compartment or under a seat in many states. Mace and pepper sprays are legal but they are often kept somewhere that is not easily accessible in an emergency - at the bottom of a bag or a purse. Like rape alarms, deterrent sprays must kept within easy reach – on the dashboard, for instance. Know how to use them - the canisters have to be unlocked before they can be used so know how they work.

Sergeant Marshak's advice is that if you are attacked and decide to resist there is no point being half-hearted about it - you will have to overcome natural inhibitions against poking someone in the eyes or trying to break a bone. It only takes 14 lbs of pressure to break some of the small bones in the feet so stamp and kick hard. Go for the body's vulnerable spots - the nose, eyes, knees and groin. A car ignition key can be a useful improvised weapon. Do not worry about playing fair - grab anything that is to hand such as a torch or a steering lock.

Fighting back is not about beating an attacker it is about creating an escape opportunity and you might only get one chance so use it and get away. Resistance may only make an attacker even angrier so make it count - hit and run.

Follow-home Crimes

There have been a growing number of incidents of women being followed home in their cars and attacked. In most cases it is someone they know or have met, either in a bar or in a shop.

Stay alert, check the mirrors frequently and be aware of who or what is around the car. Has the same vehicle been behind you for a number of miles? If you think you are being followed;

- **Do not drive home**
- **Do not panic.** Stay alert and tell yourself to relax. Sometimes the pursuer only aims to scare and after a while he will get bored
- Make sure **all doors are locked** and the windows closed
- Do not accelerate
- **Stay on the freeway** as long as you can to avoid stopping at lights or being hemmed in
- If you are not on a freeway or if you have to exit because it is taking you to an unfamiliar area, **keep to the main streets**
- **Drive to a police station** if you know where to find one or to a **busy location** and ask for help

Road Rage

> *'Anger blows out the lamp of the mind.'*
>
> Robert Ingersoll, American orator.

America did not 'invent' road rage but it was the first country to give the phenomenon a name and although not entirely justified, it does have a bad reputation in this respect. In fact, the conditions for road rage exist in every developed country - crowded roads, pressured lifestyles and short fuses – and all of them suffer from the odd incidence of lost tempers.

Who Rages?

In 1997 the AAA Foundation for Traffic Safety conducted the Mizell Study which estimated that between 1990 and 1996, 218 people were killed and another 12,610 injured in more than 10,000 road rage incidents. The Mizell study showed that most of the violent aggressive drivers were men aged between 18 and 24. Women account for only 4% of aggressors. However, individual cases showed that men of all ages could get angry and dangerous when behind the wheel. One of the cases in the study was a 75-year-old man. On February 20th, 1994 the 54-year-old Donald Graham from Massachusetts became involved in an on-going feud with 42 year old Michael Blodgett along several miles of Interstate. Eventually the pair pulled on to a side road and got out of their cars. Graham went to his trunk, pulled out a crossbow and killed Blodgett with a 20-inch arrow. Graham was an accountant and a church deacon.

Road Rage

Why Rage?

Please - Grow Up!

Speaking to the House of Representatives Committee on Transportation and Infrastructure in 1997, the Chief Executive of the AAA Foundation for Traffic Safety quoted some of the reasons given by road rage offenders:
'He hit my car so I shot him.'
'Nobody gives me the finger.'
'He was playing his radio too loud.'
'He kept honking and honking his horn.'
'She was driving too slowly.'
'I would never have shot him if he hadn't rear-ended me.'

Arnold P. Nerenberg is a clinical psychologist in Los Angeles County and he has identified five triggers for road rage attacks.

1. **Endangerment.** This includes cutting someone up, tailgating or running into the back of another car. A survey in 1996 found that cutting up was the Number One irritant for drivers. Another annoyance is failure to signal when turning.
2. **Driving too slowly.** Lane hoggers who sit in the overtaking lane are particular targets.
3. **Taking someone else's parking spot.** A frequent cause of arguments when two cars compete for the same space.
4. **Showing anger.** If someone gets yelled at they yell back and soon the whole situation spirals out of control.
5. **Breaking the rules.** A surprising number of aggressors are law-abiding drivers who get wound up when they see someone flouting the rules.

It seems *everyone* has a breaking point.

These are just the triggers. The root causes of road rage are much harder to identify. The aggressor may have just had a frustrating day at work, a relationship may have broken up or a huge bill may have just arrived. Driving is now more about getting from A to B in as short a time as possible, rather than cruising along and enjoying the scenery. So when someone frustrates that goal he becomes a potential target. Whatever the reason, road rage starts when someone drives into another's bad day and even a sideways glance when alongside at a red light can be a sufficient trigger.

Avoid Being Attacked

There are a few things that can be done to reduce the risk of a road rage attack:
* **Use signals and do not cut up** other drivers
* **Do not block the overtaking lane**
* **Keep a safe braking distance**
* **Only use the horn for warning, not as an expression of anger**
* **Dip headlights** when required to do so
* **Do not be distracted by a mobile phone**
* **Do not allow the car alarm to wail incessantly** if it goes off

If an incident develops, there are steps the victim can take to calm the situation:
* **Avoid eye contact.** A dispute becomes personal when the eyes meet.
* **Seek help from the nearest police officer**
* get away If another driver is becoming dangerously aggressive
* **If there is no escape, keep the doors locked** and only open the window a crack to speak to the other driver. Keep calm and do not be provoked

Keeping Your Cool

There has been a 7% increase in road rage incidents in America every year since 1990. Whilst several surveys have asked people if they have been the victims of aggressive driving, very few people have been asked if they would admit to committing it. The only sources of information are the minority who are arrested. Given that even a church deacon is capable of killing someone in a roadside row, it is wise to acknowledge that there are things everyone can do to keep their own anger under control:

- **Do not take it personally** if someone holds up the journey
- **Accept that your can arrive late.** Will the world come to an end if the office's meeting starts at 9.05 rather than 9 o'clock?
- **Make the interior of the car a relaxing environment**. Listen to music with a beat slower than your heartbeat. Turn the air-con on
- **Driving is a team activity.** Co-operative behaviour is repaid in kind. Driving in congested traffic is a test in diplomacy and communication. Pass that test
- **Empathise**. Put yourself in the other driver's shoes and try and understand his needs

Carjacking

The United States Department of Justice's Bureau of Justice Statistics defines carjacking as, 'completed or attempted robbery of a motor vehicle by a stranger to the victim. It differs from other motor vehicle theft because *the victim is present and the offender uses or threatens force.'* (Author's italics).

American cars are being fitted with evermore-sophisticated anti-theft devices. Some models are almost impenetrable to all but the most resourceful and determined thief. However, this has had an unforeseen consequence; it is now easier to steal the vehicle while the owner is still in it and so the incidence of carjacking has increased. Why waste time trying to jemmy open a door or over-riding an ignition system when you can point a gun at someone and force them to hand over their car? Furthermore, the car remains undamaged from any enforced entry, which means that it is less conspicuous to the police if used in other crimes (such as a get-away car) and it retains its value if sold on.

Every year around 26 Americans are killed by carjackers. It is difficult to assess how many carjackings there are in America every year because there is no such offence on the statute books. Offenders are charged with robbery or armed robbery. The National Crime Victimisation Survey (NCVS) estimates that between 1992 and 1996 there were just under 50,000 carjackings a year. Half of those attempts failed but of the successful ones, 92% involved weapons. The most used weapon was a gun, followed closely by a knife.

Favourite Carjacking Spots

Parking lots, shopping centres, gas stations, car washes, convenience stores, ATMs (Cashpoint machines), fast-food drive-thrus - basically anywhere where the car is stationary with the owner (and the keys) inside or nearby. Carjackers also like to be near a slip road on to a freeway for a quick getaway.

A more risky location for carjackers, but one that many will try, is at traffic lights. One of the robbers will pull open the unlocked driver's door and force the occupant to get out before driving away. This method allows for a quick getaway but has the disadvantage of too many witnesses.

They will tend to target lone victims and, statistically, young men are more vulnerable than women. The NCVS suggests this is because young men take more chances and go to higher risk areas.

The 'Bump' Carjack or the Phoney Fender Bender

The carjackers will bump a car from behind at low speed, often at a stoplight, to trick the target into pulling over to discuss the 'accident'. One of the robbers will then steal the vehicle while his accomplice makes off in the other car.

How to Avoid a Carjacking

- When leaving their car unattended, **slide the front seats as far back as possible** to leave no room for anyone to hide in the back
- Before getting in, **check the back seat**
- **Park in well-lit, un-isolated areas**
- **Look out for people loitering** in the vicinity
- **If suspicious** of someone do not go to your car - **walk or run away**
- **Have your keys in your hand** as you approach your car so you can get in as soon as possible. The other benefit is that *if* you are threatened you can hand them over quickly without being assaulted while finding them
- Once inside the car - **drive off immediately**
- **In cities** drive with the **windows wound up** and the **doors locked**
- **Do not get penned in by congestion or traffic lights**
- **If bumped** from behind **switch on your hazard lights** to acknowledge that you are aware of the contact. **Switch on your interior light** so the driver behind can see you signal to follow **and head for somewhere crowded and well lit,** preferably a police station if you know where it is. Sergeant Pam Marshack is a specialist in women's safety with Delaware State Police. She says that you shouldn't worry about leaving the scene of an accident as it is your safety that is paramount
- **If you are near home do not go there**
- If the car is too badly damaged to drive away it is unlikely to be a carjacking because the robbers like undamaged vehicles

If you do find yourself cornered by a carjacker:

- **DO NOT RESIST.** Give up the keys and let them have the car. It is replaceable, you are not
- **Do not argue with the robber**
- If you are forced to drive the car, you may **consider crashing** it at a busy intersection so people will come to your aid and call the police

An additional piece of advice; there have been incidents where parents have left their children in a car with the keys still in the car while they nip into a shop, only to come out to find it stolen with the children still inside. **Take the kids and the keys with you.**

Police Impostors

This is not a common problem but there have been some incidents of robbers travelling in vehicles similar to unmarked police cars. If it does not have clear markings or if it does not display any flashing blue lights (usually on top or behind the radiator grill) and you are suspicious, switch on your hazard lights and signal him to follow you. Drive to somewhere busy and well lit. If you can, go inside a store or a gas station and speak to the 'officer' there. If there is nowhere to go, keep the doors locked and open the window just enough to speak to him. Ask to see his photo identification and examine it thoroughly. Genuine police officers will understand your precautions.

Gangs

A popular 'game' among gangs in America is to drive around at night with no lights. They wait until another motorist flashes them to tell them their lights are switched off and he becomes their random target for the evening, either for robbery or a beating. The practice has become so widespread that some police forces have circulated memos to local rental agents warning of the risks. So if you see a car without lights after dark, do nothing.

Hitchers

'The beckoning thumb of the hitch-hiker can be a lure to disaster in disguise.'
J Edgar Hoover, Director of the FBI, 1924-72

Hitching is a dying art in America because people are more concerned about personal safety. Fear of crime has increased dramatically over the last 30 years. Anyone who has seen the movie The *Hitcher* in which Rutger Hauer plays a psychotic hitchhiker will probably never pick anyone up again. Equally there are horror stories of hitchers who have been attacked by drivers. The truth is that most thumbed rides are pretty uneventful.

The History of the Hitch

The expansion of the road network, the proliferation of cars and the growth of the economy in the first half of the 20th Century meant hitching became an easy and convenient way of getting around. Cheap travel was no longer just for hobos jumping on and off freight trains.

The Depression forced more and more Americans on to the road in search of work and the rationing of gasoline during the Second World War increased the popularity of hitchhiking. In the 1940s Ralph Schimpf escaped from Ohio State Penitentiary and was eventually arrested in Nebraska. Neither state could provide the transport to take him back to jail so he was allowed to hitch there on his own - which he did.

Young women who worked in armaments factories, office workers, soldiers returning to base - they all stuck out their thumb for a ride. There were those, however, who saw hitchhikers as potential murderers, drug addicts and Communist infiltrators. In the 1950s the director of the FBI, J Edgar Hoover, launched a massive publicity campaign warning the public of the dangers of picking up hitchers. One poster warned:

'Don't pick up trouble! Is he a happy vacationer or an escaping criminal? A pleasant companion or a sex maniac? A friendly traveller or a vicious murderer? In the gamble with hitchhikers your safety and the lives of your loved ones are at stake. Don't take the risk!'

Despite J Edgar Hoover's best efforts, hitching remained an accepted form of transport until the early 1980s when a string of assaults, rapes and murders hit the headlines. Mostly, it was the hitchhikers who were the victims. Then, students, who tended to make up the bulk of hitchers, became wealthier and bought their own cars so they no longer needed to thumb rides.

So today the image of the hitchhiker has changed; he or she is no longer seen as a student, a soldier or a worker but a latter day highwayman. It is against that background that you must perform your own risk assessment in deciding whether to pick up a hitcher or whether to thumb a ride yourself.

With the vast distances to be covered in America some drivers are grateful for the company. It can be difficult to weigh up a potential passenger in the few seconds you have when travelling at 40 or 50 miles an hour. If you pull over and then have doubts, make up some story that you are not going where they want to go. The same goes for hitchers; only get in the car if you are sure about the driver.

There is no federal law prohibiting hitchhiking although it is illegal to thumb rides from certain locations such as on freeways. Local laws vary; sometimes you cannot hitch while standing on the road surface. Sticking out your thumb is also sometimes illegal, in which case the accepted custom is to *smile* at passing traffic. The policing of hitchhikers is inconsistent and often at the whim of the officers.

A sign saying where you want to get to is usually essential. Gas stations and truck stops are good places with the added advantage that you can approach drivers individually. Turnpikes can be good spots to thumb rides *if* the cashiers let you. They will sometimes let you stand where the cars slow up to pay. Other times they will tell you to move on or call the cops. Among the best places to hitch rides are right on the state borders where there is a 'no-man's' land between police jurisdictions. Each would rather leave it to the neighbouring force with the result that hitchhikers are often left unmolested.

Hollywood Hitcher

The Hollywood star, Kirk Douglas, once found himself thumbing a ride after his car broke down. It was the start of his career and he was already a recognisable face. A young serviceman pulled up and Kirk got in. The driver's jaw dropped when he recognised who he had picked up. Eventually he blurted out, 'Do you know who you are?!'

Where Can I Find Out More?

American Woman Road and Travel; 2424 Coolidge Rd, Suite 203, Troy, Michigan 4808. (☎ 248-614-0017; www.awroadandtravel.com). This excellent website contains all manner of useful information and articles on safety and security for women. All the advice is just as pertinent to men, however.

Drivers.com; PDE Publications Inc, 310-5334 Yonge St, Toronto, Ontario, Canada. (☎ 1-800-DRIVERS (374-8377) www.drivers.com)

National Highway Traffic Safety Administration; 400 7th St SW, Washington DC 20590. (☎ 1-888-DASH-2-DOT (327-4236); www.nhtsa.dot.gov)

Woman Motorist; PMB 240, 2674 East Main St, Suite D, Ventura 93003-2899. (☎ 805-641-2400; www.womanmotorist.com)

✦ Crooks, South Dakota, to Lawyers, Virginia - 1,300 miles ✦

Preparation for a Journey

'Every mile is two in winter.'
George Herbert, *Jacula Prudentum,* 1651.

One principal is universal – whoever and wherever you are –

⚒Plan and Prepare⚒

Whether planning a trip of a couple of hundred miles or a couple of thousand, there are a few precautions that can ensure it is trouble-free. Do not wait until you are on the road before you start thinking about your planning. Even if you do encounter problems, a little preparation can make sure a drama does not become a crisis.

Before You Leave - Checking The Car

Here is a checklist of things to do before you even turn the ignition:

- Check the levels on **all the fluids** - oil, coolant, brakes, transmission, battery, power steering, windshield washers (If you will be travelling in a cold region, make sure the washer fluid contains anti-freeze and not just water)
- **Tyres.** Make sure there is adequate tread and they are the correct pressures (including the spare). If you will be driving in snow, call the local visitor bureau to see if you will need snow tyres or snow chains
- **Battery.** If the battery is more than four years old it could struggle to hold a charge in cold weather so get it tested at a local garage
- Test all **belts and hoses** for signs of wear and leaks
- Replace the **windshield wipers** if they are split, streaking or skipping
- Make sure all **lights** are working

What to Take

Here is a list of all the essential items that should be carried on board any road tripper's vehicle:

- **Maps**
- **Blankets**. Even if driving across the desert - the nights are cold
- **Warm clothing.** As above
- **A torch** and spare batteries

- **A first aid kit**
- **Drinking water.** The Bureau of Land Management and the National Park Service recommend at least one gallon per person, per day in the desert
- **Mobile phone.** This could save your life if you break down – see below
- **Replacement fluids** – oil (10W-40 which is good for most vehicles), antifreeze and gasoline
- **Music**. Carry a selection of CDs or tapes because there are vast stretches of wilderness in the United States where you will not be able to pick up a radio station
- **Books and toys** if you are travelling with children
- **Cat litter.** A surprising accessory but vital when you sink a wheel into mud or slush. The litter can provide traction when you are trying to get your car out. (Carry the gravel type rather than the paper pellets) Cat litter is also useful for soaking up oil and fuel spills
- **A jack** and a jack stand to hold the car in position once it is off the ground. The danger when the car is balanced on the jack is that it could topple off - not a good thing when you are working underneath. *Never work under a car supported only by a jack.* A pair of jack stands will cost about $20. The weight of a car can push jack stands into soft ground, so place a foot square (30 cm X 30 cm) piece of plywood under the stands to spread the weight
- **A tyre iron** or lug wrench for undoing the wheel nuts
- **A two-foot hollow pipe.** Often the wheel nuts need a little force to undo and a pipe slipped over the handle of the tyre iron gives some extra leverage
- **Reflective warning signs** and roadside flares
- **Rags** or paper towels
- **A funnel** - or try a plastic drinks bottle with the bottom sliced off
- **A set of screwdrivers**
- **Pliers**
- **Adjustable wrenches and spanners.** Although, ideally, you should only use the correct size of spanner to avoid chewing up the head of the nut or the bolt.
- **Jump leads**
- **A spare tyre.** Many cars now carry 'Space Saver' tyres, which are narrower than proper tyres so they take up less space in the trunk, as the name suggests. They are only designed to be driven at less than 50 mph and should not travel more than 50 miles. Similarly, many sports cars carry no spare tyres at all.
- **A Swiss Army knife** is another useful item to carry

Mobile Phones

A mobile or cellular phone, as it is more commonly known in America, is an absolute must for any driver. With such vast expanses of wilderness, a cell phone is a potential lifesaver and network coverage is extensive - even in the most seemingly isolated areas.

On many networks in America you can still call the emergency services even when you cannot get a signal. Dial *611 (the local carrier) and asked to be put through to 911.

Many car rental companies now offer phones with 911 already programmed into the speed dial. Hertz phones are free of charge until they are used - there is no standing charge - and calls are billed at the local rate.

Foreign visitors who wish to use their own mobile phones in the United States will have to check they are compatible with the American cellular network. Only Tri-Band phones will work - check your owner's manual or ask your local dealer if you are unsure whether your phone is Tri-Band. You can buy Tri-Band phones outside America so it is possible to buy a compatible mobile before you go or hire one for a short trip from your normal service provider.

Global System for Mobile Communication (GSM) is the umbrella organisation for mobile phone networks around the world. Its website shows which networks are compatible with each other across the globe. For more information, contact **Global System for Mobile Communication** at 6-8 Old Bond Street, London W1 6NU (Tel 44 20 7518 0530; www.gsmworld.com).

Signing up for a mobile in America is as easy as anywhere in the world with the same variety of rates and contracts; provided you can clear the necessary credit checks and demonstrate proof of residence.

Route Planning – Maps

Do your research. A good source of route information is **Mapquest.com.** You can type in your departure point, destination and anywhere you would like to stop in between, and Mapquest will come up with a route map, directions and driving distances. It is also worth investing in a United States road atlas - you can order one from your local bookshop before you go.

Rand McNally and National Geographic publish the most comprehensive road atlases. All good book shops should carry state maps so you can start planning your journey before you travel to the United States. Once you are in America the major bookstores like Barnes and Noble will have extensive stocks of maps and atlases.

The American Automobile Association - Triple A

The American Automobile Association, or Triple A as it is more commonly known, was founded in 1916 and now boasts 36 million members across America and Canada. You will join through a state club, called a chapter, so membership fees will vary, ranging from $35 to $80. The basic Emergency Road Service (or ERS) covers the following:

- 30 minutes free assistance at the scene of a breakdown or towing to an approved garage
- 24 hours coverage
- Battery service
- Tyre service
- Fuel delivery service
- Lockout service
- Winching service

Some state clubs have different policies on charging for additional call-outs above a certain number. In addition to the basic repair, other services may be offered. East Tennessee, for instance, guarantees your cheque for up to $250 to pay for repairs at an authorised garage and can provide a bail bond of up to $5,000 to get you out of jail for a motoring offence. So, check your membership contract.

You can call Triple A for help on one national number by dialling 1-800-AAA-HELP (1-800-111-4357).

For membership information call 1-800-874-7532 or contact the organisation at the AAA National Office, 1000 AAA Drive, Heathrow, Florida 32746-5063. You can also log-on to www.aaa.com.

Safety information can be obtained from the AAA Foundation for Traffic Safety, 1440 New York Avenue NW, Suite 201, Washington DC 20005.

Surviving the Elements, Animals and Accidents

'Every sky has its beauty, and storms which whip the blood do but make it pulse more vigorously.'

George Gissing, *Winter*, 1903.

In no other country could you expect to encounter such extremes of weather or terrain on one road trip. In the morning you could be driving across a desert, hoping the engine does not overheat and in the afternoon you might be winding along mountain roads while trying to peer through the snow and slush smeared across the windshield. The North American climate can provide some tremendous driving challenges - hail stones which smash through the windshield, rain which swills frogs on to the road, winds which can toss trucks into the air and heat which can turn a car into a mobile kiln. The American weather and terrain can challenge even the most experienced driver and this chapter will offer advice on how to cope.

Car-ma Chameleon

So, does the colour of a car make it safer?

The National Highway Traffic Safety Administration published a study of car colours and reported that red, the colour of fire engines, is one of the least visible colours. The most visible colour at night is white but not during the day. A beige car will not be so obvious in arid states like Nevada or Arizona. A green car may merge into the background in Sequoia National Forest. So different cars are more or less conspicuous in different conditions.

For further information, see the website www.colormatters.com where visitors can ask questions and swap anecdotes.

So, is there a 'safe' colour for a car, given that so many factors come into play? The NHTSA, with agreement from optometrists, concluded that the safest colour for a car is one that falls in the very middle of the spectrum -

Lime yellow.

Whether you can bring yourself to drive a lime yellow car is another matter altogether.

Surviving the Elements

Should I Stay or Should I Go?

Every year, hundreds of Americans are killed or injured because they did not know what to do when caught out in their cars by extreme conditions. Some stayed put when they should have got away and some tried to get away when they should have stayed put. The Oahu Civil Defence Agency, on Honolulu, offers this helpful summary of what to do:

Earthquake - Stay in the car
Hurricane - Avoid driving
Flood - Get out of the car
Lightning - Stay in the car
Tornado - Get out of the car
Blizzard - Stay in the car
Summer heat - Stay out of a parked car
Developing emergency - Await instructions from radio or television

Hot and Bothered

America is a country of extremes and in the period of one holiday, you could encounter its full array of territories, terrains and meteorological moods.

On 10th July 1913, the highest ever temperature in the United States was recorded at Stovepipe Wells in Death Valley, 56.7C, (134F). It was so hot that day that birds fell dead from the sky, according to a plaque at the local general store.

Death Valley, California, is the hottest place in America with summer temperatures of around 35C (95F) and often topping 48.7C (120F). If the name Death Valley does not give you a clue as to what to expect, a few other place names leave the visitor in no doubt - Furnace Creek, Stovepipe Wells, Devil's Golf Course. Even some of the animal names offer a warning about the nature of the Valley - the killdeer and the mourning dove.

The really 'hot' states, generally, are Texas, New Mexico, Arizona, Utah, Nevada and California. The desert is a harsh environment and people sometimes think that just because Death Valley and the Mojave Desert are within a day's drive of big cities like Los Angeles or Las Vegas there is no need to worry about taking precautions. Park rangers in the desert regions regularly rescue hapless tourists who have under-estimated the conditions.

Let someone know your travel plans and the time you expect to arrive. If you change your itinerary, keep people informed. Take time to learn about the area before you go and check the weather conditions with local visitor centres or National Parks offices. Be conservative when working out your travel plans in a hot region - you might be surprised just how much effort everything becomes in the heat. You may also find that you cannot bear to stay in the car as long as you thought - even with the air conditioning on - so plan shorter driving shifts and more frequent rest breaks.

If you plan to spend any length of time in the desert, there are a few items you should take with you to cope with any problems:

- **Proper clothing** - sunglasses and a hat are vital. Some parts of the Mojave and the salt flats of Utah are white and can magnify the already blinding glare from the sun. Also pack warm clothes - people are often surprised by how cold it can get at night

- **Sunscreen** - You will burn within minutes without proper protection. The US Food and Drug Administration recommends the highest Sun Protection Factor (SPF) of 30 for desert regions and it advises that new arrivals should limit their exposure to one hour a day. If you are driving in an open-top car the risk of skin damage is even greater because the cooling wind will disguise the damage being done by the sun's rays

- **Fluids** - Drink plenty of water and avoid alcoholic drinks that dehydrate you. As diuretics, tea and coffee may also lead to fluid loss

- **Food** - Carry a cooler box if you have room. Chocolate becomes brown glue within minutes in the desert and will be less than appetising when you stop for lunch. Similarly hot orange juice tastes disgusting.

- **Spares and repairs** - extra fuel, fan belts, a tyre, and a jack.

Make sure your car is up to the journey. Engine temperature and fuel consumption will be your two biggest concerns. It is likely that you will have the air-conditioning turned up full so remember that you will be burning gas at a faster rate. Gas stations are rare in the desert. Be prepared to travel a few hundred miles between fill ups.

If the car overheats, do not attempt to continue if steam is coming out from under the hood. That means your cooling system is boiling. Pull over but **do not open the radiator cap.** If you do you will be sprayed with scalding water. Wait for the radiator cap to cool which may take a while.

Blowouts are more likely in hot weather because the air pressure inside the tyre increases and the tyre itself will be picking up the heat from the baking tarmac. So check tyres (including the spare) are in good condition before setting out on a desert drive and consider driving with them slightly below normal pressure.

If the worse does happen and you break down and find yourself stranded, this is the advice from the Bureau of Land Management:

- **Stay with your car and make yourself visible** - A car is easier to spot from the air than a person, so do not wander off

- **Avoid walking during the heat of the day** - If you must move, do it during the morning and evening when your body is better able to conserve its

moisture. Walk slowly to conserve energy
- **Try to avoid eating** - Digestion uses up the body's water
- **Breathe through the nose** - rather than the mouth which lets a lot of moisture escape
- **Shelter** from the sun

Cold Comfort

Mostly the hazards caused by heat tend to cause discomfort and inconvenience while the hazards of driving in the cold tend to cause accidents.

Robert McCool, from the Community Injury Prevention Programme in Kentucky, says, 'There are three things that affect your chances of having a collision - you, your vehicle and the roadway. Winter weather changes each of these three factors, usually in ways that reduce safety.'

There is not a lot you can do about the condition of the roadway but you can prepare yourself and your car.

Preparing Yourself

Wear several layers of clothing that you can peel off to suit the temperature. The most important item of clothing is a hat as most of our body heat escapes through the head. Should you need to do any repairs or maintenance to the car, such as removing a flat tyre, they will be nearly impossible without a good pair of gloves.

The hot and the cold regions of America share two hazards for the unsuspecting visitor - dehydration and sunburn. You can lose fluid in a dry cold as much as you can in a desert as your body works harder to keep itself warm. So, drink plenty of fluid. Snow reflects the sun's rays back at your skin and, if you are at high altitude - such as in the Rockies - the thinner air does not offer as much protection from the sun, so use sunscreen and sunglasses.

Preparing Your Car

Follow the steps listed in the *Preparation* chapter. Nevertheless, if you are planning to drive in cold weather, you should make sure you have these additional items on board:
- A tow rope
- Something brightly-coloured which can be spotted some distance away. If you are stuck, tie it to your car's ariel
- Chocolate
- Water
- A sign saying, HELP, in brightly-coloured letters to put in the window if you get stuck
- Snow chains. Make sure you have them on board for when you need them. You could be turned back from some mountain roads if you do not have

snow tyres or chains fitted. (See below).

Remember an older battery is less efficient in cold weather so get it load-tested at a local garage to check that it can hold a charge.

Another hazard is produced by your car in cold regions - carbon monoxide. Carbon monoxide poisoning is more likely in the winter because people are driving with their windows closed, having run the engine while stationary to warm it up and the thinner air may make the engine produce more harmful gases. A damaged exhaust increases the risk so get it checked regularly. The symptoms of carbon monoxide poisoning are sudden tiredness, yawning, dizziness and nausea. The only cure is plenty of fresh air so stop the car and get out as soon as you can **and do not wait in a stationary car while it is warming up.**

Setting Out

Give the engine time to warm up before you drive off. While it is idling clear the snow and ice from the windows, hood and lights. After a few minutes rev the engine slightly until the heater and window de-mister have warmed up. Make sure the windscreen washer fluid contains anti-freeze but beware of using the washer with the windscreen wipers at high speed on very cold days: the speed of the wipers combined with the cold can freeze the fluid on the windscreen.

To start moving on ice or snow, drop the engine revs. If the car has a manual gearbox, try moving off in second and let the clutch out very slowly. If the car is an automatic, accelerate gradually or select position 2 rather than Drive, on the gear lever.

Test your brakes at low speed to find out how much traction there is. Your stopping distances will be increased so leave space from the vehicle in front. If you do have to stop suddenly, pump the brake pedal - locked wheels do little to stop a vehicle so release the brake pedal as soon as it begins to skid and then apply pressure again.

Snow and Ice

Skidding

In a skid the rear of a vehicle starts travelling faster than the front and starts swinging around. Therefore, the key to stopping a skid is to slow the rear wheels or to speed up the front. The methods for stopping a front-wheel drive vehicle and a rear-wheel drive vehicle in a skid are different.

Front-wheel Drives. Apply a little more gas so the front straightens up.

Rear-wheel Drives. Take the foot off the gas to allow the natural braking of the engine to slow the rear end.

Many roads in America are closed in winter or restricted to vehicles capable of coping with the conditions, such as four-wheel drive vehicles or cars fitted with snow tyres or snow chains. Any road atlas will indicate which routes are likely to be affected. You should also check with local visitor centres for any restrictions.

The routes most often affected are through the Colorado Rockies and the Sierras in California. The Great Plains may also be subject to heavy snowfall, even blizzards, as the wind whips up the snow across the exposed ground. Stopping distances will increase by up to ten times so allow a huge margin of error. To maintain traction on slippery roads use a higher gear and lower revs.

The North Dakota Department of Transportation warns motorists **not to use cruise control in slippery conditions.** It can delay your response to a skid and cause an instant loss of control. Snow tyres have small steel studs sticking out of them to improve grip in the snow. They are not legal in all states because they damage the road surface but they are permitted in the pacific coastal states.

Snow chains are more suited to ice and packed snow. They are like a wire ladder wrapped around the tyre. They are cheaper than snow tyres but the disadvantages are that they can be difficult to fit and if they come loose while you are driving they can rip chunks out of your bodywork. The chains also bite into your tyres and cause damage over time. You can be fined for driving with snow chains when there is no snow because, like snow tyres, they damage the road surface.

The biggest problem with both snow tyres and snow chains is that they can lead to over-confidence in slippery conditions. They are not designed for high speeds anyway - snow tyres should not be driven above 75 mph, while chains are likely to snap or puncture the tyre. So, drive conservatively.

A Cold Con

Dave Parker, and his group of fellow travellers, fell foul of a common scam worked on roads subject to winter closures.

'We were driving a rented Mitsubishi Mirage and we wanted to drive the Tioga Pass road through Yosemite National Park in California. It was January and we were turned back by Rangers who were only allowing four-wheel drives or vehicles with snow chains through.

We eventually found a store selling snow chains and bought a set. While we were reading the instructions on the box in the parking lot, we were approached by a Ranger who offered to fit them for a $20 fee. We could see other Rangers fitting chains to other cars. So we paid the guy and he put the snow chains on. A couple of miles down the road one came off, fortunately without damaging the wheel arch. We limped back to the entrance to the Tioga Pass where we explained to the Ranger on duty that a colleague of his had not fitted our chains properly. He told us the guy was not a National Park Ranger, just someone wearing the same fluorescent bib and uniform but without the crucial National Parks insignia. These guys never actually say they are Park Rangers they just leave their victims to assume they are because they are wearing very similar uniforms. They make a hash of

> fitting snow chains and take the money. The real Park Ranger repaired our snow chain, although it was not his job, and let us through. So beware of phoney Rangers in parking lots.'

Snow chains can be very fiddly to fit so take your time to do the job properly or take your car to a local garage. You might find that these 'Rangers' who approach you in parking lots do fit them properly - it is up to you if you want to take the risk.

Listen to the weather bulletins for regular updates, because conditions can change quickly, and heed any advice given.

If You Are Snowbound...

※ **Do not leave your car** - a vehicle is easier to spot than a person is. Beware of disorientation, especially in white-outs. The wind chill in a blizzard can freeze the skin in seconds and people have been known to die within feet of their shelter

※ **Put a 'Help' sign in the windscreen** and tie something bright to the aerial

※ **Do not run the engine** for more than a few minutes at a time to keep warm. If the exhaust is blocked by snow, you will suffer carbon monoxide poisoning. Minor frostbite is preferable to death from asphyxiation

※ **Avoid activity that makes you sweat.** As you cool down the sweat chills on your skin

※ **Curl up in the blankets** you will be carrying for just this situation

※ **Dial 911** on your mobile phone for emergency help

※ **Hug your passenger** and share their body heat

Driving Across Ice

Ice is another hazard to beware of - both on the road and on water. Bridges in America display signs which tell you they are the first things to freeze in cold weather so be particularly careful when crossing them if the temperature drops. Your grip could be fine one minute and non-existent the moment you put your wheels on the bridge.

Ice on water is another danger area, whether you are in a vehicle or on foot. The Minnesota Department of Natural Resources (www.dnr.state.mn.us) offers some useful guidelines for dealing with ice. It recommends the following thicknesses for travelling across ice:

※ 4" (10cm) is the minimum for travel on foot

※ 5" (12.5 cm) for snowmobiles and All Terrain Vehicles (ATVs)

※ 8"-12" (20-30.5 cm) for cars and small trucks

The guidelines also point out that factors other than thickness can cause ice to be unsafe. Generally, do not try driving on ice, however thick you think it might be. **There is no such thing as 100% safe ice.**

What To Do If Your Car Falls Into Water

- Do not panic
- Open a window and climb out through it
- If your car is fitted with electric windows they will fuse and jam. The pressure of the water on the doors will make them almost impossible to open so wait until the water reaches your head, hold your breath and open a door. By then, the pressure inside and outside the car should be equal
- Alternatively, try breaking a window or the windscreen with a heavy object such as a steering lock. You can buy spring-loaded punches for making holes in metal and they are handy to carry in the car for breaking glass in this kind of emergency. Place the punch in the corner of the window for the best effect
- The weight of the engine will pull the front end down. So the greater the fall or if the water is deeper than about 15 feet, the greater the risk of the car settling on its roof. If the car does sink nose first, an air pocket will usually form in the back. Try to climb into it if you are unable to escape immediately

Getting out of the car is one problem. Getting out of the water is another if you have fallen through ice. The water absorbed by your clothes could add to your weight by up to 60 lbs. The advice from the Minnesota Department of Natural Resources is to turn towards the direction you came from, as the ice will be stronger from where you came, and lay your hands and arms flat on the unbroken ice. If possible, use a sharp object, such as a bunch of keys, to gain a purchase on the ice. Kick your feet to work your way back on to the surface of the ice. If it breaks, repeat the action until you are out. Once you are out roll away from the hole to spread your weight - do not stand or walk.

Warning. Recovery from immersion in cold water can be deceptive. There is a potentially fatal condition called 'after drop' which is when cold blood on the body's outer extremities starts moving around other organs as the circulation gets going again. So do not remove any clothes or blankets you have been given even if you think you have warmed up sufficiently.

Wet and Windy

☂ Rain ☂

A Florida thunderstorm has to be seen to be believed. Sometimes the rain is so heavy there is nothing a driver can do other than pull over and sit it out. The roads are awash, vehicles leave wakes and windscreen wipers, even on their fastest settings, cannot clear the water to offer any visibility. (Some state laws, such as in Alabama, require you to switch on your headlights whenever you use your wipers - although this does not include intermittent usage).

Light rain can present unexpected dangers in the United States. In areas with very little summer rain, a film of oil and dirt builds up on the road surface, especially on hills and intersections where engines tend to work harder. A light rainfall can lift that film off the road and make it dangerously slippery. Heavier falls, in late autumn and winter, wash the road clean of any residue. So, beware the early showers.

Getting bogged down

Mud, slush, snow and sand can all trap the unwary motorist. Drivers of big cars should be especially careful because the weight helps them to sink into soft ground. Desert roads can catch out a lot of people: the strips of ground at the road side may be designed for vehicles to pull over but the sand is often very fine and deep.

To avoid becoming bogged down, keep at least two wheels on one side of the car on the road surface. If the vehicle does sink, use the cat litter (mentioned in the *Preparation* chapter) for traction. Alternatively, the floor mats will give the wheels something to grip. Use a low gear to increase the torque and avoid pressing the accelerator too quickly otherwise the wheels will spin and the car will sink even further.

Hydroplaning

The risk of skidding in the wet increases with every mile an hour over 35 mph. At speeds below 35 mph, most tyres will squeeze water out from between the rubber and the road. Above 35 mph the tyres start to ride on top of the water until, at 55 mph, they are not in contact with the road at all and hydroplaning. At this point, the car has no traction and the slightest puff of wind or kink in the road can send it careering off the highway.

So what can you do? Take your foot off the accelerator and allow it to slow down naturally. There is no point in using the brakes because the car has no traction. If the car skids when you have some traction, correct according to whether you have a front-wheel or rear-wheel drive as outlined above. If you are completely hydroplaning then this book cannot help you. All you can do is ride out the skids and hope.

Prevention is always better than cure so slow down and make sure you have a good tread on your tyres because hydroplaning is almost guaranteed when the depth of the water exceeds the depth of the tread.

Tornadoes

The mid-western states are particularly prone to tornadoes and they can form in a matter of minutes. The winds can exceed 150 mph. Tornadoes like hot and humid conditions and mostly form in the Mid-West. Tornadoes can measure anything between ten feet and a mile and a half wide and will smash anything sticking up above the ground. Listen to weather forecasts if you think the conditions for a tornado are forming and act on any advice given. **You will not be able to outrun a tornado in a car.** If you can get to a building, head for the basement or the innermost rooms, preferably one without windows. Cover yourself with bedding, mattresses and clothing but bear in mind you might only have seconds to do this.

If you are unable to find a building **get out of the car** and find a ditch, a culvert or an underpass. Try and get as low down as possible. Tornadoes pass very quickly but their destructive power is awesome.

Hurricanes

While tornadoes are very localised spirals of wind, hurricanes are larger storms. A hurricane is a spinning storm with a hole in the middle so after a couple of hours it will be back to wreak more havoc. Unlike tornadoes where the key to survival is to get as low as possible, when a hurricane hits it is best to be on high ground to avoid the flooding. Listen for broadcasts that will explain evacuation procedures and routes but if you are unable to get away find a brick building.

If one is coming your way, **get out of the car and get indoors.**

Flooding

Floods are the biggest weather-related killers in the United States, according to the National Weather Service. A car can be washed away in just two feet of water.

Never attempt to drive through moving water on a road because it could be deeper than it looks, more powerful than it appears and it could be concealing debris which might damage and stall the car. If the exhaust is submerged the engine will choke and stop.

Flash floods are a big danger in the deserts and the National Parks Service advice is to stay out of flood washes - the natural channels created by running water. When they are dry, the washes might seem like attractive tracks for dirt bikes or off-roaders but they can turn into raging torrents in minutes.

If you are in a vehicle that is stranded – Get out and Get Away - Quickly!

Lightning

The good news is that when lightning strikes, a car is just about the safest place you can be. You are protected by what is known as the Faraday Cage effect: in other words, the energy of the lightning strike is dissipated around the vehicle's metal body and down into the ground. You might notice some strange effects such as the windscreen wipers moving or the lights glowing as the car's electrical systems receive a brief charge.

Mist and Fog

San Francisco Bay's rolling mists are legendary. In fact, the author did not see the Golden Gate Bridge in its entirety until his third visit to the city. Keep lights dipped in fog because full beam only reflects back on the driver.

Night Rider

Nearly half of all fatal accidents in America occur in the hours of darkness.

Be visible at night. Be the first to switch on your lights and the last to turn them off - they are there to make you visible as much as to help you see what is ahead. One of the biggest causes of accidents in darkness is over-driving head lights. In other words driving too fast to be able to stop within the distance illuminated by the headlights. Lights on full beam normally illuminate an area about 350 feet in front of the car. Dipped beams will shine about 200-250 feet ahead.

The laws on headlights vary from state to state but the rules in Alabama are typical across America. You must dip your lights within 500 feet of an on-coming vehicle and within 200 feet if you are behind it. Lights must be switched on half-an-hour before sunset and be kept on until at least half-an-hour after sunrise. They must also be turned on when visibility is less than 500 feet.

If you break down at night, pull as far off the highway as you can and switch on your hazard lights. If you do find yourself a reluctant pedestrian, carry a torch and walk on the left-hand side of the road towards the on-coming traffic.

Up in the Hills

The United States contains some beautiful undulating terrain that can be a challenge to drive through. Those rolling, winding hill roads can also conceal any number of hazards - animals, other cars, pedestrians. So ease off the gas and drive cautiously. It may be tempting to shift in to neutral and to coast on a long downhill stretch but this is illegal in many states because you are not considered to be in control of the car. **Never coast downhill.**

A combination of blind bends and poor weather conditions can make hill or mountain driving particularly hazardous. Beware of swinging out too wide on mountain bends because you could be faced with a vehicle coming in the opposite direction. If going up hill remember that the engine loses 10% of its power if it is also powering the air conditioning so it could struggle and overheat on a steep climb. Keep a steady speed and try to avoid too many gear changes, which increase the wear and the tear on the gearbox.

If going downhill select a low gear - even if the car is an automatic. The natural braking of the engine will slow the car to a manageable speed and the gears will not wear out whereas the brake pads could.

If your brakes do fail, try pumping the pedal to get some pressure back into them. (Although this may not work with anti-lock brakes. Put the car into a low gear and apply a little emergency brake (hand brake) - not enough to lock the wheels. Steering the car into a side barrier will also help slow its momentum. Do not steer too sharply into the barrier because the car could simply bounce back into the road.

Steep hills in America have escape roads for just this sort of emergency. They are clearly signed with distances to the next one and they are steep inclines covered with a deep layer of gravel to bog down the wheels. Escape roads are often at the apex of bends allowing the vehicle with failed brakes to steer straight on and allow the gravel and the incline to bring it gently to a halt. A level or uphill intersecting road may have the same affect.

If all that fails and you think you are about to go over the edge, try to steer into an object that slows the vehicle down but avoid all but the smallest trees as they do not give at all. **If the car comes to rest over the edge of a drop, do not make any sudden moves.** Most of the car's weight will be over the front where the engine is. Climb very slowly out of the front doors if they are not over thin air. If they are, climb carefully into the back of the car and out of the rear doors.

Long Distance Driving – Fighting Fatigue

Imagine driving the 411 miles from London, England, to Glasgow, Scotland - that is a day's drive. Now imagine getting in your car the next day and driving all the way back again. The day after that you repeat the trip to Glasgow. Driving from one side of the United States to the other could be the equivalent of driving from London to Glasgow and back every day for eight days. It can leave you exhausted. The monotony of some areas can also lead to boredom and tiredness: in states like Kansas you can drive in a straight line for hours without moving the steering wheel. In fact, there is an urban myth that engineers put kinks in Wyoming's highways just to give drivers something to do. The novelty of the Kansas wheat fields will wear off after a couple of hours and the Texas landscape becomes little more than a beige blur.

If you are looking for a cure for tiredness, remember this; **coffee does not work.** Coffee may give you a short burst of energy but it is borrowed energy and the short period of extra alertness just means you will be even more tired later on.

☞ **Keep your eyes moving.** After a while you can slip into Highway Hypnosis - a blank stare at the road ahead without registering anything that is going on. This is a particular danger on long, straight roads and at night when oncoming lights can lure you into a trance. The tell-tale signs, apart from crashing, are late braking and slow responses. To prevent this, your eyes should be kept constantly moving. This can be achieved by frequently checking your mirrors.

◁Watch Your Posture. Keep your head and shoulders back and push your bottom against the back of the seat. Keep your legs flexed at an angle of about 45° and *not* fully extended.

◁Keep Your Body Involved in the Driving. Try and avoid using cruise control, vary the speed, chew gum or smoke a cigarette (illegal in some states in the summer), flex your muscles, slap your thighs (one at a time), sing or talk to yourself.

◁Adjust the Car's Environment. Keep the interior temperature cool, even in the winter. Change the radio station, tape or CD frequently and avoid soft music that can lull you to sleep.

Other ways to stave off fatigue:

◁ **Leave early**
◁ **Eat before you go** - but not a huge meal which could make you sleepy
◁ **Take rest breaks** even if you do not feel tired
◁ Every so often **take a long break** - a couple of hours
◁ **Have a nap** if you feel you need it, but no more than 20 minutes
◁ **Try a Wal-Mart parking lot** which are open 24 hours and are well lit if you cannot find a rest area, service station or **motel**
◁ **Take nutritious food** for the trip and **lots of water**

Ultimately, though, there is only one cure for fatigue - a good night's sleep.

Surviving the Wildlife

Oh Deer!

The five most common explanations made to the North Carolina Highway Patrol by drivers who have put their pickup trucks into the woods:
1. A deer ran into the road.
2. A deer ran into the road.
3. A deer ran into the road.
4. A deer ran into the road.
5. I was stopped at a stop sign but I had to start up again real fast and run my pickup into the woods because otherwise it would have been smashed by this deer that ran into the road.
P.J. O'Rourke, Republican Party Reptile, Picador, 1987.

Collisions with animals are a common hazard on America's roads, particularly on those long country highways and in the wilderness. No one can quite agree just how many accidents involve animals. The succinctly named National Highways Traffic Administration's Fatal Accident Reporting System (FARS) reported

275,000 collisions with animals in 1995. Yet, the Insurance Information Institute estimates that there are half a million collisions with deer alone every year. An unfortunate by-product of effective conservation and animal husbandry in America has been an increase in the number of accidents: the deer population has increased from 10 million in the 1980s to 20 million today. More animals equal more collisions.

The range of animals killed on America's roads would be enough to stock a zoo. In Florida, the author has seen dead alligators at the roadside. In other parts of the Everglades, the grasshoppers are so numerous it is impossible not to drive over them. In the Mojave Desert, snakes can be seen slithering across the road. They are easy to drive over without squashing but elsewhere other animals are harder to miss: bears in the forests and, of course, deer are all hazards waiting around the next blind bend.

So how can you avoid hitting an animal?
- **Dawn and dusk** are the danger times, particularly for deer.
- **Look out for road signs** warning of animals.
- **Sound your horn rather than flash your headlights**, if you do see an animal in the road. Flashing your lights could cause it to fixate on your beams.
- **Brake rather than swerve**, if you think you are going to hit it. Swerving could confuse the animal as to which way to run. It may be hard to accept but hitting the animal is preferable to swerving into a tree or an on-coming vehicle.

I Can't Bear It!

Bears are more than a hazard on the roads. They love breaking into cars at campsites and stealing food. Despite numerous warnings and signs telling people NOT to keep food in their cars, damage costing tens of thousands of dollars is done to cars in National Parks every week. In Yosemite in California, for example, the Visitor Centre plays a video of a bear breaking into a car and viewers are always amazed at the destruction the animal causes.

The bear is strong enough to smash windows, bends doors off their hinges and tear the interior to pieces in its search for food. If you park your car while you go off and visit an attraction, your car should be safe; bears will avoid crowded car parks in daylight. It is at night when they like to roam in search of food. Bears are attracted by any strong smells, not just food. Therefore, the advice from the National Parks Service is:

Store all food in the special bear-proof lockers provided at National Park campsites.

Perfumes, toiletries, toothpaste - in fact anything with a smell - should also be removed from cars overnight.

Bears love breaking into cars to steal food

Surviving Accidents

The priority of the first person at the scene of an accident is *not* treating the victims. The first thing to do is to make the scene safe and secure to ensure no one else crashes into the victims or vehicles already involved.

- **Park your vehicle off the road with its hazard lights flashing.**
- **Send people out to warn on-coming traffic.**
- If you have **road flares,** lay them out a couple of hundred feet on either side of the accident but only after making sure there is **no risk from leaking fuel.**
- **If injured people are lying in the road, protect them by parking vehicles on either side.** The barrier vehicles should also turn on their hazard lights.
- **Switch off the ignitions** of any vehicles involved to reduce the risk of fire.
- **Call for the police, fire and ambulance.** Do not assume someone else will have done it. It is better that the emergency services receive duplicated calls

rather than none at all. Use a mobile phone if you have one or an emergency call box if you are on a major highway. Look for the arrows on the small wooden posts at the roadside, which will point to the nearest telephone: people's instinct is to walk back in the direction that they have come from but the nearest telephone might actually be ahead of them, in the direction that they were travelling.

These steps should only take a couple of minutes and should ensure the situation is not made worse by further collisions. Once the scene is secure, attention can be given to the victims.

A common fear among many Americans is that they may be sued if their attempts at first aid make things worse. There have been cases where accident victims have sued good Samaritans who tried to help. There was even one case where an off-duty doctor was taken to court because accident and emergency treatment was not his specialist field and he made an error of judgement.

However, most states have Good Samaritan laws to protect people from legal action when they help at the scene of an accident. A few only offer protection to people helping at car accidents, not other types of accident.

Whatever your legal position, your priority should be to protect the victims until professional help arrives, not to treat them.

- Attend to any **unconscious accident victims first**: the people making the most noise may not be the most seriously injured.
- **Do not move injured people** - there might be a risk of aggravating a neck or back injury. Eighty per cent of people hurt in road accidents suffer some kind of head injury. If they suffer a head injury, it should be assumed they have a related neck or back injury. Only if the injured person is inside a burning vehicle should you move them.
- **Ask the victim if they want assistance.** If they say 'No' then do not offer it, even if you think they need it. If you give unwanted help you could invalidate your protection under the Good Samaritan laws
- **Talk to the injured person,** reassure them and be encouraging. Hold their hand.
- **If they are bleeding, use a compress** rather than a tourniquet which can cause tissue damage by cutting off the blood supply. Apply as light a pressure as possible to head wounds in case the skull is fractured
- **Do not be tempted to apply advanced first aid techniques**, such as splinting broken limbs, if you are not trained. There is a risk of causing more damage. Wait until the paramedics arrive
- **If a person is unconscious** but appears to be breathing normally, roll them

on to their side **in the recovery position** to prevent them from swallowing their tongue or inhaling vomit

If the victim has **stopped breathing then apply mouth-to-mouth resuscitation and heart massage (CPR)**.

The Aftermath of an Accident

Once the casualties have been dealt with the police will ask you for a witness statement. (Although you are not required to report the accident to the police if there were no injuries or if no property was damaged).

- If the accident did result in death, injury or damage to property above a certain value you may be required to **notify the Department of Motor Vehicles (DMV)** and establish financial responsibility within a certain period of time. The attending police officer will advise you of your responsibilities. A report to the state DMV will be *in addition* to any report filed by the police and the insurance company.
- Generally it is advisable to **report all motor accidents to the police,** whether they are called to the scene or not. You are required to report accidents involving all domestic animals, except cats, and some wild animals such as deer.
- If the police are called **do not move any of the vehicles** unless they are causing an obstruction. Then **take photographs** or make a sketch of their positions.
- If you were involved in the accident, **do not admit fault** (or even apologise), do not offer to pay for any damages and do not discuss it with any of the other parties. It is the job of the police and insurance companies to decide who was to blame.
- **Find any witnesses** and get their names and addresses.
- From any other involved parties you will need to **get names and addresses, licence plate numbers, vehicle registration and insurance details.**
- **Do not sign anything** other than a traffic ticket issued by the police, which you are required to sign by law.
- Make a note of the **name and badge number of the attending police** officer and get the **number of the accident report** as well as a copy.
- **Contact your insurance agent** as soon as possible to discuss whether to file a claim through your own company or pursue a liability claim against another party. Record all communications in writing.
- Finally, if the unthinkable happens and **you are arrested, exercise your right to silence until you have spoken to a lawyer.**

Where Can I Find Out More?

Weather Information

The National Weather Service: 1325 East-West Highway, Silver Spring, Maryland 20910. (☎301-713-0090; www.nsw.noaa.gov)

For information about weather and climate across the United States, USA Today provides a detailed guide on **www.usatoday.com/weather.** The site provides details of the weather in all major cities and the national parks.

The State Visitor Centres also provide information on weather, road conditions, accommodation and attractions. A useful website that offers access to all of the state websites is **www.travelingusa.com/dirstate/ tourism** and add the name of the desired state at the end of that address.

There is also a full list of the toll-free telephone numbers for information about road conditions for all 50 states at the end of the American Road system chapter.

Natural Hazards

National Park Service: Department of the Interior (also incorporating Bureau of Land Management), 18th and C St NW, Washington DC 20013.

National Parks Service (☎1-800-365-2267 for campsite reservations. 1-301-722-1257 from outside the United States; www.nps.gov)

Bureau of Land Management (☎202-452-5125; www.blm.gov)

✦ Windyville, Missouri, to Calm, Missouri, 300 miles ✦

Garages, Gas, Grub & Goodnight

'The squeaky wheel gets the grease.'

Proverb

Garages

Risible Repairs

If something does break, a little improvisation can keep you going - or at least within the law - until you can get a proper repair at a garage:

Indicators. If a bulb fails, use the one from the fog light

Leaking radiators. Chewing gum is good for plugging small holes. If you break a raw egg into the radiator it will disperse and then hard-boil around any cracks and so block them

Broken fan belts. Tights or stockings serve as good temporary replacements

Wiper blades. If the blade on the driver's side splits, take the one from the passenger side. Alternatively, take the blade from the rear wiper

Leaving lights on. Do not attempt to start the car straight away. Wait for 15 minutes before turning the ignition - a good battery should regain its charge

Recharging the battery. Drive around in third gear, if the car has a manual transmission, the high revs will recharge the battery

Rusty bolts. Pour cola drink over them and wait 10 or 15 minutes before attempting to undo them. (Sugar-free drinks will not work!)

Changing wheels. If, somehow, you lose the bolts, take one bolt from each of the other three wheels. It is possible to drive safely for a short distance with three bolts holding each wheel

Finding A Reliable Mechanic

If an aircraft can fly hundreds of thousands of miles every year and have a service life of 40 years, there is no reason a car travelling about 15,000 miles a year cannot last for nearly as long. The secret to a long automotive life is good maintenance - whether you do it yourself or it is done at a garage.

If you do need to take your car to a mechanic, you will want to be sure he is reliable and honest and that you are not being ripped off. Anyone can say they offer a great service but the real test is whether they can get their customers to say it. So ask around - **talk to friends and neighbours.**

The **following institutions** may also be of help in finding a reliable mechanic:

✕ *The Better Business Bureau,* which is an American equivalent of a Trading Standards Department, will have records of any complaints against local garages

✕ *Triple A* is another good recommendation - the organisation approves more than 4,000 repair shops across America

✕ *The National Institute for Automotive Service Excellence, or ASE,* vets and approves reliable mechanics and the certificates should be clearly displayed

✕ *The Automotive Service Association* operates a code of ethics which reputable garages will abide by

✕ *The Local Division of Standards,* in some states, requires repair shops to post a bond, sometimes in the region of $10,000, to cover customer litigation

Checks and Precautions

Below is a list of checks, actions, and cautionary steps to ensure that a mechanic delivers the level of service expected:

✎ **Obtain a guarantee in writing** before you agree to any repairs. Honest mechanics will have no fear of this and it is reasonable to expect warranty of at least six months - anything less than a 90-day warranty should send alarm bells ringing. Ensure the warranty covers parts *and* labour because a part may fail not because it is faulty but because it was not fitted properly

✎ **Be specific** and describe any symptoms in as much detail as you can. Avoid vague instructions and *never tell the garage to do 'whatever is needed'* - you might as well write out a blank cheque

✎ **Ask for written details** of the work to be done *and* estimated costs

✎ Ask for the hourly labour charge and ask for an estimated time for the job. At least then you can pin the mechanic down to a ballpark figure

✎ **Obtain a full explanation** of the work to be done. Popular scams include 'finding' more serious problems while carrying out routine servicing

✎ **Question any jargon or unfamiliar terms.** Beware of a mechanic playing on your ignorance; if he suggests changing the clutch fluid, walk away. There is no such thing

✎ **Get a second opinion if necessary.** Do not agree to the work if you are suspicious - take it to another garage

✎ **If any parts are replaced, ask to see the old ones** so you can verify whether they look damaged or worn and that the old one has actually been removed. Some manufacturers insist removed components must be returned under their warranty agreement so ask to see them before they are sent back

⟡ **Ask to see the boxes and invoices for the new components** to confirm that you have received the brand of part being charged - do not pay top dollar for a bargain-basement part

---

Phrases to Ring Alarm Bells

🔔**The Teardown.** If a mechanic says your car needs a teardown then prepare for a very big bill. The word means the mechanic will have to tear down the whole engine and completely rebuild it. It is a drastic remedy, only necessary when there is something very seriously wrong. If a repair shop says such extensive work is needed, ask for a detailed breakdown of what will be done and how much it is likely to cost - both for parts and labour. If you have any doubts, get a second opinion before agreeing to a teardown.

🔔**Being 'Back-Ended'.** Being 'back-ended' means being presented with extra costs you were not told about when you agreed to the service. The term applies to buying a car from a dealer as well as to getting repairs at a garage. Sometimes mechanics will tell you they found 'unexpected' problems once they got to work and decided to 'fix' them without telling you.

Your Rights

States offer car owners some basic consumer rights in auto-repairs. Those offered by Massachusetts are typical: the Attorney General's Auto Sales and Repairs Regulations apply to all garages offering repair services, bodywork and retail services. They do not apply to gas stations which offer minor repair services, like changing bulbs, fan belts and oil filters.

Car owners' basic rights include:
- *The right not to be misled.* A mechanic cannot lead a customer to believe repairs are necessary when they are not
- *The right to be informed.* A mechanic must inform the owner about charges for estimates or diagnosis, storage charges and rights to the return of any old or damaged parts that will be removed
- *The right to a written estimate* before any work is carried out. The estimate must list the specific parts and the labour. The repair shop does not have to provide a written list of charges if they are already displayed where they can be clearly seen. The garage is also exempt from providing a written estimate if it is unable to diagnose the problem, if the car is brought in outside usual business hours or if the work is carried out off the premises
- *An excess of the estimate* of more than $10 should be communicated to the customer if it is likely to occur
- *The final bill must be itemised* and list parts and labour, unless the repairs

are carried out on a flat-rate charge clearly displayed in the repair shop
* *Any work that does not meet trade standards* must be repaired at no charge

Unsatisfactory Work

Comebacks. Cars that are not fixed properly and taken back to the repair shop are known as 'comebacks' in the trade. *Every mechanic (and customer!) wants to avoid a comeback* - it makes him look bad and it eats into the profit margin. Take the car out for a **test drive** (preferably with the mechanic) before paying for any major repairs. If the problem persists always try to **speak to the same mechanic** who worked on the car and if he refuses to look at the car immediately, ask to **speak to the manager**. **Remain calm** - it may just be an honest mistake rather than an attempted rip-off but a customer should make it clear that he knows his rights and point out that the business would not want to damage its reputation.

If the manager refuses to look at the problem, **cancel any payment** that may have already been made. Be aware, though, that most states allow garages to withold cars until outstanding payments have been settled so be prepared to leave without the vehicle if still not satisfied with the work and no compromise can be found. If it is possible to leave with the car, however, other repair shops might be reluctant to deal with work done by someone else. The original garage might also be entitled to cancel any warranties if another works on a car.

If still not satisfied, enlist the help of the local **Better Business Bureau** that will offer the services of a mediator to try to resolve the dispute. However, mediation does require the consent of both sides so if the repair shop refuses to co-operate a customer may have to consider other options such as **accepting his losses, sending a demand letter or even taking legal action.**

The 30 Day Demand Letter

There is a possible solution that stops short of all-out court action - the 30-Day Demand Letter. This can be used in any dispute between a trader and a customer and not just in auto-repair disagreements. Each state's version of the 30 Day Demand Letter is available through its own Better Business Bureau or local consumer groups.

A trader *must* respond to such a letter within 30 days or face punitive damages and costs. In Massachusetts, for example, a business that fails to respond will find that the damages awarded against it are tripled. The letter will encourage the trader to settle out of court but it also lays down the amount of damages should the case go to court. Ideally, the letter should be sent by recorded delivery ('certified delivery' in the US).

The letter *must* include the following information:
- Your name and address
- A description of the unfair, deceptive or sub-standard service
- An outline of the injury or cost suffered
- The relief being sought, including the amount of money to be recovered

If the repair shop replies within the 30 days the customer must then decide whether to accept any offer made. If a court subsequently decides that the repair shop's offer was reasonable then you will have to accept it. If the repair shop does not reply within 30 days or if the court rules that any reply was not made in good faith then the customer could be awarded more than the original damages sought plus costs.

Below is a sample 30 Day Demand Letter for Massachusetts. Other state consumer agencies will have their own templates and will be able to explain the relevant legislation under which you are making a claim.

Your name and address.
Date.
Name of business.
Business address.

Dear -
Under the provisions of Massachusetts General Laws, Chapter 93A, Section 9, I hereby make written demand for relief as outlined in that statute.
On or about (date), the following unfair or deceptive act occurred:
(Explain what happened)
This unfair or deceptive act or practice is, in my opinion, declared unlawful by Section 2 of Chapter 93A which reads as follows:
(Quote text or section although you do not have to copy out the actual regulations or laws to support your claim. However, try to be as thorough as possible in listing the regulations you believe were violated)
As a result of this unfair or deceptive practice, I suffered injury or loss of money as follows:
(Give details of the injury or money or property loss)
Therefore I demand the following relief:
(List the relief or damages being sought)
Chapter 93A gives you the opportunity to make a good faith response to this letter within thirty (30) days. Your failure to do so could subject you to triple damages, attorney's fees and costs if I decide to institute legal action.
Yours Sincerely,

Your name.

Source; Massachussetts Office of Consumer Affairs and Business Regulation website, www.state.ma.us/consumer/Pubs/demand.htm.

January 2002.

Gas

I wipe the pipe, I pump the gas,
I rub the hub, I scrub the glass.
I touch the clutch, I mop the top.
I poke the choke, I sell the pop.
I clear the gear, I block the knock.
I jack the back, I set the clock.
So join the ranks of those you know
And fill your tank with Texaco.

Theme song from Milton Berle's Texaco Star Theatre, 1948-55.

America's first gas station was opened by the Automobile Gasoline Company in St Louis, Missouri, in 1905. By the time of the Golden Age of American motoring hundreds of thousands of gas-pump attendants, in crisp white overalls, were filling up the gas-guzzling spaceship-style vehicles, checking the oil and water and cleaning their windshields. The first self-service gas stations opened in California in the 1940s. At the time, the oil companies launched a vigorous campaign against self-service stations, claiming that there was an increased risk of fire and explosion when an untrained person operated a gas-pump. For a while the strategy worked but then came the 1973 oil crisis. Car makers produced more efficient and smaller cars which did not need their oil topped up so frequently, the popularity of paying less in return for filling for oneself grew, and improved technology meant one cashier could monitor several pumps at once. By 1990 less than a third of gas stations offered attendant service. Now only New Jersey, where there are no self-service pumps, and a few rural stations are the last bastions of the pump attendant.

The quality and efficiency of gas stations varies tremendously in America. It is not too difficult to find a 24-hour gas station and most are open seven days a week, although the more isolated areas may have limited opening hours. Some gas stations are part of extensive shopping complexes offering everything from cinemas to dry cleaning. Others are struggling independent outfits where the pumps date back to the old days. These may have no display link-up to the cashier's office but more worryingly they may have no automatic cut-off so beware of over-filling the tank.

Gas stations can also be Aladdin's caves of goodies to suit every taste - from the sickliest Danish pastries to Elvis compilation cassettes to garish key rings and even ATMs and internet terminals. Most will have restrooms. Drivers who did not buy any gas but who used the facilities, such as asking for directions, using the restroom, and topping up with water used to be known as IWWs - Information, Wind and Water - and they were considered a drain on profits. Now, though, gas stations offer so many other services that gas may be a small part of their business.

The Cost of Gas

A US gallon is smaller than an imperial (UK) gallon by about 20%. So, while an imperial gallon equals 4.7 litres, a US gallon represents 3.8 litres.

Gasoline is cheap in the United States compared to Europe - usually in the region of $1.20 a gallon or $0.32 per litre - which makes for a motorist's dream and an environmentalist's nightmare. Depending on the type of car, it is possible to travel coast to coast on about $100 worth of gas. That compares with $200-$300 to make the same journey by plane, train or bus.

The more isolated the gas station, the more expensive the gas, so you could be paying around $2.20 a gallon in the desert towns where competition is limited. Furthermore, in some parts of the United States there are no gas stations for a hundred miles or so. Always try to fill up before heading into the wilderness and it is best to keep the tank topped up once there to avoid an expensive fill-up or running out of gas altogether.

In California it is an offence to run out of gas. If carrying a spare can in the trunk, the container must be of an approved design that will not break, leak, or even burst at high altitudes. Plastic containers are prone to the danger of static electricity sparks.

Paying

America has a fear of cash and a love of plastic. Many pumps have card swipes for credit or debit cards. Drivers simply swipe their card, wait for authorisation, select the grade of gas and fill up. The pump prints out a receipt when they are done.

As a precaution against non-payment, such pumps require a cash-paying customer to guess how much gas he will need, say $20-worth, to then pay the $20 in cash and then fill up. If the sale comes to less than $20 the driver is given change but the pump will automatically cut off once $20 is reached - so it is usually less hassle to pay with a card.

Types of Gasoline

Since 1996 all gasoline has been unleaded and it comes in three grades -
• Regular (87 octane), • Mid-grade (89 octane), and • Super (92 octane).

The octane rating has nothing to do with the power the gasoline provides for the engine so putting super unleaded in the tank will not turn a junker into a hot-rod. Car engines are designed for a particular grade of fuel and the octane-rating determines the rate at which the gasoline burns in the cylinder. The owner's manual will explain which is the optimum grade for your car - stick to that grade.

Grub

Americans love their food so the foreign visitor will be spoilt for choice when it comes to eating. Whether the choice is always good quality food is another matter. Almost every freeway and interstate exit will lead the traveller into a neon forest of signs advertising motels, hotels, restaurants and fast food outlets.

Names like McDonalds and Burger King are worldwide brands but as an internet search for 'US restaurant chains' revealed, there exist a huge number of nationwide chains unfamiliar to foreign visitors (nearly 300 links, in fact): travellers can choose from *Armadillo Willy's, Bugaboo Creek Steak House, Diamond Dave's Mexican Restaurants, Mr Goodcents Pizzas, Souper Salad,* and *Yia Yia's* to name just a few.

It is important to maintain a varied diet and to avoid the easy option of always heading for the same old restaurants because their menus are familiar. When many miles are being covered, especially at night, it is vital to maintain energy levels with some complex carbohydrates (rice, potatoes, beans, pulses, wholegrain bread, etc). The quick-hit sugary highs from snacks and sweets will be followed by sleepiness as the body over-compensates and blood sugar levels plunge from a sudden high to below normal levels. Large and protein-rich meals are also best avoided because of their soporific effect – this time caused by blood moving to the digestive tract to help break down the meal. Another couple of reasons for taking the healthy option while driving are to avoid gaining a typical American waistline (the US has the highest obesity rate in the world) and to keep yourself regular after spending so much time in a sedentary position.

Having said all that, American burgers are the best in the world and well worth savouring. Other not-so-healthy delights for your on-the-road diet should include the seafood offered by *Red Lobster* and the Mexican cuisine of *Taco Bell*. If feeling really devilish and it is sugar you need then there are always *Dunkin' Donuts, Krispy Kreme Donoughts* or the ice cream sundaes offered by *Dairy Queen*.

For a comprehensive list of restaurant chains in the United States and links to their websites, visit **www.virtualvoyages.com /resource/restrnt.htm**.

Roadkill Cookoff

Cars and cuisine meet head on in Marlinton, West Virginia, every September with the **Roadkill Cookoff**. It is legal, in West Virginia, to take home and use any animals run over on the highway so the annual event could be seen as a testament to a waste-not-want-not, hippy way of life rather than having anything to do with the colour red, necks and a slightly warped sense of humour. West Virginians had been cooking squashed critters for years and the state legalised the practice because so many people were doing it anyway. Now the *Roadkill Cookoff* boasts such culinary delights as *Thumper Meets Bumper, Broken Chicken Wings* and *Fragged Frog*.

For more information about the Roadkill Cookoff, contact the West Virginia Division of Tourism, 2101 Washington St, East Charleston, West Virginia 25305. (Tel 1-800-225-5982; www.callwva.com).

The Diner

No road trip is complete without at least one trip to an American diner. The diner is *the* archetypal piece of roadside Americana.

That the *very first diners* started out as surplus railroad dining cars is, in fact, a myth. The first diner was Walter Scott's Pioneer Lunch Wagon, set up in Providence, Rhode Island, in 1872. Walter offered a mobile eatery with a walk-up service at the counter on the outside and seating inside. Soon everyone was jumping on the luncheon wagon and these mobile eateries started appearing all over the north-eastern United States. They became known as 'diners' when much later, in the 1920s, some entrepreneurs did start using retired railroad dining cars.

Diners used to be more than restaurants - they were meeting places, roadside community centres where travellers and locals would mix and swap news. The food was often just an added bonus. Customers would sit at the counter and enjoy a cup of Java, a *tall stack* of pancakes, *eggs over easy* or a *sun kiss* - diners even had their own culinary jargon.

They were also examples of great design. Pre-war diners took the best features of European Art Deco while the post-war designs reflected the American passion for the streamlined chrome and aluminium of the jet age.

Booths became a feature as owners tried to attract more families and female customers. Rock 'n' Roll saw the introduction of the private jukebox in many of those booths and diners-as-meeting-places attracted a new generation.

McDonalds

Then in the early 1950s a catering equipment salesman called Ray Kroc bought out a diner owned by two brothers, Richard and Maurice, at San Bernadino, on Route 66 in California. He found they had refined their business so they could produce consistently good quality food, in high volume and at reasonable prices. The brothers were already on the road to riches when Ray came along in 1952; they operated 12 franchises and the San Bernadino restaurant, alone, was turning over $350,000 a year. Mr Kroc imitated their business model and kept the business name used by Richard and Maurice **McDonald** and the result was a success that spread first locally, then across the States and eventually across the whole world.

Soon everybody was at it and the diner evolved into the fast-food outlet we know today, losing most of its character along the way. More recently, though, the story has come full circle; the old-style diner has made a comeback as people hanker for a taste of classic American heritage. The older diners, which clung on, are back in favour and new ones are opening, enabling travellers to live the road trip to the full.

Diner Dictionary

Diners developed their own language and waitresses would be heard telling the cook to 'Sweep the kitchen' or 'Cremate it!' Here are some of the phrases used in diners.

Adam's ale	Water
B & B	Bread and Butter
Black and White	Chocolate soda with vanilla ice cream
Boiled leaves	Tea
Cremate it	Toast it
Cow paste	Butter
Hen fruit	Egg
Hot one	Chilli
House boat	Banana split
Flop two	Flip two eggs
Let the sun shine in	Unbroken egg
Lighthouse	Bottle of Catsup (ketchup)
Over easy/easy over	Fried eggs, turned
Pitch till you win	Eat all you can
Shivering Eve	Apple juice
Sun kiss	Orange juice
Sweep the kitchen	Hash browns
Vermont	Maple syrup
Wax	American cheese
Yellow paint	Mustard

Goodnight

With thousands of hotels and motels to choose from, it is possible to follow a very flexible itinerary on a road trip in America. There is no need to book ahead, the traveller can simply find somewhere to stay at the end of the day. There is usually a wide choice of accommodation clustered around freeway exits and it is not uncommon to see a hoarding promoting a motel for anything up to 200 miles further down the road. Furthermore, accommodation in the United States is of good quality and reasonably priced, starting as low as $25 per room.

Camping

Kampgrounds of America - or KOA - runs hundreds of campsites across America, Canada and Mexico. The organisation caters for holidaymakers who want to stay in tents, cabins, cottages or Recreation Vehicles. KOA also operates a Value Card that offers members a 10% discount on camping fees and a 15% discount on Budget car rentals.

Motels (Motor-hotels)

Rates are usually displayed on neon signs outside the motels so it is possible to cruise around comparing prices before making a decision. Operators will often try to tempt customers with offers such as a 'free continental breakfast' or a swimming pool. Unfortunately, the pool may be an enlarged paddling pool and the continental breakfast usually consists of a muffin or a doughnut and a polystyrene cup of warm coffee picked up from reception. Motels and food outlets tend to be grouped together at the major interstate and freeway exits so it is best to head for a local restaurant or diner before hitting the road in the morning.

Free continental breakfast

Motel facilities tend to be fairly standard. Most rooms offer a television, air conditioning, an en suite bathroom, and a telephone. (Not forgetting the ubiquitous Gideon Bible). There is very little to choose between the different motel chains and the individual motels of chains are pretty much the same as one another.

Motel or Hotel?

The big advantage of motels is that a guest knows what to expect. If he likes Days Inn then he can pull off at the next Days Inn sign and not have to worry about quality or level of service or vast expense. The disadvantage is blandness. A long road trip can become a blur of identical rooms. If the accommodation is part of the holiday experience rather than just a bed for the night, then the traveller should consider paying more for a hotel with more character and a higher level of service.

Location is another factor to consider. Motels are often found in unattractive service areas close to the main highways. They are great for hopping on and off the interstates but not so convenient for people who want to do more with their time - a trip to the cinema or a meal in a classy restaurant.

Hotels require a little more navigation to find but they are better for town or city centre locations and closer to the main attractions. Unlike motels, hotels often need to be booked in advance and are less suitable for a make-it-up-as-you-go-along holiday. The problem with making an advanced reservation is that there is always the risk of losing a deposit if plans change. If you are not on a particularly tight budget and are looking for inns and hotels with character look for the series of accommodation guides called *Country Inns, Lodges and Historic Hotels* to various regions of the US.

Prices

Hotel rates in America are quoted per room not per person. Singles – where they exist – are only slightly less than doubles, so it is much more economical to travel with a friend or two.

An inexpensive hotel room should cost less than $100 a night but in such a competitive market there are always offers and discounts available. A decent motel room should cost between $25 and $40 for one guest and a further $8-$10 for each additional adult.

Rates for both motels and hotels used by tourists tend to be lower in mid-week - Monday to Thursday and it is always worth haggling, especially late in the day when the manager will be keen to fill the rooms for the night. Smart business hotels tend to have lower rates at the weekends. It is always worth trying to negotiate a cheaper rate by asking for a smaller room or just by haggling: the basic room rate quoted to customers is called the 'rack' rate and this is generally considered negotiable. Another difference between hotels and motels is that in a hotel, guests pay at the end of their stay, while in a motel it is customary to pay in advance.

Taxes

As with all goods and services in the United States, the prices displayed *do not* include taxes. Local tariffs will vary from state to state depending on the levels of sales tax or whether a bed or occupancy tax is charged. Generally, though, expect to pay another 10-15% in taxes on top of the advertised room rate.

Booklets of Discount Vouchers

It is always worth stopping at the first visitor centre or rest area when entering a new state and picking up a booklet of discount vouchers. The booklets offer deals on local hotels, motels and restaurants and can be great money savers. Be prepared for blank looks from some hotel and motel staff, though, because their head offices do not always seem to keep them informed of new promotions. However, most will accept the evidence of the voucher when it is presented and give the appropriate discount.

Where Can I Find Out More?

Maintenenance

The American Automobile Association (Triple A); 1000 AAA Drive, Heathrow, Florida, 32746-5063. (☎ 1-800-874-7532; www.aaa.com)

The Council for Better Business Bureaux; 4200 Wilson Blvd, Suite 800, Arlington, Virginia 22203-1838. (☎ 703-276-8277; www.bbb.org).

The following two organisations set the standards which repair shops and mechanics must meet;

The Automotive Service Association; PO Box 929, Bedford, Texas 76095-0929. (☎ 1-800-272-7467; www.asashop.org)

The National Institute for Automotive Service Excellence; 13505 Dulles Technology Drive, Herndon, Virginia 22071. (☎ 703-713-3800; www.asecert.org)

These two websites offer useful tips on car maintenance and dealing with garages;

American Woman Road and Travel at **www.awroadandtravel.com and www.eHow.com**

Food

This website links to the sites of nearly 300 restaurant chains across America; www.virtualvoyages.com/resource/restrnt.

The American Diner Museum; 110 Benevolent St, Providence, Rhode Island 02906. (☎ 401-331-8575; www.americandinermuseum.org)

The American Diner Directory is also available from the museum at $27.95 ($23.95 for members) plus $4 shipping.

Accommodation

Hotel bookings on the internet; Hotel Reservations Network; www.180096hotel.com.

Campsites

Kampgrounds Of America; KOA, PO Box 31734, Billings, Montana 59107-1734. ☎ 406-248-7444; www.koa.com

Hotel Chains

Best Western 1-800-528-1234
Embassy Suite Hotels 1-800-362-2779
Hilton Hotels 1-800-445-8667
Holiday Inns 1-800-465-4329
Hyatt Hotels 1-800-233-1234
La Quinta Hotels 1-800-531-5900
Marriot Hotels 1-800-228-9290
Quality Inns 1-800-228-5151
Radisson 1-800-333-3333
Ramada Inns 1-800-228-2828
Sheraton Hotels 1-800-325-3535

Motel Chains

Budgetel Inns 1-800-428-3438
Comfort Inns 1-800-228-5150
Days Inn 1-800-325-2525
Econo Lodge 1-800-553-2666
Friendship Inns 1-800-453-4511
Embassy Suite Hotels 1-800-362-2779
Hampton Inns 1-800426-7866
Rodeway Inns 1-800-228-2000
Super 8 Motels 1-800-800-8000
TraveLodge Hotels 1-800-578-7878

Hostels

Hostelling International/American Youth Hostels; 733 15th Street, Suite 840, Washington DC 20005. ((1-800-909-4776; www.hiayh.org).

Bed and Breakfast

B&B Central Information; PO Box 829, Madison, Tennessee 37116. ((615-868-1946; www.bbonline.com)

✦ Greasy, Oklahoma, to Mechanicsville, New York - 1,550 miles ✦

Glossary

What does that mean? Just as Eskimos are said to have innumerable words for snow, it is fitting that a society so in love with the car should have so many different words associated with road travel. Here is a glossary of words and phrases you might come across in the United States.

'American'   'English'

'American'	'English'
Autopay	Direct debit
Better Business Bureau	Trading Standards
Beltway	Ring road
Certificate of Title	Document signifying vehicle ownership (log book)
Checking Account	Current account
CDW	Collision Damage Waiver
Comeback	A car which is inadequately repaired and 'comes back' to the repair shop
Compact	Small car
Credit Union	Building society
Crosswalk	Pedestrian crossing
Divided highway	Dual carriageway
Driveaway	A car delivery
DUI	Driving Under the Influence
Expressway	Motorway
Fender	Bumper
Freeway	Motorway
Grade Crossing	Level Crossing
Gridlock	Traffic jam
Hazmats	Hazardous Materials
HGN Test	Horizontal Gaze Nystagmus Test - to check the vision of a drunk driver
Hood	Bonnet
LCV	Long Combination Vehicle (Articulated lorry)
LDW	Loss Damage Waiver
MOV (or HOV)	Multiple (or High) Occupancy Vehicle (Car share)
Muffler	Exhaust

'American'	'English'
No Passing	No Overtaking
No Standing	No Parking
Parking Brake	Handbrake
PAI	Personal Affects Insurance
Parkway	Motorway - but landscaped with trees
Pavement	Road surface
Pink Slip	Document signifying ownership of vehicle
PIP	Personal Injury Protection
Pull-off	Lay-by
Ramp	Slip road
Rest Area	Service station with vending machines, information and toilets, but no gas or restaurants
Rotary	Roundabout
RV	Recreational Vehicle (camper)
Savings Account	Deposit account
Sedan	Saloon car
Sidewalk	Pavement
Station Wagon	Estate car
SFS Test	Standardised Field Sobriety Test - Set of roadside tests to establish whether a driver is drunk
Stick shift	Manual gearbox
Stop lights	Traffic lights
Stroller	Pushchair
SLI	Supplementary Liability Insurance
SUV	Sports Utility Vehicle (A four-wheel drive)
Superhighway	Motorway
Tagged	Summonsed for a traffic offence but not stopped
Tags	Licence plates
Teardown	A drastic repair - where the engine is 'torn down' and rebuilt
Thruway	Motorway
Trailer	Caravan
Transmission	Gearbox
Trunk	Boot
Turnpike	Toll road
U-Haul	Small (rented) trailer
UMP	Uninsured Motorist ProtectionUrban

'American'	**'English'**
Business District	City centre
Vascar	Type of speed gun
Windshield	Windscreen
Winnebago	Recreational Vehicle (trade name)
Work Zone (or Area)	Roadworks.
Yield	GiveWay

OK to sign you up for CDW, SLI, PIP, LDW as well as giving you the UMP?

Information and Conversions

Surfing USA

You can access a whole range of information through each state's official website. From there you can access agencies like the Department of Motor Vehicles, the Department of Insurance or you can find out local weather and road conditions.

Simply type www.state.(State Abbreviation).us

So, for example, Vermont's website would be *www.state.vt.us*

Alabama AL	Maine ME	Oklahoma OK
Alaska AK	Maryland MD	Oregon OR
Arizona AR	Massachusetts MA	Pennsylvania PA
California CA	Michigan MI	Rhode Island RI
Colorado CO	Minnesota MN	South Carolina SC
Connecticut CT	Mississippi MS	South Dakota SD
Delaware DE	Missouri MO	Tennessee TN
Florida FL	Montana MT	Texas TX
Georgia GA	Nebraska NE	Utah UT
Hawaii HI	Nevada NV	Vermont VT
Idaho ID	New Hampshire NH	Virginia VA
Illinois IL	New Jersey NJ	Washington WA
Indiana IN	New Mexico NM	Washington D.C. DC
Iowa IA	New York NY	West Virginia WV
Kansas KS	North Carolina NC	Wisconsin WI
Kentucky KY	North Dakota ND	Wyoming WY.
Louisiana LA	Ohio OH	

Gas

An American gallon is about 20% smaller than an imperial gallon.

Imperial	American	Metric
1 gallon	1.2 gallons	4.5 litres

Oil

Imperial	American	Metric
1 pint	1.2 pints	0.57 litres

Distance

1 mile is 1.609 kilometres; 1 kilometre is 0.621 miles.
As an approximate method of conversion; multiply by eight and divide by five to convert miles to kilometres. To convert kilometres into miles, multiply by five and divide by eight.
1 yard is 0.9144 metres; 1 metre is 1.094 yards

Temperature

To convert Fahrenheit to Celsius, Fahrenheit minus 32 and divided by 1.8
To convert Celsius into Fahrenheit, Celsius times 1.8 plus 32.
Fahrenheit = Celsius:

32°F=0°C; 41°F =5°C; 50°F =10°C; 59°F=15°C; 68°F=20°C;
77°F=25°C; 86°F=30°C; 95°F=35°C; 104°F=40°C; 113°F=45°C

56.6°C - the hottest temperature ever recorded in the United States. Stovepipe Wells, Death Valley, CA - 10th July, 1913.

Weights

America	Metric	Metric	America
1 ounce	28.35 grams	1 gram	0.035 ounces
1 pound	454 g	1 kilogram	2.205 lbs
100 lbs (1 US cwt)	45.36 kg	1 tonne	2,205 lbs
1 US ton (a 'short' ton)	907.2 kg		

(An imperial ton is called a 'long' ton in the United States and equals 2,240 lbs. A short ton equals 2,000 lbs)

Public Holidays

1st January - New Year's Day
Third Monday in January - Martin Luther King Jr Day
Third Monday in February - Presidents' Day
March - Good Friday
April - Easter Monday
First Monday in May - May Day
Last Monday in May - Memorial Day
4th July - Independence Day
First Monday in September - Labour Day
Second Monday in October - Columbus Day
11th November - Veterans' Day
Last Thursday in November - Thanksgiving
25th December - Christmas Day

Opening Hours

Banks - 9am-5pm weekdays. (Some stay open until 6pm and open on Saturdays)
Post Offices - 8am-4pm weekdays. (Some stay open until 5.30pm. Opening hours on Saturdays are local decisions)
Shops - 10am-9pm, generally
America is a 24 hour society and you will generally be able to find what you need at any time of day or night.

Daylight Savings Times

The clocks go forward one hour at 2am on the first Sunday in April.
They go back one hour on the first Sunday in October.
Arizona and Indiana do not observe Daylight Savings Time.
Spring forward, Fall back.

Electricity

Visitors from all countries, except Japan, will need adapters to operate electrical appliance from home in the United States. The supply is 110-115 volts, 60 cycles AC.

RVs can be fun to rent

Vacation Work publish:

	Paperback	Hardback
Summer Jobs Abroad	£9.99	£15.95
Summer Jobs in Britain	£9.99	£15.95
Supplement to Summer Jobs in Britain and Abroad *published in May*	£6.00	–
Work Your Way Around the World	£12.95	–
Taking a Gap Year	£11.95	–
Taking a Career Break	£11.95	–
Working in Tourism – The UK, Europe & Beyond	£11.95	–
Kibbutz Volunteer	£10.99	–
Working on Cruise Ships	£10.99	–
Teaching English Abroad	£12.95	–
The Au Pair & Nanny's Guide to Working Abroad	£12.95	–
The Good Cook's Guide to Working Worldwide	£11.95	–
Working in Ski Resorts – Europe & North America	£10.99	–
Working with Animals – The UK, Europe & Worldwide	£11.95	–
Live & Work Abroad - a Guide for Modern Nomads	£11.95	–
Working with the Environment	£11.95	–
Health Professionals Abroad	£11.95	–
Accounting Jobs Worldwide	£11.95	–
The Directory of Jobs & Careers Abroad	£12.95	–
The International Directory of Voluntary Work	£12.95	–
Live & Work in Australia & New Zealand	£10.99	–
Live & Work in Belgium, The Netherlands & Luxembourg	£10.99	–
Live & Work in France	£10.99	–
Live & Work in Germany	£10.99	–
Live & Work in Italy	£10.99	–
Live & Work in Japan	£10.99	–
Live & Work in Russia & Eastern Europe	£10.99	–
Live & Work in Saudi & the Gulf	£10.99	–
Live & Work in Scandinavia	£10.99	–
Live & Work in Scotland	£10.99	–
Live & Work in Spain & Portugal	£10.99	–
Live & Work in the USA & Canada	£10.99	–
Drive USA	£10.99	–
Hand Made in Britain - The Visitors Guide	£10.99	–
Scottish Islands - The Western Isles	£12.95	–
Scottish Islands - Orkney & Shetland	£11.95	–
The Panamericana: On the Road through Mexico and Central America	£12.95	–
Travellers Survival Kit: Australia & New Zealand	£11.95	–
Travellers Survival Kit: Cuba	£10.99	–
Travellers Survival Kit: India	£10.99	–
Travellers Survival Kit: Lebanon	£10.99	–
Travellers Survival Kit: Madagascar, Mayotte & Comoros	£10.99	–
Travellers Survival Kit: Mauritius, Seychelles & Réunion	£10.99	–
Travellers Survival Kit: Mozambique	£10.99	–
Travellers Survival Kit: Oman & the Arabian Gulf	£11.95	–
Travellers Survival Kit: South Africa	£10.99	–
Travellers Survival Kit: South America	£15.95	–
Travellers Survival Kit: Sri Lanka	£10.99	–
Travellers Survival Kit: USA & Canada	£10.99	–

Distributors of:

Summer Jobs USA	£12.95	–
Internships (On-the-Job Training Opportunities in the USA)	£18.95	–
How to Become a US Citizen	£11.95	–
World Volunteers	£10.99	–
Green Volunteers	£10.99	–

*Plus 27 titles from Peterson's, the leading American academic publisher, on college
education and careers in the USA. Separate catalogue available on request.*

★ **Vacation Work Publications, 9 Park End Street, Oxford OX1 1HJ** ★
Tel 01865–241978   Fax 01865–790885

**Visit us online for more information on our unrivalled range of titles for work,
travel and gap years, readers' feedback and regular updates:**

www.vacationwork.co.uk